A Progressive's Case for Bitcoin

A Path Toward a More Just, Equitable, and Peaceful World

C. Jason Maier

Foreword By Peter McCormack

Bitcoin Magazine Books
Nashville, TN

ISBN 979-8-9876363-0-5 – (paperback)
ISBN 979-8-9876364-1-2 – (ebook)
ISBN 979-8-9876364-8-0 – (hardcover)

BITCOIN MAGAZINE BOOKS

Published by Bitcoin Magazine Books
An imprint of BTC Media, LLC
438 Houston St. #257 Nashville, TN 37203
Address all inquiries to contact@btcmedia.org

Printed by Amazon
Formatting by RMK Publications, LLC

A Progressive's Case for Bitcoin

Acknowledgments

Writing a book like this is only possible with the help and support of an entire community. Throughout this journey I have been surrounded by the most supportive and helpful people, and I am truly grateful.

I owe a huge thank you to my wife, Carolyn, for her unyielding support and motivation through this entire process. I also owe a huge thank you to my best friend, Doron, for orange pilling me and for encouraging me to write this book!

Peter McCormack changed my life by supporting me and my idea for this book. Without him, you would not be reading these words. Dozens of others have lent their support, agreed to interviews, or have offered helpful thoughts about various drafts and parts of this book. Any list would be incomplete, but I must mention Mark Stephany, Troy Cross, Anita Posch, Alex Gladstein, Lamar Wilson, Margot Paez, Dennis Porter, Lyn Alden, Kent Halliburton, Lee Bratcher, Dawdu Amantanah, Neil McCormack, and each and every one of my Kickstarter supporters! Through writing this book, I've learned there is a growing community of progressive Bitcoiners for which I am grateful.

Lastly, I would like to thank my two beautiful children who have inspired me in ways they could never know.

Table of Contents

Foreword

When Jason Maier wrote to me in June 2022 telling me he was writing a book about Bitcoin for progressives, I knew he was writing the most important book about Bitcoin for conservatives. Let me explain.

Bitcoin is an apolitical tool for human freedom, and to achieve its full potential, it must avoid becoming a partisan issue. I have been working on Bitcoin for six years, making hundreds of podcasts, and during that time I have noticed how underrepresented progressives are. Bitcoin has been more broadly accepted by those on the conservative side of the political spectrum, but this new technology lives under a cloud of regulatory threat. It desperately needs people like Jason working on educating progressives on why Bitcoin should be embraced so it will earn bipartisan support.

I first discovered Bitcoin in 2013. A friend of mine introduced me to the Silk Road, a marketplace where you could use this new Internet money to buy drugs. Intrigued by the opportunity, I headed to Local Bitcoins and sent some guy a photo of me holding a picture of my name with the date. About an hour later, I received my first Bitcoin, which I immediately sent to my Silk Road wallet and used to buy some weed. At the time I didn't have the faintest clue about how Bitcoin really worked, much less that in a decade it would become my life's work. All I knew was that if I entered a string of letters and numbers in a computer, an hour later someone else would now "have" it, and in return I would get what I wanted.

The Silk Road closed a few months later, and I watched as the price of one Bitcoin climbed to $1,200 and then crash back down. I assumed without the marketplace and because its value had cratered Bitcoin was dead and forgot all about it. But four years later, my mother was dying from cancer, and we wanted to try one last treatment: cannabis oil. While the laws regarding cannabis had become more liberal in America, unfortunately at the time this treatment was still illegal in the U.K. But because of my experience with the Silk Road, I had a workaround I could pursue. So I bought some more Bitcoin, found a provider, and ordered the treatment. Sadly, although the treatment offered her some relief, Mum passed away, but the experience pushed me to learn more about Bitcoin.

It might sound odd to say that my interest in Bitcoin was spurred in large part because of cannabis oil, but the experience really rankled me. It wasn't just that I was angry that a plant that was decriminalised in large parts of America was not legal in the U.K. It was the broader notion: if the government was wrong about something like this, what else could they be wrong about? And if this technology helped me address a policy error by my government, could it help other people around the world?

Like many other Bitcoiners, this second touch sent me down the rabbit hole. In 2017, I started a podcast called What Bitcoin Did, which quickly introduced me to communities discussing libertarianism and Austrian Economics. For the first time, I found myself tackling important questions regarding the role of government and money. It was only after studying Bitcoin's technical design and understanding what sound money is that I realise that Bitcoin is the most important tool we possess for building an open and fair society.

I watched the world become more polarised in the 30 years since I first used the Internet. I have struggled to understand whether this is because the Internet has changed the media's incentives or whether it is the broader access to information that has allowed people to challenge commonly held beliefs. Either way, we have become more divided, with new battlelines drawn on every issue.

Over the years, as my podcast audience has grown, so has awareness and adoption of Bitcoin. Increasingly I have had listeners write to me questioning why I only have conservatives and libertarians on the show and why I don't spend more time talking to progressives. I realised that Bitcoin adoption was spreading to progressive circles, and the podcast needed to represent this shift. My producer and I henceforth have made a concerted effort to feature more progressives on the show to discuss how Bitcoin aligns with progressive policies.

Bitcoin is too important to become just another partisan issue; to become another thing for politicians to fight over to advance their career objectives. This is why Jason's book is so important. The book you are about to read will explain why Bitcoin should not be a partisan issue, how it supports progressive policies, and why it should be embraced by anyone who supports human freedom wherever they are on the political spectrum.

As the world has become increasingly polarised by political, social, and economic issues, we have seen the divide between rich and poor grow. We have witnessed financial crimes go unpunished and reckless behaviour in the financial sector wreak havoc on the hard-working people who are the economy's foundation.

While each election sees new messaging from our political parties vying for power, the issues in the financial system remain unsolved regardless of who is in power. Successive governments across the political divide have abandoned the idea of running a surplus, and increasingly borrow money to pay for the things they can't afford. Central bank policies have compounded the issue, and a low interest rate environment has allowed the richest to accumulate a significant percentage of the country's wealth. For me, it has become increasingly clear that left versus right arguments have become a cloak for policies that benefit only one group – the ruling class.

As democracy fractures, we need a revolution that swings back the power to the electorate over the elected, and I believe that Bitcoin is the most important tool for achieving this and creating a truly flourishing society.

Money should not be a partisan issue. At its core, it is simply a neutral tool that allows society to produce, innovate, and function. The productive parts of society require good money, which enables prudent saving and the fair allocation of resources. But our current financial system and the money we use are broken. Our monetary system is controlled and exploited by a small group of people who can manipulate the economy for specific political reasons. Nor are we alone in this: the problems are magnified in smaller countries with even weaker institutions. Even as we witness double-digit inflation in Western liberal democracies, countries such as Lebanon, Venezuela, and Turkey have seen their economies collapse as a result of much higher levels of inflation.

These economic issues are why many people seek alternative forms of money that no central authority or government can control. You only have to look at the data to see that when a country reports a massive rise in inflation, Bitcoin adoption in that part of the world tends to increase. Bitcoin is a safety net and tool that the world's most needy rely on, which is another reason we need to protect it from becoming a partisan issue.

While Republican states such as Wyoming and Texas have embraced Bitcoin and politicians in those states have become advocates, across the aisle some Democrats have been working against Bitcoin. Whether this is ignorance or malice, we should work towards educating those in power on both sides as to why Bitcoin should not become the latest battleground for partisan politics. We will have failed if Bitcoin is seen as a tool of the right or the left.

Many on the right have recognized the benefits of Bitcoin. But the beauty of Bitcoin is that it aligns with a wide range of progressive policies too. A key pillar of progressive policy is wealth inequality, which is often addressed by higher redistribution through taxation. But a policy to combat wealth inequality that does not address inflation will ultimately fail, as inflation impacts the poorest in society the most, with even low inflation increasing the divide. The Foundation for Research on Equal Opportunity published a study on the compounding impact of inflation on the poor and found "earners in the bottom decile experienced inflation that was 71 percentage points higher than for the top decile."[1]

Similarly, progressives have pushed harder to address climate change, but their policies have often exacerbated grid instability or targeted demand reduction in a world of growing demand. This has led to higher energy prices, energy poverty, and in greater instability in energy grids. But the economic incentives involved in Bitcoin mining help support environmental goals by allowing for the overbuild of renewable sources. This introduces interesting new use cases all over the world, where there are over 770 million people living without electricity.[2] For example, in Africa Bitcoin miners are working with mini-grid providers to change the economics of brining electricity to rural communities.

It isn't just inflation and environmental issues. Bitcoin supports human rights, activists in autocratic regimes, marginalised communities, and much more – all of which Jason explains in this book. This is why *A Progressive's Case for Bitcoin* is an essential book for conservatives. It is vital for conservative politicians and their constituents that Bitcoin's power is recognised by both sides of the political aisle. It should not be hindered by becoming the latest battleground for votes.

We know that Ted Cruz cannot convince Elizabeth Warren that Bitcoin is a force for good. Only an army of progressive voters will do this, and Jason's book may be the best way to build this army. Whether you are a progressive or conservative, you should ensure that his book reaches as many progressives as possible.

Bitcoin is the most important tool right now for fixing the parts of human civilisation damaged by the misaligned incentives of money that are controlled by the few. Bitcoin is money controlled by nobody. Its incentive structure creates the fairest money we have ever had and Bitcoin should be available to everyone.

Peter McCormack
Bedford, England
February 13, 2023

Chapter 1: Why This Book?

How a Poster Led Us Here

I hadn't really been into Bitcoin for very long before I gained the nerve to put a small Bitcoin poster above my desk at work. I was a little nervous displaying my interest in such a public way. I worked at a school where nearly all of my colleagues would consider themselves liberal to one degree or another. Because Bitcoin wasn't really on their radar I didn't know what to expect, but I had a rough idea. Some people would assume I had fallen for a scam and would politely hint that I was an idiot. Others would just laugh and ask if I was serious. I secretly hoped that the poster might help me find other Bitcoiners to talk to.

But the reaction I got was completely different. The poster had been up for only 10 minutes when the first co-worker to see it gasped, mouth open, looking at me as if I had committed a crime. I don't remember her exact words, but the tone and substance were unmistakable, akin to Elizabeth Warren's Twitter feed: "How could you? You're ruining the environment! It's so wasteful!" If she had been wearing pearls, they would have been clutched.

Because I had done a fair bit of reading already, I already knew that learning about Bitcoin meant diving headfirst into books, podcasts, and videos explicitly geared toward the libertarian/conservative side of the political spectrum. Some resources might claim to be politically neutral but contained not-so-subtle winks and nods to the political right. My experience quickly taught me I had to be open-minded so I could learn from people who had something to teach me about Bitcoin but who would probably disagree with me about most other things I cared about. Being a progressive learning about Bitcoin could be lonely, but I just figured that was the price of admission.

But my co-worker's reaction to my poster made it clear that progressives are not just a minority within the Bitcoin community, but have also been exposed to false narratives about Bitcoin by liberal politicians and other progressive thought leaders. These stories could stop people who shared my political convictions from learning about and even adopting Bitcoin. That experience and subsequent ones with other liberal-leaning co-workers and friends made me worry about the potential for 40% of the country winding up convinced that Bitcoin was only for Republicans. If that happened and Bitcoin became a wedge issue that divided people even more, it would be impossible to convince people on the left that they should even consider using Bitcoin.

It is a long and complicated story to understand how Americans became so polarized, but we are. What might surprise partisans of every stripe is my belief that Bitcoin represents the best hope we have for *overcoming* the economic, political, and even social problems that divide this country. But if Bitcoin joins the long list of items we have become polarized over, it would not just be bad for Bitcoin – it would be bad for the country and the people I care about. I knew something had to be done, and so I set out to write this book.

Is Bitcoin Even Political?

In a perfect world, there would be no need for this book, because in its most basic form, Bitcoin is just some interesting math and a few hundred lines of computer code. It is apolitical, completely neutral, and doesn't favor any one group over another. It isn't built to support or attack a particular political party. Progressives don't have, and shouldn't need, a better case for or against Bitcoin than conservatives. Bitcoin is just a tool. Through history we have come to understand that tools and technology aren't inherently right or wrong – it's the ends that the people put them to that lead to good or bad outcomes. Thus, writing a progressive case for Bitcoin should be as absurd as writing a conservative case for hammers.

But because Bitcoin exists in a political world that, at least in the United States, is polarized, there is a need for this book. Bitcoin is used by people, and people have a way of making things messy and more complicated than they have to be. Unfortunately, both the culture and narrative around Bitcoin cater to those on the right of the political spectrum. I say "unfortunately" not as a critique of the people or policies on the right, but to lament that Bitcoin as a tool became politicized in the first place. Despite what should be a welcoming adventure, a progressive person beginning their journey down the Bitcoin rabbit hole will face hurdles, misinformation, and judgment.

It is a difficult road I have had to travel and my goal is to help clear the path for you. I want progressive people to know that Bitcoin can be seen as a tool for *good* in the world and it is not only okay to own and use it, but that progressives *should* turn to Bitcoin if they want to advance their goals. If we are lucky, Bitcoin could become one of the very few things that aren't needlessly politicized and polarized because both sides of the spectrum recognize its inherent value and see how it could be used to benefit society. This book is being written with the hope that one day a book like this won't be necessary because the case for Bitcoin won't need to be political at all.

I want progressives to understand that Bitcoin can be a powerful tool for good in the world and they *should* turn to Bitcoin to help shape a more just, equitable and peaceful world. In the chapters that follow you will learn how Bitcoin can promote sustainable, green energy while stabilizing the grid. You will learn how Bitcoin can cut out (i.e. disintermediate) predatory, too-big-to-fail banks as financial middlemen. You will learn how Bitcoin can provide financial security to billions of unbanked and underbanked individuals across the world, provide financial freedom to historically disadvantaged groups both in the United States and abroad, and help secure freedom for the growing

70% of people on this planet that live under autocratic rule.[3] You will learn how Bitcoin can help address wealth concentration and also hold politicians accountable for the policies that exacerbate wealth inequality. You will learn how Bitcoin can advance the cause of peace and make war less common.

And to top it off, you will learn that Bitcoin is *already* doing each one of those things today.

Bursting the Political Bubble

Going back to 2009, the very first group of people to get excited about Bitcoin were computer nerds. These programmers, hackers, and geeks liked Bitcoin because it represented an interesting and exhilarating new technological innovation. Notwithstanding the demographic makeup of that group being almost entirely white and male, it wasn't (and isn't) a particularly partisan group. But the second group of people to get excited about Bitcoin were small-government libertarians who saw the new technological innovation as a way to separate money from the state and achieve their goals of reducing the role of government in the individual's life. It's fair to say that their view of Bitcoin, like everything else, is entirely wrapped up in their politics.

But while the ends to which Bitcoin is used have moved on from its initial championing by libertarians, in lots of ways the narrative hasn't. Now to be clear, I don't want to make a case that the libertarian case for Bitcoin is wrong. The arguments in this book do not require that they are. My point is that by using Bitcoin both libertarians and progressives can achieve their goals.

The problem with the current narrative is the best books to learn about Bitcoin assume that the reader not only wants to learn about Bitcoin but also agrees with all the right-wing political stuff being slipped in. But one is not intrinsically connected to the other. It's perfectly logical to be both interested in Bitcoin and have a liberal outlook. There should be room for the progressive narrative as well.

My journey down the Bitcoin rabbit hole did burst the political bubble I lived in, but like the reaction of my co-worker did so in a surprising way. Like all of us, I watched the news I agreed with and spent time with friends that I agreed with. If I watched Fox News, it was as a joke, and I couldn't take in more than a couple of minutes before needing to change the channel. But on some level, I knew that this wasn't healthy. I told myself that I was reflective about my beliefs and opinions, but I never really took a sincere step out of my comfort zone or my echo chamber. It was just confirmation bias on repeat every day. And when you think about it, what incentive did I have to change my behavior? I was *right* after all. And being right is easy and kind of fun, too.

But learning about Bitcoin helped me reconsider my approach. While discovering all that Bitcoin had to offer didn't change my values, it did open up my mind. I was able to read books written by people I disagree with on fundamental political issues. I now regularly listen to interviews with people that are on the opposite end of the political spectrum from me. Instead of insulating myself from those viewpoints, learning about Bitcoin forced me to consider alternate ideologies.

By listening to hours of podcasts and audiobooks I got to know better the people behind what I was hearing. My experience is that a good many people that represent the public face of Bitcoin would be characterized as conservative by progressive listeners. But listening to them also reveals that they deeply care about the fact that the world isn't fair and that our current system is rigged against the little guy. As a group, they come to different conclusions than most liberals about how to mitigate the effects of that unfairness, but they start from the same place of concern and are genuinely sincere, thoughtful, and principled individuals. That doesn't mean that I agree with their solutions, but it does mean that I don't think these are evil people.

For example, consider Scott Melker, one of the many prominent voices in the Bitcoin space. In a 2022 interview with fellow conservative author and entrepreneur Jeff Booth, he offered the following unexpected observation:

> *If you're a liberal...if you're on the far left side, Bitcoin should literally be the dream you should be pushing to every person... If you believe in helping the average person, you should be an ally not an enemy.*[4]

This exchange is perhaps a little odd: two conservative people discussing what liberal people should think about Bitcoin. But even more remarkable is what they were saying: Bitcoin's importance in creating a more fair and just world.

It is admittedly all too common in the Bitcoin space that a public discussion between two Bitcoiners likely means a conversation between two people on the right side of the political spectrum. But there's not a progressive I know that would disagree with the idea of creating a more fair and just world. So why is it that some high-profile liberal politicians resist Bitcoin? Could it be that there need to be more liberal voices in the Bitcoin space to better critically assess such claims? I think so, which is why I wrote this book.

Learning about Bitcoin has not just led me to learn things from people I disagreed with politically but made me a more open-minded person – a progressive value I cherish. Often I found myself empathizing with someone's perspective without agreeing with their politics or changing my principles. Never before in my adult life had I allowed myself to listen to so many people that I disagreed with. But the common thread I had with all of these people was a deep interest in Bitcoin and how it might make the world a better place. That helped me pop the political bubble I was living in.

I encourage you to do the same. This is not the only book about Bitcoin you should read. Expose yourself to other books after you read this one. Most of the others you pick up will have some nasty things to say about socialized medicine or government handouts, but you can get through that without too much trouble. You can expose yourself to ideas you don't agree with and have confidence that you will still be a progressive when you're done. In fact, by examining your beliefs more fully, you may even become a better progressive because of it. What I guarantee is that you'll become even more knowledgeable about Bitcoin (I have included a list of recommended resources in the Appendix).

Resetting the Game

Like many nerdy people, I regularly gather with my friends to play strategy board games. If you've played Settlers of Catan, you've started the journey and are on the right track. Some of the most interesting and challenging of these strategy games, like Terra Mystica, include a component of asymmetry. For example, the blue player may start with more money, but the red player is able to produce resources more efficiently. These asymmetries make playing the games more challenging and interesting. This isn't like Monopoly where each player starts with exactly the same things. Each time you play is a different experience and some people find the more challenging rule set fun.

But over time, it is discovered that the benefit available only to the red player is a little too helpful. The game isn't really fair and therefore not that much fun. So, the game makers publish detailed booklets filled with special rules that level the playing field. The booklet says the red player is still able to produce resources more efficiently but starts the game with -5 points. Each of the other players is given some sort of equalizing handicap also. And if we're to trust the makers of the game, who didn't quite get it right the first time, then everything is fair and fun again.

Trusting liberal politicians to pass and enforce laws to nudge the systems we live in to fairer starting points is like publishing the booklet of special handicaps for asymmetric games like Settlers of Catan. The solution is well intentioned, but unsatisfying and ultimately not very effective. Of course, we should vote and march and fight to make the world a little more fair, but we have been doing that for a very long time, and every time even if we remedy the old unfairness we create a new one as a result.

The economic policies that liberals support are well-intentioned attempts to tweak the system from within the system. They are just little handicaps published after the fact because we notice the game we're playing isn't actually fair. Examples abound: Increase the Minimum Wage, Ensure Universal Health Care, Fund Early Pre-K, Tax the Rich, Regulate the Banks, Support Labor Unions, Provide Access to Student Loans, and so many more. These are policies that help people and I'm happy to support them all. But I think you can work on improving the current system without closing your eyes to other options too. Each of these just makes the current system a little less unfair, but not one moves us closer to a different and fundamentally fairer system. But changing to a Bitcoin system is like starting over with a new game that is fair from the very beginning.

Changing the money we use will not solve all of our problems completely. But adopting a Bitcoin standard could be an important first step to help make the world more fair, equitable, and peaceful. These are progressive ideals that every liberal person I know strives for. These ideals are also very much part of the ethos behind Bitcoin.

I'm all the way liberal. I'm also all in on Bitcoin. I feel great about both of those things coexisting within me. If you also consider yourself a progressive liberal, then you might be a lot like my co-worker who didn't like my Bitcoin poster. And if, unlike my co-worker, you're open to learning more about Bitcoin and a better future, then I wrote this book for you!

A Peaceful Revolution

I consider myself a progressive person because I look around the world and I see that it is not just, fair, equitable, or peaceful. I have always looked for ways to make the world better, and I have always done that from within the systems I recognized as broken. For most of my adult life, I have expected the government (one example of a broken system) to make rules and laws that nudge the system closer to justice, fairness, equity, and peace. Isn't that the best we can hope for?

One reason why I encourage you to learn about Bitcoin is so you can question the current system through another lens. Learning more about how and why Bitcoin works is only one half of the journey. Bitcoin also provides an opportunity to examine the unexamined, study the water around us, and ask tough questions about the systems we have always lived with. It presents the opportunity to ask questions we never really ask. What is money? Who controls it and how? Who should control it? Learning about Bitcoin empowers you to imagine what things might be like if we replace a structure we intuitively know is unjust but have never had the vocabulary to question before.

The idea that the monetary system might one day be all the way fixed has never seemed like a real possibility. The idea that the entire system could be replaced – the water around us that we don't notice – has never been a possibility either. Yet while many of my liberal friends are very adept at pointing out systemic inequities, proposals for systemic *change* to replace the systems that cause those unfairnesses are few and far between. Certainly financial and monetary systems are systems that one doesn't usually examine, but a better understanding of Bitcoin interestingly offers you a better understanding of the systems it seeks to replace, and why incremental change won't fundamentally address its unfairnesses. It also allows you to imagine, perhaps for the first time, a world without those inequities.

The world is controlled by political, social, economic, and military systems that both create and depend on the hegemony of the United

States dollar. Unfairness, inequity, and violence are woven into the fabric of these systems. They are inexorable parts of those systems, not just unfortunate externalities that exist on top of otherwise healthy structures. To take just one example, wealth inequality is not just an unfortunate thing that happens because some greedy people break the rules and get away with it. It is a necessary and integrated feature of a system that depends on a hegemonic United States dollar being a global reserve asset (see Chapter 7). But now, for the first time in human history, we have a potential monetary invention that could overhaul the system, not just tweak it from within to be a little more fair.

In my experience, the more a person knows about the legacy financial system, the more they dislike it. Henry Ford is credited, most likely incorrectly, with having said, "It is well enough that people of the nation do not understand our banking and monetary system, for if they did, I believe there would be a revolution before tomorrow morning."[5] Bitcoin could be the nudge to help you learn about our banking and monetary system and start a peaceful revolution.

About This Book

In this book you will find, in equal parts, the things I think are wrong with our current financial system and the ways I think Bitcoin provides an opportunity to explore an alternative system. This book is intended to be a solid introduction for the curious person. It is written without assuming any technical knowledge, and a deeper technical understanding of Bitcoin should be sought in other resources. The book is written from an American perspective both because I wish to remain authentic to my personal experience, and because of the importance America plays in the international monetary system. You will see that throughout the book I use the common convention to refer to the monetary network, the invention, and the concept of Bitcoin using a capital B. References to the actual digital token, bitcoin, will be lower case.

In Chapter 2 I introduce the twin questions of "what is money?" and "what is Bitcoin?" The first is a question people don't often ask in their everyday life, and you may find some of the answers presented in the chapter surprising. Our explanation of Bitcoin is a brief introduction, and more details about the how and why of Bitcoin are reserved for subsequent chapters when they are explicitly needed. As such, you should not worry if they don't feel like an expert on Bitcoin when you are done reading this chapter. Nevertheless, there is enough of an exposition that you will understand the potential Bitcoin has to reshape our relationship with money and why progressives should care a great deal about it.

Chapter 3 is the longest and possibly most important chapter in the book. In it, we explore the relationship Bitcoin has with the environment. The main theses of the chapter are that the environmental damage from Bitcoin is misunderstood and often overstated, while at the same time there exist new and exciting opportunities to help the environment that Bitcoin is uniquely positioned to take advantage of. You will be encouraged to check your initial assumptions about both energy consumption and energy creation so you can appreciate the fundamental ways in which Bitcoin is actually good for the environment.

In Chapter 4 we present Bitcoin as a viable alternative to too-big-to-fail banks and describe the advent of Bitcoin as a protest against the predatory and unfair banking industry at large. We provide details about how a person can store and transact their Bitcoin assets without needing to trust centralized third parties like banks. The chapter explores the ways in which the banking industry has become enmeshed with our government and exactly how this deep relationship favors the wealthy and connected while taking advantage of regular people. In contrast, we describe the ways in which Bitcoin is a more fair, transparent, and equitable alternative to banks as we currently experience them.

In Chapter 5 we take a deep dive into ways that Bitcoin can help poor and marginalized people around the world. We study the ways in which Bitcoin's permissionless and censorship-resistant properties are important tools in helping disenfranchised and marginalized communities in America and abroad. For billions of people who are unbanked or live under the threat of authoritarian rule, Bitcoin helps secure basic property rights and financial independence that couldn't exist without it.

Chapter 6 examines the surprising ways that the inflation of government-created money has contributed to wealth inequality for more than 50 years. The chapter offers the opinion that Bitcoin could be a more fair and equitable system by which to create and distribute money. You will not be asked to abandon your personal understanding of what causes wealth inequality. Instead, you will be asked to consider a wider perspective about how the wealth inequality we see in our society is a systemic issue created by the type of money we use.

Chapter 7 offers a fairly comprehensive examination of what is wrong with our current system from a global monetary perspective. The chapter is a look behind the curtain at how and why the US dollar maintains its privileged status as the world reserve currency. But more importantly, the chapter provides a sobering look into the consequences of such a system for regular folks in America and beyond. We conclude this chapter by arguing that Bitcoin could serve as a more humane and neutral reserve currency.

We explore in Chapter 8 the ways in which Bitcoin can help make war less common and less deadly. Important to this conversation is a discussion of how wars are paid for under the current monetary system and how having a fiat-paper money system has allowed governments to pay for war when they might otherwise have avoided them. The aspirational conclusion to this chapter is that under a Bitcoin system, nations would only be able to afford, and therefore go to, war if it were a transparent priority supported by an engaged populace.

Chapter 9 provides one vision of what the world will look like when Bitcoin is more widely adopted. The chapter, explains how Bitcoin could offer, for the first time, a chance to use money that isn't controlled by a specific nation and how it might interact with our current government systems to promote progressive values.

Chapter 10 concludes the book by offering a call to action where you are encouraged to continue learning about Bitcoin and involve yourself with the progressive Bitcoin community.

Chapter 2: Why Bitcoin?

The Current System Is Broken

In the fall of 2021, the nation's imagination was captured by a coin that didn't even exist. But the coin wasn't digital. It wasn't bitcoin. The coin that grabbed the headlines and sucked up the oxygen at water coolers for a few short weeks was a fantastical trillion-dollar platinum coin. In our shared imagination, the platinum coin was emblazoned with a fierce-looking bald eagle and was supposed to save our Federal government, and, by association, the world economy, from certain calamity. And for a very short while, it was all anyone following the news could talk about.

By the end of September of that year, it was clear that negotiations to raise the federal debt ceiling were not going well. In an all too familiar display of political showmanship and economic brinkmanship, Congressional Republicans refused a vote to raise the debt ceiling. Democrats were being forced into a position to vote alone on a bill to raise the debt ceiling, a move that would open them up for relentless attacks by Republicans for spending money the government didn't have and plunging the country deeper into debt. Democrats were understandably reluctant to go it alone, but it was plain that Senate Leader Mitch McConnell and the rest of the Republicans were willing to sit quietly as the Democrats held the hot potato.

In reality, such a vote would only allow the government to pay for the debts it had already incurred through expenditures voted on by both parties over the preceding decades. It does not authorize new expenditures. Testifying before Congress in late September, Treasury Secretary Janet Yellen warned in no uncertain terms that the Federal government defaulting on its debts would be catastrophic and cause a self-inflicted crisis.[6] If Congress failed to act, the consequences were both clear and dire. The government defaulting on its debt would most certainly plunge the world into a downward economic spiral. The damage would be widespread and long lasting, and the global depression that would ensue would be difficult to combat with US monetary policy since it would be precipitated by the loss of confidence in the dollar. In his congressional testimony, Federal Reserve Chair Jerome Powell confirmed that the Fed would not have the power to combat such an economic collapse should it happen.[7] The politicians were playing chicken with the economy of the entire world.

Of course default wasn't an option; Democrats couldn't let such a devastating global depression happen on their watch. But the Republicans sat quietly on their hands and waited for the Democrats to authorize the debt ceiling increase on their own. They would get the best of both worlds: the United States wouldn't default on its debts and they would have some political fodder to use during the next election cycle. As difficult as the politics of it were, Democrats were going to have to clean up the mess.

Or maybe not. This is where the trillion-dollar coin comes in to save the day. Democrats wouldn't have to vote to raise the debt ceiling if the US Treasury minted a small platinum coin, gave it a face value of one trillion dollars, and deposited it at the Federal Reserve. Such a move would prevent the catastrophic debt default by padding the treasury's account balance by one trillion dollars created out of thin air, and the debt ceiling debate goes away without anyone having to vote on it.

To be clear, nobody was proposing that $1 trillion worth of platinum be mined from the ground to create a coin. Such an amount doesn't exist. The ability to mint such a coin is a hack that manipulates the wording of the Coinage Act, which (after being amended in 1982) gave the Treasury Secretary additional authority and discretion about how and why coins and money are created.[8] The proponents of #MintTheCoin were fully aware that this solution was just a gimmick. Maybe they couldn't tell that the problem and their solution were really the same thing: printing money to solve problems.

If the very idea of minting a one trillion-dollar coin seems silly to you, you're not wrong. If the plan feels a little bit like a seven-year-old cheating at Monopoly with a $1,000,000,000,000 bill and trying to keep a straight face, you're closer to reality than you think. In this case, the seven-year-old is still holding the magic marker used to change the bill's denomination when she asks if you have change for a trillion.

But as silly as it is, the idea received a lot of attention. The plan was seriously discussed by the US Treasury and gained support from Nobel laureate Paul Krugman.[9] Multiple members of Congress, eager to remove the debt ceiling as a political weapon, supported the plan. The hashtag #MintTheCoin dominated Twitter for weeks.

The coin – an absurd solution to an absurd problem – was the inevitable culmination of an absurd monetary system that we will explore throughout this book. The fact that it was never minted is telling as it might have finally pulled back the curtain on the fact that the United States dollar is pretend money, created from nothing, to prop up a financial system that is built like a house of cards. Perhaps creating a fake trillion dollars with a single physical coin was a little too "on the nose" when the preferred method is to copy and paste almost $14 trillion dollars into existence since the economic crisis of 2008.[10]

Ultimately, minting the coin wouldn't have saved us. It would not have fixed the failing economic system that would have allowed for its creation. It would not have fixed the failing political system that necessitated its creation. It may have helped a few politicians win easier re-elections, but otherwise the net effect would be to merely kick the can down the road – the moment when we all have to pay. It's no mistake that the proposed image of the fantastical one trillion-dollar platinum coin featured 13 stars and a swooping, fierce-looking bald eagle.[11] While the depiction of the coin contained the symbols of dominance, aggression, and power, the fact that we even were discussing such a coin is, in every sense, the epitome of weakness.

The answer to "Why Bitcoin?" has many answers. But the story of a gimmick platinum coin that is supposed to fix everything answers the question well enough: the system of easy money is broken and our political system is unable to solve it. By reading this book you are sure to learn a lot about Bitcoin, and there is a good chance – like most people – that the more you know about it, the more you will like it. But you will also learn a lot about our current financial system that people don't usually think about. What you learn will make sense because you can *feel* something is wrong with the system; you always have. What's more, for the first time you may feel like there is an actual solution to work toward.

The debt ceiling stalemate of 2021 was nothing special or new. These inane debacles of conservative obstructionism have been happening regularly since 2011. The magic platinum coin wasn't new in this go-around either. It was also first introduced in 2011. In the over ten years since, there have been many other moments when the absurdity of our financial system was on full display for anyone willing and able to pay attention. And in the time that passes between me writing these words and you reading them, there will surely be more. Rich, powerful, and connected people understand that the system is broken, but they aren't incentivized to fix the system because they know exactly how to benefit from it. Many regular people assume this is the way it has to be. But for the first time, with Bitcoin, there is an alternative.

What Is Money?

For many people, their first sense of Bitcoin is that it is magic internet money – something easily ignored and certainly not worth the time needed to understand it. Many of the people I talk to about Bitcoin say that their "plan" is just to ignore it until it goes away. As we will learn throughout this book, that isn't really an option. Most people also laugh when presented with their first opportunity to exchange "real money" for bitcoin. But bitcoin is real money; better money than any of us have had in our lifetimes – and it is so much more.

Both Bitcoin the network and bitcoin the digital token can be hard to define because they don't just replace *one* thing and make it better. Bitcoin is the new, better version of gold from the ground and the paper dollar bill. Bitcoin is also the new, better version of your savings account and your checking account and your credit card. It is also the new, better way to send money internationally and to buy a cup of coffee down the block. Bitcoin doesn't just replace the hard asset money and the currency, but also the payment rails, the political monetary policy, and even the central bank – all in one fell swoop. It is a completely new thing.

To truly understand Bitcoin, you must understand the thing it aims to replace: money. What is money? Oddly enough, despite its centrality to almost everything we do, we rarely pause to consider the question. But we have to if we really want to understand what Bitcoin actually is.

In the most fundamental form, money is any object that is used for some combination of the following purposes:

1. A medium of exchange (folks can buy stuff with it);
2. A unit of account (folks can reliably use it to price stuff); and
3. A store of value (folks can buy stuff with it later).

Over the years, many different objects have been used as money: sea shells, salt, large stones, gold, and the $20 Federal Reserve Note currently in your wallet. If you're reading this book in prison, you might use cigarettes or packets of ramen as money. I encourage you to reflect on how and why people naturally converge on forms of money based on the time and circumstances they find themselves in and how technology has *always* played a role in the development of new money. Some things make better money than others. As we will see, the paper money and its digital copy you use every day is the latest form of money, but it isn't the best – in fact it is far from the ideal.

To be considered a good form of money – something that accomplishes the three purposes listed above well – an object must have some combination of the following fairly intuitive properties:

1. Durability (It has to last, not spoil or deteriorate);
2. Portability (You have to be able to move it around);
3. Divisibility and Aggregability (You need to be able to buy little things and big things too);
4. Fungibility (The units need to be uniform);
5. Scarcity (If there's a lot of something, it won't maintain value);
6. Acceptability (People have to want it for you to use it); and
7. Verifiability (You don't want a lot of counterfeit money).

You or I may have other properties that we think should be added to the list. For example, I think good money should be created fairly. But this is the list that economists have used for generations. In fact, the Federal Reserve Bank of St. Louis lists these properties in the teachers' resources section of their website[12] and uses them to argue – correctly – that US dollars are better money than a cow. A cow seems like a low bar, but maybe they only want to make the arguments they can win.

Each of these properties economists use to decide how good something is as money is measured on a scale; none of them is a binary "yes" or "no." If an object fulfills many of these properties, it would make for a good form of money. From this list, it is trivial to see what your intuition already tells you. Bananas would make a horrible form of money and coins made of gold would probably serve the purpose well. But what about the $20 bill in your wallet? What about bitcoin?

In a head-to-head competition, the $20 bill easily beats bitcoin in category #6: Acceptability. But acceptability can change and has many times throughout history, and the gap is narrowing every year as more establishments accept bitcoin. It's not too hard to imagine that gap closing substantially over time. On a technicality, the dollar also has a slight edge in category #4: Fungibility. But this is only a small difference that most people would not notice, and technological methods already exist that close this gap completely.

As we will see as the rest of this section unfolds, Bitcoin walks away with the lead over dollars in all of the other categories. It's not even close. Bitcoin is not just a little but a lot more Durable, Portable, Divisible/Aggregable, Scarce, and Verifiable. These aren't properties I cherry-picked because they make Bitcoin look good. These are the old textbook properties economists have used for "good money" forever. We can add to this list the fact that since Bitcoin is natively digital and programmable, it seems like a better form of money right now and for the future. Nor is Bitcoin just better than the dollar: when comparing Bitcoin to other forms of money (e.g., gold) it still demolishes the competition across most or all of the categories. It's simply the best money that humans have ever created.

Before I explain why that is true, I want to pause and make sure we also understand what money *isn't*. You will notice that the properties listed above for something to serve as good money do not require the item to have a physical form you can hold in your hand. Nor do the properties suggest that something used as money needs to have some other intrinsic value. Nor do the properties suggest that money must be issued by a government. All three of these things are often cited as reasons why Bitcoin cannot be real money, yet none of them really have anything to do with the actual definition of money. These are things people reference because they are important to their experience with money, but they aren't intrinsic to that experience. Just like how what has served as money has changed over time, so too has our experience with money.

For example: It is not necessary for money to have a physical form that can be touched or held. Indeed, you have never held most of the dollars you have earned, spent, and saved in the last 20 years. They have just been numbers on a screen. Digital money, dollars or otherwise, is perfectly functional as money. And the same is true of

Bitcoin; just because you can't touch it doesn't mean it's not real either. Hopefully this is reassuring, since this is typically the very first argument offered by well-meaning folks when they first start to grapple with Bitcoin. But the simple fact is that you don't need to be able to touch something for it to be a good form of money.

Nor is it necessary for money to have an intrinsic value. In fact, because money is used to communicate price information from one market participant to another, it is better that it not have other use cases. Money having intrinsic value would add "noise" to the signal and make every economic decision more difficult. Imagine having to weigh every purchase you make with your money against the value of its other uses. It would cause economic activity to grind to a halt as everyone debated whether to use the money they had for purchasing goods or this other use. Some people don't realize that the numbers on their screens that represent the dollars in their bank account don't have an intrinsic value either. Bitcoin's lack of intrinsic value is another very common argument launched against it, when in fact that turns out to be a valuable feature and not a bug. The fact that Bitcoin doesn't have some other intrinsic value means it is able to provide price information for economic decisions without noise or manipulation.

Finally, it is not necessary that money be issued by a government. For many centuries it wasn't. People would use various media of exchange and stores of value without the government interceding in any way. It was only in the last couple of centuries that it made sense for governments to get into the money game when it was difficult to trust and verify the purity and weights of coinage. Stamping the king's face onto a coin served a purpose at that point. Since then, the intertwining of government and money has been so complete that most folks have a hard time imagining that money can be something separate from the government. This misunderstanding has repeatedly been manipulated for the sole benefit of the government that controls the issuance of money. But despite our experience, there is no need for money to be issued by the state to be valid. Bitcoin is the best hope humanity has of severing the ties between government and money.

At the very least it will serve as a check on how the governments discharge their responsibility as stewards of monetary policy.

The good news is that people understand the seven properties of good money listed above on an intuitive level. In other words, people do not need to read an economic textbook to recognize "good" money. They just start gravitating toward it over time. People won't need to know *why* Bitcoin is better to know that it *is* better. Our recent monetary experiment with unbacked paper money is only 50 years old, and paper money owes most of its success to the privileged legal status paper money enjoys through the governments that issue it. But absent coercion people will always choose a better form of money, as shown by the fact that they did for thousands of years by using gold. Before Bitcoin had been invented, Jörg Guido Hülsmann explained, in his book *The Ethics of Money Production*, that in the case of "gold and silver – and whatever else free men might discover and develop for monetary services... there is a natural tendency in the market to spread the use of the most useful monies over the entire world."[13] Bitcoin is better money and because of that, Bitcoin adoption is very likely to grow and spread for the foreseeable future.

What Is Bitcoin?

Answering this question will happen over the course of the book, but let's begin with the basics. Bitcoin is a secure, digital, peer-to-peer network for broadcasting a public ledger through which users are able to exchange value. If Alice would like to send Bob the value of 1 bitcoin, she would submit that transaction to the network to be approved. Every 10 minutes a bundle of transactions called a block gets validated by a miner and appended to the end of what's known as the block chain. The miner (just a powerful computer) is only allowed to do so if it has proven it has "worked," i.e. expended some amount of real-world energy. There will be more about this in Chapter 3. At this point a vast, decentralized network of nodes (just small computers) scattered around the world all independently verify that the transactions in the latest block, and work the miner did, are all valid. If they are, the nodes update the world-wide public ledger by adding 1 bitcoin to Bob's wallet and subtracting 1 bitcoin from Alice's. All the nodes on the Bitcoin network will now agree about how many bitcoin Alice has and how many Bob has. That's Bitcoin in a nutshell: tick tock, next block.

The fact that the nodes verifying valid transactions are decentralized and distributed all over the world may seem like a small point, but it is one of the most important components of how Bitcoin works. There is no centralized authority to enforce rules. There are no gatekeepers – all participants are considered peers on a level playing field. Decentralization has immense implications; for instance, because you do not need permission to participate in the Bitcoin network, your transactions on the network cannot be censored. If someone disagreed with how you wanted to spend your bitcoin, they would have no power to block you because tens of thousands of other nodes have broadcast and approved your transaction. As we will see throughout this book, *permissionless transactions* and *censorship resistance* are critically important for not just supporting but advancing a host of progressive values.

Amazingly, Bitcoin does not just allow people to transfer information through a network of computers. It allows people to transfer actual value through a network of computers. Writing in 2008, the year before Bitcoin started, Jörg Guido Hülsmann understood how important this distinction is. "[N]ew information technologies have been unable to create any new monies," he wrote. "They have been able to develop various new instruments to access and transfer money. [But] these new electronic techniques... must not be confused with the creation of electronic money."[14] While this was true when Hülsmann wrote it, the landscape changed on January 3, 2009, when the Bitcoin blockchain began with what is commonly referred to as the *Genesis Block*.

Let me explain the difference another way to illustrate its importance. If I know a secret word and I choose to tell you it, then we both now know the secret word. This is an exchange of information.

Extrapolated to the digital world, this is what the internet offers: the ability to exchange information over space and time by using a network of computers. Despite the initial skepticism the internet occasioned – and there was plenty – there is no way you could possibly imagine your life without this idea of exchanging information through computers. The internet has completely changed the world.

Now let's imagine that instead of a secret word, I am holding a very shiny rock, and through some mutually agreeable scenario I hand the rock to you. You now have the rock and I don't. This is different from the exchange of information because in that instance we *both* get to keep the information. But this instance represents an exchange of value. Prior to 2009, an exchange of value was not possible over a network of computers, but now – thanks to Bitcoin – it is. I can directly send you value – a digital "shiny rock" – over a computer network so you "have" it and I do not.

Satoshi Nakamoto is the pseudonymous name for the person or people that invented Bitcoin. On October 31, 2008, Satoshi released the Bitcoin whitepaper, which was a technical document describing how Bitcoin would work. Three months later in January of 2009, Satoshi implemented the protocol described in the whitepaper and Bitcoin was up and running and has been running ever since. To this day, nobody knows who Satoshi is, but the impact of their work is impossible to ignore.

Being able to digitally solve the problem of actually handing over the shiny rock so you have it and I no longer do is called the "double spend" problem (i.e., preventing the original owner from transferring it a second time). Satoshi was the first to solve it digitally without using a centralized authority. Before 2008 a trusted 3rd party (read: bank or multiple banks) would have to keep track of who had what and if transactions were valid. With Bitcoin, this task is decentralized. The responsibility belongs to everyone and no one at the same time. There is no need to trust a bank or some other central authority – or even worry about whether a bank will approve your transfer and allow you to use your own money. This isn't usually a problem in the United

States, but we will see in Chapter 5 how it might be in other jurisdictions.

Computer scientists call the task of getting all the nodes across the planet to agree on the current and correct state of a public ledger the Byzantine Generals problem, and it had been around for decades. Satoshi's whitepaper also contained the first solution to it as well. Without using a "trusted" 3rd party or centralized authority like a bank, they showed how money could exist in a digital form and everyone agrees about the information on the ledger.

In solving both the "double spend" problem and the Byzantine Generals problem, Satoshi Nakamoto also created (for the first time ever) the concept of digital scarcity – something on a network of computers that could not be copied and pasted. When Satoshi created Bitcoin, they implemented a limit to how many bitcoin would exist – 21 million – and there is not a single thing any computer or person on this planet can do to change that fact. There is more about this in Chapter 3.

A natively digital item that you can't reproduce, no matter what resources you choose to devote to the problem, is a novel invention, and the gravity of this advance is hard to understate. Rivaling the "you can't hold it in your hand" issue for newcomers to Bitcoin is the mistaken belief that it can't have any real value because it is digital – and therefore can be reproduced the same way a forward from Grandma or a cat meme can be copied and shared around the world. The fact that a thing – a bitcoin – can exist as a digital object and also be a scarce object is a fascinating fact that most people struggle to comprehend. Those who do have a chance to glimpse the future.

If you consider yourself a life-long learner, then you're going to really like Bitcoin. The advent of Bitcoin is a marvel in mathematics, economics, game theory, cryptography, and computer science. There is a plethora of second-order effects on geopolitics, the energy industry, monetary policy, and many other aspects of society – many of which we explore in further detail throughout the book. Satoshi

Nakamoto would rightly be a candidate for a Nobel Prize in Economics, a Nobel Peace Prize, the Abel Prize (the highest honor given to a Mathematician), and the Turing Award (the highest honor given to a Computer Scientist). Bitcoin may end up being the most influential invention created in your lifetime.

What is truly astonishing is that after creating such an immense and powerful new tool, Satoshi Nakamoto gifted it to the world. After releasing Bitcoin as an open source software that anyone can verify and use, Satoshi stuck around for a couple of years to answer questions and then disappeared. But not knowing who created Bitcoin just reinforces its central features. It is an open and accessible network that runs across computers all over the world with no leader in charge of it. In fact, Bitcoin's lack of a leader is what makes it different from any other form of digital currency that has been developed since. It is one of the many reasons people all over the world trust it as the next form of money.

Bitcoin Is Better Money

When you purchase a bitcoin, or even a fraction of one, you are investing in a monetary network. Because, as we will explain in the chapters that follow, bitcoin is the token that secures and governs the entire Bitcoin network. Because the Bitcoin monetary network is open, globally accessible, and censorship resistant, investing in it makes great sense for many people. Indeed, this is how most people, at least in America, first come to understand Bitcoin – as an investment meant to increase their wealth measured in dollars.

But as a progressive, this isn't how I think about Bitcoin at all. For me, Bitcoin isn't about making more dollars. I try to encourage those around me to understand that Bitcoin is first and foremost a better form of money. Bitcoin's improvement on money is the first-order effect of this still-new technology, while many of the other benefits discussed later in this book are corollaries of that.

Nor is it just my opinion that Bitcoin is a better form of money – it's better based on the properties economists cite in describing what makes good money that we looked at earlier in this chapter. We already discussed "acceptability," but what about the other properties of good money?

1. **Durability**. Gold doesn't tarnish, decay, or erode. This is one of the major reasons that it has been used for money by almost all cultures throughout most of recorded history. It is intuitive that a monetary technology that is meant to be used as a store of value should not lose its value over time. Gold is much better at this than the US dollar, and that is why it is considered in traditional investment circles to be a great inflation hedge. But Bitcoin is even better. Because Bitcoin is maintained and secured in a decentralized way, there is no single point of failure. As long as electricity and computers exist, so will the public Bitcoin ledger and all of the wealth stored on it. Nor can the bitcoin that exists on the public ledger deteriorate or be edited in any way. We will see why this is the case in Chapter 3.

2. **Portability**. Anyone can access the Bitcoin network from anywhere in the world, which means your secured bitcoin that you own in New York is also owned in London and Tokyo at this very instant. You just need to bring the private keys (think: password) and you can access that value no matter where you are. This means you can get on a plane and travel halfway around the world with all your value intact. To be sure, you're not "bringing" your bitcoin with you; they are simply accessible at your final destination already. Now imagine the alternative: you are welcome to try and board an international flight with a large amount of gold or dollars in your possession, but you will not have them when you land! They are simply not portable. But unlike gold, bitcoin can be zipped around the world frictionlessly without involving a bank. It is faster, cheaper, and more secure than transporting value in any other form.

3. **Divisibility and Aggregability**. Gold really isn't divisible in any practical way as the amount of gold that you would need to buy a pack of gum is likely to be lost with the lint in your pocket. A dollar bill

is better because it can be broken into 100 parts (two decimal places), each of which is called a penny. But as you already know, handling more than a few of these pennies at any one time is cumbersome – you're more likely to walk past one laying on the street than you are to stop, bend over, and pick it up. Bitcoin is better. A bitcoin can be broken into 100 million parts (eight decimal places), each of which is called a satoshi.[15] Unlike pennies, satoshis don't take up space and aren't hard to digitally "count" and use as a medium of exchange. Because an app on your phone handles Bitcoin transactions, it is as easy to spend a couple of satoshis as it is to use your credit card. This opens up new possibilities for "streaming" incredibly small amounts of money over time that simply doesn't exist in the current system. Imagine sending a small fraction of a penny to a podcaster every minute while you listen to their content. This is actually possible with Bitcoin, and currently is happening. On the opposite end of the spectrum, it is fast, easy, and secure to send large amounts of bitcoin when it is required. Values of over $1 billion are regularly sent over the Bitcoin blockchain almost instantly for fees that are less than $2.

4. Fungibility. Despite falling short on many of the properties of good money, well into the 19th century cowry shells were used in many parts of the world as money.[16] But even then people freely acknowledged that one obvious issue with seashells is that they are not fungible. Some are larger than others and some are prettier. Some are pristine while others are damaged. There are similar issues with using diamonds as money, too. But fungibility of a monetary good – the ability to swap out one unit for another – is an important feature because it allows for trade and commerce without friction. Dollars are fungible; if you receive a $5 bill as change from a store, you don't really care which $5 bill from their drawer the cashier gives you. Bitcoin is equally fungible. All bitcoin are considered equal by the protocol, so if Alice sends 1 bitcoin to Bob, he doesn't have to worry about which coin she sends.

5. Scarcity. Every year the world's gold supply grows at the low rate of about 2% when new gold is mined and refined into existence. Compared to other precious metals, gold is in its own category; for example, the percentage growth for platinum year over year is closer to 100%.[17] The growth of US dollars is slower than most fiat currencies, but they aren't scarce, and more are being printed each year at an increasing rate. On the other hand, Bitcoin is by definition scarce. The supply of bitcoin is hard capped at 21 million, with no potential to produce more. We will explore more fully why this is the case in Chapter 3. And by 2024 the global supply of bitcoin will grow by less than less than 1% each year. Eventually that number will reach 0% because the supply of new bitcoin programmatically decreases every four years.

6. Acceptability. We discussed Bitcoin's acceptability above, but it is worth noting that the Bitcoin network is spreading each year. Perhaps you've noticed a local business that accepts bitcoin for payments or maybe you've heard of a famous athlete that is accepting part of their salary in bitcoin. You may even have heard about countries like El Salvador that have adopted it as legal tender.

7. Verifiability. Have you ever been frustrated when a business won't take anything larger than a $20 bill? Do you have the expertise and access to the machinery needed to verify that your gold necklace is really pure gold? How much time, energy and effort do you think has gone into making $100 bills harder to counterfeit? Bitcoin is an improvement on all of this. With most other forms of money there is a need to either trust somebody or invest effort to verify that it is legitimate. But with Bitcoin there is no need to trust. Simple computer code allows you to verify the bitcoin you spend and receive is valid. In fact, it's done automatically by computers all over the world every time a transaction is verified.

Bitcoin is better money. And as the subsequent chapters will show, this fact has real implications for the things that matter most to progressives.

Chapter 3: Why Bitcoin Is Good for the Environment

Everything Old Is New Again

By listening to mainstream commentators and politicians, it might be easy to conclude that Bitcoin is ruining the environment. Some big banks, knowing Bitcoin is a genuine threat to their industry, like to put out pieces criticizing Bitcoin from any angle they think will resonate with people.[18] It's worth considering where these attacks are coming from and what motivations exist to produce them. It is also worth considering that criticizing the energy use of a new revolutionary invention is a move from an old, tired playbook. It seems to be a go-to criticism for anything that might upend the status quo. For example, in 1999 *Forbes* published a piece warning of the environmental dangers of computers and the internet.[19] Just think about how the world would change for the worse if we snapped our fingers and returned to a personal computer and internet-free world.

The point isn't that computers have no environmental impact – they do. But we also have to consider the environmental impact in the context of the vast social and economic benefits computers have provided humankind. I don't just mean in the affluent West, but the benefits provided to all 8 billion people on the planet. And we need to consider the fact that the worst criticisms and forecasts levied in 1999 never really came true and that those criticisms might have been an attempt to scare people away from a new, powerful tool. Something similar is happening all over again with Bitcoin.

I'll be honest. It is frustrating to me when misinformation about Bitcoin is spread. It gets tiring to respond to the same lines of attack repeatedly. This is exacerbated when you're emotionally invested and need to respond to friends, co-workers, and loved ones who delight in forwarding you the latest hit job that claims Bitcoin is boiling the oceans. But I do that work because I care about Bitcoin. Unfortunately, there are Bitcoiners who would like to sidestep that work entirely because they don't believe they need to worry about the environment. There certainly isn't one universal view among Bitcoiners, but there are those that think that climate change isn't real, isn't caused by humans, or isn't as serious as scientists think. There are also those in the community who think that initiatives to protect the environment are just veiled attempts by the government to control people. There are still others who think the entire focus of investors on ESG narratives (Environment, Social, Governance) is a sham. These people are being more than just silly – they are choosing to alienate a vast majority of people who, like the experts, believe that climate change is real, dangerous, and caused by humans.[20] They are making my work harder.

The amazing thing is that there is no need to run away from the debate on Bitcoin's environmental impacts. There are already winning arguments to be made, even if you believe that climate change is real. I consider myself an environmentalist and I support Bitcoin. A closer look reveals that the attacks on Bitcoin's energy use are very similar to those levied against other disruptive technologies throughout history. I am prepared, like many other inspiring people in the Bitcoin space, to address those attacks directly.

What Is the Energy Used For?

By the time you reach the Whitestone mining facility in Rockdale, TX, you would have already been driving through the dusty planes of Milam County for quite a while. The facility is owned by Riot Blockchain and consists of a series of large buildings in parallel lines, each over 1000 feet long. Upon entering one of these buildings, you are confronted with walls consisting of thousands of powerful computers running nonstop – and not much else apart from the infrastructure needed to keep the computers cool. A tangle of hardware, wires, and blinking lights fill the room. The noise, created by the fans keeping the computers cool, requires hearing protection. Even with the fans, the heat the computers generate requires dedicated mitigation techniques to keep the machines running optimally. It is an impressive and overwhelming sight.

The facility is sort of like an island. There isn't much else around, which isn't a complete coincidence. In 2008, the major employer in the town, Alcoa Corporation, fully curtailed its aluminum smelting operations,[21] which devastated the local community.[22] Since then, Riot Blockchain has played an instrumental role in revitalizing the Rockdale economy by employing hundreds of people in the town.[23]

To the untrained eye, this particular collection of thousands of computers running continuously would be indistinguishable from any other data center. Such centers exist all over the world. There are massive collections of computers running nonstop so that Google can perform an internet search for you in a fraction of a second. There are massive collections of computers running nonstop so that Amazon can sell you the latest plastic widget from China. There are massive collections of computers running nonstop so that hospitals can save lives. Computers running for air traffic controllers. Computers running for Facebook. Computers running for your Netflix account. Computers running to operate traffic lights. Computers running for your bank account. Computers running for your email account. And the computers running in Rockdale, TX? They are protecting the global Bitcoin network and all of the value secured within it.

Like all computers, these computers require electricity to run. And this fact has led a lot of people to claim that because it uses energy Bitcoin is bad for the environment. This is actually one of the more popular attack vectors some on the left have levied against Bitcoin, and I wouldn't be surprised if you've already heard the claim that Bitcoin ruins the environment for exactly this reason. If you're a decent liberal person, learning this may have already led you to dismiss Bitcoin as an unnecessary evil. I know that when I first started grappling with Bitcoin, this was the conclusion that I came to. And with my self-righteousness in full bloom, I proudly dusted my hands and walked away from Bitcoin, *knowing* I was right. But as I eventually learned, the truth is more complicated.

Civilization requires people to use energy. Since there is no way around this fact, the important questions to ask are:

1. What is the energy being used for?
2. Is it possible to use renewable and clean sources of energy?
3. Is it possible to increase efficiency?

If we are to be good stewards of the environment while caring about limiting human suffering, we will ask each of these questions in a deep and honest way. These are questions not just about Bitcoin, but any situation in which our actions intersect with energy consumption.

There are wasteful uses of energy and resources and we can all benefit from reflecting carefully about those uses. Most reasonable people agree that some things are simply wasteful: taking long showers, letting the water run while you brush your teeth, and leaving the lights on when you leave the room. Consensus about wastefulness is more difficult to achieve for other uses of energy and resources: watering your lawn, plugging in Christmas lights, or taking a flight. These are the types of things that may cause a *conversation* with an in-law. And there are some things that even the crunchiest of hippies will admit, all things being equal, are worth the energy used: keeping lights and machines on in a hospital, growing and transporting food, and cleaning and distributing water. Most people who criticize Bitcoin's energy use start with the assumption that Bitcoin is useless, not worth it, or even harmful, and therefore any energy expenditure devoted to it is wasteful. But people who truly understand Bitcoin's importance begin to see things differently.

The computers running in the Rockdale facility are known as application-specific integrated circuits (ASICs) and are designed to do only one thing – protect the Bitcoin network. Thousands of times every second, these computers consider a potential block of transactions from the Bitcoin network and run the information from those transactions through a hash function.

Generally speaking, functions are just a mathematical rule that assigns an output value to a given input value. Lots of functions from algebra are easy enough to understand. $2x + 1 = y$ will take an input (say $x = 3$) and provide an output ($y = 7$). For most simple algebraic functions it's easy to determine the input just by knowing the output. In the example above, if the output was $y = 5$, we know conclusively that the input must have been $x = 2$. However, the hash function used to protect the Bitcoin network does not work like that. It is a mathematical marvel in the sense that there is no way to determine the input just by knowing the output.

Because you can't predict the relationship between inputs and outputs for a hash function, the process has to be guess and check. Bitcoin's ASIC computers are designed to find a particular "target" output from the hash function, so each time they run the hash function, they tweak one small value in the header of the proposed block of transactions and run the tweaked block through the hash function. If the result is not the target, the computer makes another tweak and tries again. This happens thousands of times every second scaled across thousands of computers located around the world. If the output from the hash function matches the target, that proposed block of transactions gets appended to the Bitcoin blockchain and the hunt starts anew for the next block. Since the hash output from each block is embedded in the block that follows, the blocks are said to be chained together.

Mathematicians rightly consider guessing and checking to be a low-order thought process and prefer interesting and elegant solutions to math problems. But developing a problem that can *only* be solved by guessing and checking is impressive. The obvious corollary is that a person or computer who offers you a solution to such a problem has likely spent some time and energy trying to find it because there are no clever shortcuts that can be used, and this can be proven mathematically. If that wasn't impressive enough, the mathematical puzzle of the hash function adjusts the difficulty of the problem over time. If more computer power is devoted to guessing and checking, the target hash is adjusted to become harder to find. This difficulty adjustment happens across the entire network of computers protecting Bitcoin roughly every 2 weeks. As a result, it always takes the entire Bitcoin network about 10 minutes on average to find the target hash, no matter how many resources are devoted to it.

Despite the cost and time it takes to get the target hash with guess and check, once you have a solution, it is trivial for anyone to instantly verify it. A great metaphor is working to find a four-leaf clover in a large field. This takes time and work depending on the size of the field, and there's no shortcuts – you have to look across every square inch to find out if there is one. But once you find a four-leaf clover, it is trivial for another person to verify you found it. This process of taking network transactions and repeatedly guessing to find the target hash is called "proof of work." Only the computers that can provide the proof of work are allowed to append new blocks to the block chain.

Proof of work protects the Bitcoin network because it requires computers to expend resources – specifically electricity – for the right to verify transactions and append them to the block chain. A person wishing to verify a fraudulent transaction (Alice pays me 100 bitcoin even if she didn't agree to this) or change a valid one that already existed would need to spend enough money on enough electricity to control 51% of the entire computing power of the Bitcoin network. However, at this point the network of ASIC computers protecting the Bitcoin blockchain is so large and robust that for all intents and purposes this is just not possible. A person attempting to verify a fraudulent transaction would in fact benefit more by following the proper Bitcoin protocol and playing by the rules. This is because verifying a valid block of transactions results in a "block reward" for the computer that did the work, while attempting to verify fraudulent transactions results in your computer being automatically kicked off the network.

Along with transaction fees, block rewards are meant to incentivize people to validate blocks of transactions through proof of work. The block reward is a specific number of bitcoin created as part of the process of validation. These newly minted bitcoin go directly to the computer that verified the block. The original block reward in 2009 was 50 bitcoin for each block. Every 210,000 blocks, or roughly 4 years, the reward is automatically halved in an event playfully called "The Halvening." After being halved three times, today the block reward is 6.25 bitcoin per block and that amount will be halved again to 3.125 at some point in 2024. At some point in the year 2140, the last bitcoin will be minted into existence. When this happens, only the transaction fees will incentivize ASIC miners to protect the network.

The proof of work mechanism along with the block reward is how both the Bitcoin network and its currency are tied to specific real-world costs. Validating blocks with powerful computers and electricity to earn a block reward is how all new bitcoin are created. Just like finding, extracting, and refining gold takes time and energy, so does creating bitcoin. Although the ASIC computers used to validate Bitcoin transactions are called miners, the analogy to mining gold is limited. The most important job of the computers "mining" bitcoin is not to create new bitcoin but to secure the network. The newly created bitcoin are simply the payment for that important work. The fact that these new bitcoin are systematically halved every 4 years is how we know the total supply of bitcoin is capped at 21 million.

Because Bitcoin uses proof of work, it uses energy. As you can see from the description above, this is intentional. To be considered a "hard" money, the creation of new bitcoin must be tied to a real-world cost. And what do we get from using that energy? Bitcoin is a peer-to-peer network for transferring value through computers. It is a decentralized network, meaning it has no owner or hierarchy and exists with equal access to everyone across the globe. Because of this decentralization, the network can't be shut down, no one can freeze funds or censure transactions, and no government or corporation can control it. Proof of work secures the value in the network and allows users to transfer billions of dollars of value across the globe almost instantly.

Proof of work also secures the issuance schedule of new bitcoin into the future, so we know exactly how much bitcoin will be created in any given span of time. This is an important property of Bitcoin that allows it to send accurate price signals through noise. No other monetary system shares this property. We don't know how many dollars will be printed in 2031 nor how much gold will be mined from the ground in 2043. Along with the difficulty adjustment, proof of work ensures that all bitcoin are created on schedule until the limit of 21 million is reached. This algorithm makes Bitcoin the scarcest, hardest money ever invented.

Proof of work with a difficulty adjustment is the essential breakthrough that allowed Satoshi to develop a purely peer-to-peer system to transfer value. It is also the mechanism that allows people across the globe to hold their value through self-custody instead of relying on 3rd parties or a centralized authority. Proof of work provides billions of people access to value that is not confiscatable by dictators, armies, or banks. This is an incredibly important aspect of Bitcoin that we discuss in depth throughout the book.

This is also an answer to our first question: What is the energy being used for? Without energy there is no proof of work. Without proof of work there is no Bitcoin or all of its important knock-on effects. Using energy to secure the Bitcoin network is an important use of energy for all of the reasons I've listed above. Through the course of this book, we will dig deeper into many of those reasons.

Understanding that Bitcoin is an *important* use of energy may be enough for some readers. But there is more to learn because Bitcoin is already making the world greener and will continue to do so in the future. We now turn our attention to our second question: Is it possible to use renewable and clean sources of energy? As you will see, the answer to this question is already a resounding "yes" for Bitcoin. But as Bitcoin welcomes more progressive voices to its community, we will have the power to shape an even greener future.

Bitcoin Is Already Green and Becoming Greener

At the time of writing, over 55% of the energy used to mine bitcoin comes from green sources – namely wind, solar, geothermal, nuclear, and offset carbons.[24] No other company or industry even comes close in terms of the share of green energy already used today. Ulta Beauty is 8% green, Walmart is at 13%, and Lockheed Martin 22%.[25] Globally, a small but growing 29% of all electricity is produced from renewable sources.[26] Using 29% as a baseline means that Bitcoin isn't just greener than other companies but might be a model for other industries. In truth, Bitcoin is way ahead of the curve when it comes to green energy, which may be surprising to people who only get information about Bitcoin from hostile sources.

The reason Bitcoin's electricity use is already green has everything to do with economic incentives and the industry's ability to consume energy differently than any other consumer of electricity. In order to be profitable, the computers securing the Bitcoin network must run as efficiently as possible and consume the cheapest possible energy. Bitcoin miners run on increasingly thin margins and operate in an industry with nearly perfect competition. If the electricity they use is too expensive or the machines they use are too inefficient, they have no choice but to turn off as mining becomes more expensive than the bitcoin reward. Electricity constitutes almost all of the marginal cost needed to run a Bitcoin miner. Because renewable energy is by far the cheapest electricity available,[27] miners seek it out to remain profitable, and this trend will surely continue since both solar and wind power are getting dramatically cheaper every year.[28] Conversely, the cost of electricity produced from most fossil fuels has remained constant in recent years, with electricity produced from petroleum being the most variable and costliest.[29]

To be clear, most Bitcoin mining operations are not choosing wind and solar power because they are tree-hugging hippies. They are doing so because it is the cheapest form of electricity available to them and the only way for them to remain profitable is to keep the cost of electricity low. And because of the dynamics of green energy production, sometimes the electricity Bitcoin miners use even has a negative price, incentivizing the use of green energy even more. This undoubtedly sounds counterintuitive or even impossible, but isn't hard to understand in the context of supply and demand. Let me explain.

If energy is being produced that nobody is using, the price decreases. Sometimes it decreases so much that the price dips below zero. In quite a few cases Bitcoin mining is a nonrival user of electricity. This means that Bitcoin mining is able to use electricity that nobody else wants or is able to use. But how is that possible?

Every bit of electricity that is generated must either be used immediately or stored in some sort of battery. This is independent of where and how the electricity is produced, and there are no exceptions. This has been the way since people started tying keys on kites. The very moment you create electricity you either store it in a battery or send it off to be used by a customer. In the case when neither of those options is possible (or profitable) the newly produced electricity is simply wasted.

It is important to know that storing electricity at a scale that would benefit the grid is costly and technologically complicated. Luckily recent advancements are making it easier and cheaper every year. but storing excess energy still requires an intensive capital investment with a very uneven and uncertain payoff mechanism. Likewise, transporting electricity to customers is also fairly limited because high-voltage power lines can only transport freshly produced electricity about 300 miles.[30] This is a limitation of physics. Any surplus electricity produced in Niagara Falls is simply impossible to transport the 400 miles it would take to reach the power-hungry populace of Manhattan.

As it happens, both of these problems do happen from time to time. Sometimes more electricity is produced than what is needed at that moment. Other times electricity is produced in locations where it can't be used and is too far away from the people that want to use it. With some surprising regularity both happen at the same time. Such moments are when the cost of electricity is driven down, sometimes to negative territory. On average wholesale prices for electricity turn negative about 4% of the time. But in some windy and sunny regions electricity is negatively priced for 6 hours a day.[31]

It isn't surprising that green sources of energy like solar and wind are major players in this dynamic. The amount of electricity that is generated by burning fossil fuels can be controlled precisely at the source. But we can't control when the sun shines or when the wind blows, and we can't control where the sun shines or where the wind blows. What should green energy producers do if they find their solar panels or wind turbines are producing more electricity than the customers close to them need at that moment? The sun can't be turned off and the wind can't be stopped. You either waste that electricity or you use the newly generated electricity – the stuff nobody else is competing for – to mine Bitcoin.

In this scenario the Bitcoin miner is not draining electricity that was meant for other uses. Bitcoin mining isn't taking away electricity that would otherwise be used by orphanages and hospitals. Throughout this chapter we will see that because of the nature of Bitcoin mining, the industry is uniquely positioned to take advantage of excesses in power production. The consequences of this fact are dramatic both in terms of how our power grid is likely to be reshaped and stabilized in the coming decades and the positive effects it will have for the environment.

For example, consider what is happening right now with respect to Bitcoin miners. They are small, nimble, and location agnostic. They can move to find cheap electricity – and they do. Bitcoin miners are very happy to soak up all of that extra electricity produced by the sun and wind. But when demand increases or the supply goes back down, the price of electricity will go up. In that scenario, Bitcoin miners turn off their machines when running them is no longer profitable, leaving the electricity for the people and things that need it.

This is a unique ability of Bitcoin miners. They are able to soak up excess power when it's not needed by others and flip a switch to immediately shut down when the power is back in demand. No other customer of electricity provides such a stabilizing demand response force for the power grid. As it turns out, the guess and check process of mining Bitcoin to secure the network is exactly what allows for this better than any other industry. A Bitcoin miner can be shut off immediately and does so without wasting any of the work it has previously done because the guessing is literally random. A Bitcoin miner running for 5 minutes technically isn't any closer to validating the next block than when it started. Turning it off doesn't waste that 5 minutes of work because the miner was guessing randomly by design, not making progress on a linear task. When it is turned back on the machine will immediately begin working with optimized efficiency once again. There are no assembly lines to shut down or start up. Nor are there any wasted, partially processed materials that must be discarded. There aren't teams of factory workers that must sit around idly while electricity is expensive. There are no real-world time limits for how long the process can be shut down. It is just a computer that can be turned on and off in perfect concert with the demands of the electricity it will or will not use.

Compare this demand response to other data centers full of computers that are used to keep our civilization running. Can you imagine if the massive collection of computers running Netflix shut down each time there was a heatwave and increased demand for electricity near their data center, which might be thousands of miles away from your living room? It's safe to conclude that Netflix's business model does not incentivize it to shut down for any reason. Unlike Bitcoin, Netflix is willing to take a short-term loss on their electricity costs to preserve uninterrupted service. The same is true for any other data center that you can imagine. The server running your email account cannot take a break because of a temporary spike in demand for electricity. Google isn't shutting down in a situation like this. Neither is Facebook or the computers running traffic lights in your city. Bitcoin is just built differently.

Mining Bitcoin has proven to be the best demand response vehicle to help stabilize our electricity grid, allowing for the increased use of intermittent sources of electricity like wind and solar. With near-perfect precision, Bitcoin miners are able to dial up and down their energy consumption in response to both the supply and demand of electricity, both of which are intricate and dynamic. Simply put, if you want enough solar and wind energy for a population, it is important to overbuild the supply because the sources are intermittent. In order to monetize the extra power when the sun shines or the wind blows while also having the option for perfect demand response at a moment's notice, you need Bitcoin.

The potential of this demand response is not just theoretical. It's happening in real life. Bitcoin mining facilities are dynamic consumers of electricity and are able to respond to demand fluctuations on the time scale of minutes or hours. Many of these sites dial up or down their electricity usage multiple times in a given month. But sometimes the need for demand response is the result of an emergency. Yet even in those cases Bitcoin is the best option available to provide that responsiveness.

Consider what happened on July 9, 2022. A heat wave hit the southern United States, which put an incredible strain on Texas' ERCOT power grid. The need for air conditioning dramatically increased demand for electricity in Texas. In response, multiple Bitcoin mining operations across Texas immediately shut down their operations for about 12 hours during peak demand times. It is estimated that about 1000 megawatts were released back to the grid precisely when it was needed[32] – enough energy to completely power over 66,000 homes across Texas during that time.[33] This quick action on the part of Bitcoin miners not only reduced and eliminated blackouts across the state but quite literally saved lives from the oppressive heat. Various Bitcoin mining operations continued to shut down throughout that week. No other consumer of electricity could even consider such a move, yet several different Bitcoin miners, all in competition with one another, were incentivized by price signals to power down and stabilize the grid. In extreme circumstances like this, extra power returned to the grid ultimately saved lives.

It turns out that not only is Bitcoin an *important* use of energy but an industry that is uniquely incentivized to use green energy. But that's not the whole story when it comes to Bitcoin and energy, and we now turn our attention to our final question: Is it possible for Bitcoin to increase efficiency?

The Imbedded Incentives for Efficiency

So how much energy does Bitcoin use? A meager 0.2% of the world's energy consumption is used by Bitcoin. Each year Christmas lights use more energy than Bitcoin does.[34] And while Bitcoin's energy is significantly greener than other industries, even if we managed to eliminate all of Bitcoin's energy usage, it would not put a dent in the effects humans have on our environment. We would still have about 99.8% of our energy consumption to contend with. That doesn't mean that we shouldn't ask whether Bitcoin could use even less energy or increase its efficiency – indeed, we turn to that question in the very next paragraph. But progressives should keep in mind just how little energy Bitcoin uses and how green the energy it uses already is.

Most reasonable people will agree that, if all else is equal, it makes sense to use the most energy-efficient machine that will accomplish a given task. You don't have to believe in human-made climate change to subscribe to this viewpoint. You just have to agree that being wasteful is bad. Notice I'm not passing a judgment about what uses of electricity are wasteful and which aren't. Of course, this book is my attempt to convince progressives that the (small) amount of energy it takes to secure the Bitcoin network is exactly the kind of technology you *should* spend energy on. I'm simply saying that if you decide to use electricity to accomplish something, you should try to use the energy as efficiently as possible.

One way then to think about energy efficiency is to answer some personal questions. Is the refrigerator in your kitchen the most energy-efficient refrigerator currently available on the market? What about your clothes dryer? What about every other appliance in your home? It is likely that you use appliances each day that use electricity inefficiently compared to the latest available version on the market. If your TV is more than 6 months old, there is currently one you can buy that will do the same job and use less electricity. This is because technology is deflationary – we should expect to have more energy-efficient products available to us over time. Technology constantly creates more energy-efficient refrigerators, clothes dryers, TVs – and Bitcoin mining ASICs.

We have already established that using computing power to secure the Bitcoin network is important and valuable work and the electricity that Bitcoin mining uses is predominantly green and incentivized to become even more so over time. But are Bitcoin mining machines efficient in doing the important work they are meant to do? Like refrigerators, the answer is yes – and increasingly so over time. The difference is that while individual consumers are not incentivized to swap out major appliances just because a slightly more efficient model has come to market, the same (happily) cannot be said for Bitcoin miners.

In 2013, the Bitcoin hardware company Bitmain released its first ASIC (called the Antminer S1).[35] This machine represented a huge leap forward in efficiency for mining Bitcoin. At that time, most Bitcoin mining was done on personal computers or by using high-powered graphics cards that were not designed specifically for the purpose of mining Bitcoin. With the release of the S1, Bitcoin mining suddenly became more streamlined and efficient, and by using this new application-specific machine, miners were now using electricity much more efficiently – about 500 million hashes per joule. This is a measurement of a machine's efficiency because it identifies how much computing power (hashes) are being contributed to the network per unit (joule) of energy.[36] When the Antminer S1 was released the leading CPUs and GPUs being used to secure the Bitcoin network generally registered less than 2 million hashes per joule.[37] With one invention, Bitcoin mining efficiency increased all at once by a factor of 250.

Miners quickly started converting their operations to run on ASICs. Because the machines were more powerful, they contributed more hash power to secure the network. This, in turn, meant miners received a greater share of the "block reward" that incentivized Bitcoin mining. But the increased power is not why the industry gravitated to ASICs – it was the efficiency of the new machines. As was noted above, nearly 100% of the marginal cost to mine Bitcoin is the cost of energy. The exciting thing about the Antminer S1 wasn't that it was more powerful – it was that it was more efficient. These new machines produced dramatically more hashing power per unit of energy than the computers that were previously being used, and it wasn't even close. Because competition to mine Bitcoin is so intense and the margins are so thin, it suddenly didn't make any sense to use the less efficient machines, and CPU and GPU mining disappeared almost immediately. In 2013, Bitcoin became greener because technology improved in a way that aligned with Bitcoin's built-in incentives.

And the story continues today. Like all technology, the efficiency of Bitcoin mining continues to improve. But unlike most technologies, the folks using electricity to mine Bitcoin are constantly incentivized to upgrade to the most efficient machines. How efficiently a miner uses electricity to secure the Bitcoin network correlates almost perfectly with how much profit they will make. Since 2013, every iteration of an ASIC without exception has been significantly more efficient than the last. In a continuous process we find that older, less efficient machines are retired as they become unprofitable, with the efficiency of the entire system continually improving. At the time of writing the most recent and most efficient ASIC released by Bitmain is called the Antminer S19 XP. In less than a decade the efficiency of the leading-edge Bitcoin mining machine has increased from the Antminer's S1

500 million hashes per joule to over 45 billion hashes per joule with the Antminer S19 XP – an almost 100 times greater increase in computing efficiency.[38]

To be clear, not all Bitcoin miners are compelled to transition to the newest most efficient machines immediately because there are upfront capital investments to purchase the hardware. But over time the older machines simply can't keep up. To profitably use a less efficient ASIC you need to have access to very cheap electricity, and you only get access to very cheap electricity if you are a nonrival consumer of that energy. Embedded therefore within the entire system is an overarching incentivized commitment to overall efficiency. In fact, according to the Bitcoin Mining Council, overall efficiency in the network improved by almost 25% last year.[39] Such improvements in efficiency represent a continuation of a long trend that seems poised to continue.

Today it is uncommon for any large-scale mining operation to use machines that are more than a couple of years old. The Antminer S9 was released in 2017 with an efficiency of about 10 billion hashes per joule. This machine currently sits on the edge of profitability and can only be used with the cheapest, least in-demand electricity. Most companies are using machines like the Antminer S19, which was released in May 2020.

We have seen that Bitcoin is an important use of energy because that energy secures the first reliable, peer-to-peer, open, fair, and secure form of money that can't be confiscated, banned, or censored. Using energy for this purpose is incredibly important to our society and to our global future. We have also seen that Bitcoin's energy use is trending green and is incentivized to continue in that direction. That energy use is already much greener than most industries and Bitcoin miners are often nonrival consumers of electricity. And we have seen that Bitcoin mining uses a tiny sliver of the world's electricity while the machines used to mine Bitcoin are orders of magnitude more efficient than they were even a few years ago. That efficiency will continue to improve and, importantly, miners will be incentivized to transition to the newest most efficient machines over time.

All of this together tells us pretty clearly that Bitcoin isn't harming the environment like we have been told. But the most important argument lies ahead. Because Bitcoin isn't just neutral toward the environment – it actually helps in very interesting ways that most people don't get to read about.

Bitcoin, Consumerism, and the Environment

At the most basic level, Bitcoin has a real chance to demonetize gold and reduce the massively destructive environmental impacts of the gold mining process.[40] This would be a huge win for the planet, but it is far from the most impactful effect Bitcoin will have on the environment. There is a growing consciousness and concern among many on the left about our society's culture of consumerism. It's easy enough to find groups online that will give tips to be more "anti-consumerist" or offer up examples of greed and wastefulness in any nook or cranny one might look. The most egregious forms of decadent consumerism and waste are highlighted on websites devoted to documenting and lamenting the "late-stage capitalism" we are currently living through. These ideas all align nicely with the "Degrowth Movement" that looks to protect the environment through much the same lens and pushes back against our society's endless need to consume and grow the economy.

It is easy to pin such consumerism and waste on our human faults – our need to want more and want it immediately. We are addicted to our phones, plastic widgets, and embarrassing portions at restaurants – just to cite a few examples – and brain chemistry is where part of the blame lies. But there are systems at work that make the problem worse and it is important to understand them. All the things you buy today, from phones and refrigerators to your car, are built with planned obsolescence in mind, which means that they are intentionally designed to break or become obsolete and require replacing. This is so you will buy more phones, refrigerators, and cars and the economy will keep growing. This wasn't the case 100 years ago, but today you've undoubtedly noticed that most of the things you purchase are simply easier to replace than repair. This is why there exists an entire "Right to Repair" movement that corporations have fought tooth and nail to undermine.[41] They make sure that rather than fix the phone/refrigerator/car you wind up buying a new one.

All of this planned obsolescence and consumption is tied to the fact that we have been fed a myth that a healthy economy needs inflation. This is a topic I discuss at length in Chapter 6, but for our purposes here I simply want to point out that we are fed this myth because the US government needs inflation. The current American debt is over $30 trillion and growing,[42] representing about 130% of national GDP. A few short years ago the idea that the debt would reach 100% of GDP was seen as a crisis point.[43] The only way that the United States government can keep the system running is to roll over the debt into new loans (notes, bills, bonds) whenever it's time to pay the old ones and by devaluing the currency so that the "real" burden of the debt is reduced as the "nominal" burden grows. It's also the case that genuine appetite for buying America's debt has been steadily decreasing in recent years such that now the Federal Reserve must buy a majority of the new treasury bills and bonds themselves.[44] These purchases also help to keep interest rates artificially low, making it easier for the government to pay off its debt by keeping its interest payments in check.

There's a name for using money from new investors to pay off old investors within a system that is mathematically unsustainable: it's called a Ponzi Scheme.

What are the government's options when it comes to dealing with debt? Its choices are to do a "hard" default by simply not paying its debts or a "soft" default by printing money to pay its debts and, in turn, debasing the money supply. This debasement is actually the inflation that the government needs. The government will eventually pay off the

$30 trillion it currently owes. But by then $30 trillion won't have the same purchasing power as it does today; it will have been debased. All the while, the debasement requires having an economy made of companies that must always grow, no matter what. Otherwise the debt and inflation can't be supported.

If you stop to think about why all this consumerism, inflation, and "no matter what" growth feels so wrong, you'll quickly arrive at an answer: because it isn't natural. We live in a deflationary world. There is no doubt that technology should be making everything around us cheaper, more efficient, and abundant. This is a point made powerfully by Jeff Booth in his book *The Price of Tomorrow*. Prices should go down as a result and products should last longer. People should have what they need. And like the natural trends technology creates within our economy, Bitcoin is deflationary. This simply means that the purchasing power of bitcoin goes up over time because the supply of bitcoin is limited. But the government – which happens to have a monopoly on money creation – is printing money to fight against deflation that would otherwise be baked into the cake. In fact, since the Federal Reserve (the agency responsible for maintaining stable prices) was created in 1913, the purchasing power of one US dollar has shrunk to the 1913 equivalent of 3 cents.[45] In short, the government creates an inflationary world that causes many of the problems we see within our economic system – including consumerism.[46]

What happens when your possessions break by design and the dollar in your hand is becoming worthless? You do the smart thing: trade that melting money for the things you need. You consume. What do you do when interest rates are artificially suppressed? You do the smart thing: you borrow cheap money to buy the things you want. You consume. The entire system, from the ground up, is designed to get you and everyone you know buying more and more every year. And if you truly care about the environment, that should be pretty scary.

Bitcoin allows people to buy the things they need – shelter, food, and transportation. But because it is deflationary, it encourages people to think before they buy the things they want. Because the purchasing power of bitcoin goes up over time, it implicitly forces people to think before purchasing a new TV or an updated phone. The Bitcoin system incentivizes individuals to save, plan ahead, and buy only the things they truly need or want.

This planning ahead and saving for what you may need in the future is what economists call *lowering your time preference*. This is good for the environment because people who use Bitcoin have a low time preference and do not consume simply because they are incentivized to do so. By adopting Bitcoin, we could turn the swelling tide of needing to buy more stuff year after year. We could create an economy based on providing the goods and services that people actually need and want as opposed to an economy that is based on simply growing exponentially forever. This is essential for the sake of the planet and its finite resources.

Lower time preferences are critical for helping the environment in another fundamental way. To the chagrin of many climate activists, it has been clear for decades that politicians and industry leaders think about the environment in four year chunks, each doing only what is necessary until the next election cycle. This is no way to stave off a catastrophe that is centuries in the making. We need long-term thinking to solve this problem – decade-long plans and commitments that are designed to address human-made climate change. We need what Roman Krznaric calls in his book *The Good Ancestor* "Cathedral Thinking" – the kind of long-term thinking that allows humans to engage with projects and policies that span more than a lifetime. Throughout history, humans have worked on valued, important projects that last generations. Consider the Ulm Minster, an impressively ornate building that is currently the tallest church in the world. It took over 500 years to complete, with construction lasting between 1377 and 1890.[47] The work our civilization does to combat climate change may be another example we look back on in half a millennium. But for that to happen, we may need a whole lot of progressives using Bitcoin and developing very low time preferences.

The Path Toward a Negative Carbon Footprint

The world has set out ambitious emissions targets to combat global climate change. Meeting these targets requires that we electrify more of the things we use and use renewable sources to produce the electricity we need. If progressives want to help the environment, they shouldn't moralize about the use of energy but influence how the energy is created. Using electricity does not produce carbon. Creating it does – sometimes.

Energy companies can see the future and are vying for the best real estate on which they can develop solar or wind electricity production in the future. But one challenge is that there are no customers demanding electricity right now. Bitcoin can step in to monetize that infrastructure and act as a buyer of first resort for that electricity. In fact, without Bitcoin, it is difficult or impossible to imagine building out renewable infrastructure in a profitable way. Because renewable sources of energy are intermittent, it is necessary to overbuild these sources, which is expensive and difficult to do without a stable base load of demand. But bitcoin miners are providing the stable base load needed for new renewable projects.[48]

Humans can get pretty creative when they are motivated and Bitcoin miners are no exception. In the search for low-cost electricity, Bitcoin miners have developed methods to power their machines that synergize beautifully with reducing the amount of greenhouse gases in the atmosphere. The fundamental infrastructure of Bitcoin mining allows it to easily locate near stranded energy sources – a location that makes it difficult to transport the electricity to other paying customers. Because the machines are small and mobile, mining operations are motivated to pick up and move to where the cheapest energy is. It could be as easy as a single storage container full of ASICs dropped off right next to the power source – and it's a solution that can easily be scaled up and down depending on conditions on the ground.

Setting up an operation to create completely clean energy (with wind, solar, or hydro) that no one else is demanding is just step one. Step two is getting that energy to people who need and want it. Bitcoin bridges the gap between step one and step two by taking that cheap and negatively priced energy and immediately turning it into money. Bitcoin miners are eager to provide a steady but adjustable base load demand for renewable sources of energy as the newly produced energy comes online.

This point is extremely important. Bitcoin can be a robust customer for fledgling renewable power generation companies who don't yet have the demand needed to support the building of green energy infrastructure. Today there are hydroelectric, wind, solar, and geothermal energy projects that were made possible only because Bitcoin miners were willing to step in and support the production of that energy and monetize it at a time and place when no one else would or could.[49]

And this is a scalable solution that can be applied anywhere in the world. It is expensive to build the necessary infrastructure for renewable energy. In most cases, that new energy is being generated in locations without sufficient demand for it, meaning it might take years to recoup the capital outlay. But even intermittent Bitcoin mining of that newly generated energy means it can be immediately monetized, thereby supporting the build-out of cheap, green energy sources. These types of projects are already underway around the world in places like Costa Rica,[50] Kenya,[51] and Australia.[52] The result is that more global electricity is being produced today from green sources than would be if Bitcoin did not exist.

Nor is this just a temporary solution till demand catches up to production. We can see concrete evidence of energy-producing companies thinking hard about ways to incorporate Bitcoin mining into their operations at the outset – to both stabilize demand, but also to monetize stranded, low-demand energy.[53] It's hard to imagine that any profit-seeking company creating energy will not have some component of Bitcoin mining to supplement revenue and serve as a direct demand response stabilizing force. In the future, there is a very good chance that the line between a Bitcoin mining company and an energy production company may be completely blurred.

Bitcoin may not be a silver bullet that solves all of the difficulties with renewable energy sources, but there are lots of innovative and exciting ideas involving Bitcoin that can help make a truly green grid a likelihood in the medium term. For example, there are several well-known examples of Bitcoin mining being used in locations where oil companies flare natural gas as part of the oil extraction process. Such a process is wasteful and polluting, but it is a widespread practice across the industry, as the challenge of productively using this natural gas is well documented. The World Bank described the difficulties with using this stranded natural gas:

> *In many cases, oil fields are located in remote and inaccessible places. These sites are hard to access, and they may not produce consistent or large volumes of associated gas that operators can use. This can make it logistically and economically challenging to transport associated gas to where it can be processed and utilized.*[54]

Because it costs too much to capture or move the gas for a different use case, oil companies simply burn the gas on location, a process that does not harness its energy but does create air pollution. The image that comes to mind of an oil field littered with dozens of burning pipes pumping carbon into the atmosphere is exactly right. Those flames are simply wasted resources.

But "remote and inaccessible places" or inconsistent or small volumes of gas are not a problem for Bitcoin miners. They are more than willing to drop off a very portable container of ASICs and mine Bitcoin with gas that would have been burned off for no purpose. Using the gas to mine Bitcoin creates less pollution[55] and monetizes a previously wasted form of energy. Exxon currently has such a pilot program in North Dakota and is exploring options to expand the program to Alaska, Nigeria, Argentina, Guyana, and Germany.[56]

I think it's inarguably good for the environment when oil companies use natural gas that they would have otherwise wasted to mine Bitcoin. But even more impressive are companies like Vespene Energy[57] that have committed themselves to using the methane naturally produced in landfills to create energy and mine Bitcoin.

Methane is one of the most harmful greenhouse gases and all landfills across the world produce methane as a natural byproduct of trash decomposing within them. In a large number of cases, this methane cannot be used and is simply released into the atmosphere with little or no mitigation. Much like gas flaring in oil fields, Vespene Energy looks to change the face of landfills by tapping into and monetizing the naturally produced methane as a resource. Unsurprisingly, because bitcoin mining is location agnostic and requires cheap electricity, Bitcoin is uniquely positioned to do this work and monetize previously wasted energy. It is quite literally saving the environment and turning trash into money.

The incentives involved in this process are key. When I spoke to the co-founder and CEO of Vespene Energy, Adam Wright, he explained that landfills are highly regulated and already required to mitigate methane. Unfortunately, many do not. The infrastructure costs to do so are prohibitive and the EPA has a hard time enforcing the regulations for landfills all across the country. In many cases, the landfill operators would rather pay the fine if they are found out than invest millions of dollars in the required infrastructure to mitigate methane and help the environment. But Bitcoin changes the equation. As Adam explained, it is the carrot and not the stick that gets the landfill operators that he talks to excited about mitigating methane. Not only does Bitcoin mining on a landfill impose fewer infrastructure costs, but it can also incentivize the build-out of electric capacity to operate the landfill and even charge a future fleet of electric vehicles used on site.

Vespene's model is intriguing because they truly do partner with the local operators of these landfills. By entering into a profit-sharing agreement with local municipalities, the company is providing a public service by mitigating the methane released into the atmosphere while also giving back to the local community. But don't take my word for it. The method Vespene Energy employs was positively cited in the OSTP White House report about the implications of digital asset mining on energy and the climate. Released in September 2022, the report stated, "mining operations that capture vented methane to produce electricity can yield positive results for the climate."[58] The first pilot site started operating in 2023 with the potential to expand into hundreds of other locations all across the country and beyond.

Of course this isn't the end of the story. Enterprising individuals and companies will continue to come up with innovative ideas that support both Bitcoin mining and renewable, green energy. For example, there is a great deal of excitement around the potential in Ocean Thermal Energy Conversion (OTEC). Some environmentalists hope to generate clean sustainable energy using temperature differentials in the ocean. Not only is Bitcoin well suited to bootstrap this technology, but the recirculated heat from Bitcoin mining synergistically aids the process, making it more efficient.

Since we know that Bitcoin mining can help today with our climate crisis, I believe we are morally obligated to deploy the tools we have right now. It would be wrong for progressives to wait for "better technology" or regulations that might one day work. The incentives to engage in this type of innovation exist right now. Wasted, stranded and excess green energy exists, and mining Bitcoin is uniquely qualified to take advantage of it, promoting the rollout of more green energy by both supplementing revenue for new builds and stabilizing intermittent sources.

How We Decide to Keep Score

I will end this chapter with a brief discussion of how we decide to track the energy use of Bitcoin and why a complete understanding of "proof of work" is important to measure it correctly. When a Bitcoin miner is successful in their guess and check routine for validating a block of transactions, they have done an important service for the Bitcoin network and the users initiating those transactions. The miner has also issued new bitcoin when they are given the reward for that block. To do all this the miner needed to expend real-world energy. But by using that energy to validate a block, the miner has done a lot more than confirm a few thousand transactions and pocketed some freshly minted bitcoin. They have protected the entire history of Bitcoin transactions by ossifying the blockchain and protecting the consensus-built state of Bitcoin's public ledger.

We use the term blockchain (Satoshi called it a "timechain") because the blocks are chained together using secure cryptographic hashes. These links in the chain cannot be undone. This means that by appending a block to the blockchain, you are not just validating the transactions in a particular block (usually a couple thousand transactions), but you are also validating every transaction that exists in every block before it. This is why Bitcoin's blockchain is considered "immutable." Nobody can go back and change the public record of transactions unless they were to gain 51% of the computing power protecting the Bitcoin network, which we have already argued is practically impossible. The job of keeping track of who has what has traditionally been entrusted to centralized banks. Their method of recording entries in a ledger seems very efficient but is fraught with risks and compromise. Replacing this system with an open, public, and immutable ledger requires energy. In other words, by using energy we get to sidestep the issue of having to trust banks to correctly manage the money we use.

Because Bitcoin does all of this, the proper way to think about Bitcoin's energy use is not to add up all the electricity used to add a particular block and assign it proportionally to the transactions contained within it. Nor is it to add up all the electricity and assign it to the newly minted bitcoin. The energy used to mine any given block on the blockchain is a "cost" that should be attributed to the entire network because all bitcoin and all transactions are protected by the work that went into the latest block. Although critics of Bitcoin are quick to perform eye-catching and headline-worthy calculations that assign total energy used by individual transactions, the problem is that at a fundamental level such calculations misrepresent how Bitcoin functions.

Troy Cross is an environmentalist and a leading voice within the Bitcoin community. He has promoted the proportional method for accounting for Bitcoin's energy use because it is more fair and accurate. He has also developed an important framework for individuals to account for and reduce their carbon footprint as it relates to the bitcoin they own. I had a chance to talk to Troy about his approach which stems from the observation that the entirety of Bitcoin's energy is used to protect the entirety of the Bitcoin network. As Troy explained, "anyone wishing to make their personal stack of bitcoin 'green' simply has to contribute to the overall mining hash power using a green energy source in proportion to how much bitcoin they own."[59] It turns out to be a simple equation as the following example illustrates. If you are an environmentalist who owns 1% of all bitcoin, you simply have to contribute 1% of all hashing power used to mine Bitcoin in a green way. That's it: there is no carbon footprint on your holdings of bitcoin because the energy used to protect your stack is generated sustainably.

It is completely possible an individual could decide to sustainably mine in proportion to their holdings. A single ASIC plugged into a renewable source would likely cover a typical person's bitcoin savings. But Troy Cross wants to make it even easier for people to do the right thing. Recently he has been working with various partners to bring an easy-to-use financial instrument to market. This instrument will allow environmentally conscious individuals to purchase bitcoin that is automatically bundled with sustainably sourced hash power, making the overall carbon footprint of that Bitcoin zero. This is hard work and there are regulatory hurdles to overcome, but this project and many others like it will help shape how progressives interact with the most sound money asset the world has ever known.

To wrap up this very heavy but important chapter, here are some important points to keep in mind:

1. Bitcoin's energy usage is relatively small but also very important to society.
2. Bitcoin's energy usage is already green and incentivized to get greener and more efficient over time.
3. Bitcoin has the potential to mitigate the current trend of hyper-consumerism that harms the environment.
4. Bitcoin incentivizes the build-out of green energy by monetizing and stabilizing intermittent sources.
5. Bitcoin can achieve a negative carbon footprint by mitigating methane from landfills and other sources.
6. There is nothing stopping a Bitcoiner from ensuring their own personal stack of bitcoin is completely green and carbon-free.

Chapter 4: Bitcoin vs. the Banks

Chancellor on the Brink

In September 2011 a grassroots effort called "Occupy Wall Street" attempted to do just that as a protest against the corrupt and exploitative nature of corporations and banks. Tents popped up, signs were made, and marches were marched. Occupy was a populist movement that gained attention and supporters across the globe. Only a few years before, the Great Financial Crisis rocked the world and threatened the entire interwoven global economy. It was a scary time when everyone became familiar with the term "too big to fail" and had to ponder why exactly the government would bail out the very banks that took the unwise risks in the first place. In the end, the Occupy movement did bring some attention to the problem, but failed to achieve much else of substance.

But this isn't a story about the successes and failures of Occupy Wall Street. This is a story about how the people occupying Wall Street spoke to each other. Shortly after Occupy started, the NYPD started enforcing a rule that prohibited the use of megaphones at the protest.[60] This change in policy was an attempt to kneecap the ability of peacefully assembled protesters to communicate and organize themselves. It is important to understand that the folks protesting in the Occupy movement did not have a hierarchical structure with a centralized authority figure or a unified strategy. This was a flat organization of peers that needed to communicate information and establish consensus about what actions the group should take next. There were no leaders but a large group of people.[61] Taking away the megaphones made it nearly impossible for members to communicate. But the protesters had an impressive solution.

Whenever information needed to be communicated or a consensus reached, the community of protesters worked together. To start, one person would yell a single sentence toward the collection of people. And wait. Everybody who could hear that sentence would repeat the sentence together in a rhythmic chant that would allow each person to amplify the voice of the person next to them. After a full beat, the next group farther away would chant the sentence again. The process would continue in waves through the throng of people until the information spread to each and every member of the crowd. The original speaker would then proceed to the next sentence.

Communicating to thousands of people in this way is painstaking and horribly inefficient. Unfortunately, the prohibition on voice amplifying devices made it necessary. But they nevertheless managed to communicate, offering an inspirational image of a committed group of people working together to overcome an obstacle that was created for the sole purpose of squashing their ability to peacefully assemble. The teamwork and deep commitment to the community still give me chills when I think about it. It is unlikely many of the protesters realized it at the time, but their solution was not just good teamwork. It was modeled after Bitcoin.

The main function of a Bitcoin node is to communicate to other nodes the latest information about valid blocks on the blockchain. This is done in a decentralized way with nodes spread across the entire globe. This network of nodes is a non-hierarchical collection of peers. There are no privileged nodes, and all the information gets spread from node to node in an ever-expanding wave spreading across the entire Bitcoin network. When a node receives a block from one of its neighbors, it validates the block and then broadcasts the information for that new block to any node that is connected to it. Then those nodes repeat the process. Eventually all nodes in the network have an updated version of the blockchain and a *consensus* has been reached about the state of the blockchain. The process then repeats itself when the next block is found.

The analogy to the Occupy protesters is important. It takes extra time and effort to communicate information this way, but it is worth it if you want to preserve certain features. The Occupy movement was notable for its non-hierarchical design and decentralization. If any single protester were to be nabbed by the police, the message would still spread. There was no single point of failure. If the police wanted to stop the messages, they would have to eliminate the entire protest down to the last person or perhaps infiltrate the group undercover at an enormous scale and start chanting the wrong sentences. For obvious reasons, neither option would have been practical or possible.

Bitcoin works the same way. There is no leader. There is no one person to arrest or to silence. The information will spread through the network because Bitcoin is a collection of peers operating in a decentralized way. Stopping the information from being spread through these nodes is not practical or possible. To do so, you would have to shut down every single node or have enough computing power to dominate the network with inaccurate information. But the network of nodes is a hydra that can't be squashed. In a very real and important sense, this is exactly what Bitcoin is: an unstoppable monetary technology for everyone in the world.

There is even some evidence that Satoshi Nakamoto, whoever they were, would have sympathized with the Occupy Wall Street protesters that were using their own version of the Bitcoin consensus mechanism. When Satoshi validated the first block (often called the "genesis block"), they embedded in the code the following phrase: "Chancellor on the brink of second bailout for banks." This was the headline appearing on the front page of the *Times of London* on January 3, 2009. The choice to include the headline was much more than a timestamp. "Chancellor on the brink" was a message about Bitcoin's significance directly from Bitcoin's inventor forever enshrined in the very origin of the immutable blockchain. The message was a specific one of concern about the relationship between the government and banks. Just like Occupy Wall Street, Bitcoin was from its very inception also a protest against banks – and Satoshi's wariness about how banks and the government interact remains valid even today.

Banks' Debilitating Addiction to Risk

It is well documented[62] that in the run-up to the Great Financial Crisis, investment banks took on riskier methods to chase yield (i.e., larger profits). These risky bets primarily manifested in the form of now infamous and opaque mortgage-backed securities, credit default swaps, and collateralized debt obligations. It's beyond the scope of this book to fully document these complicated financial instruments and how they led to the whole house of cards imploding, but a decade later the poor decisions of the banks are more fully understood and it should be easy to find resources on the topic for those wishing to learn.

All things being equal, striking a balance between risk and reward is fundamental to investing, and there is nothing wrong with taking on risk. In theory, those taking greater risks should be rewarded with the potential for earning higher returns, as they also run the risk of greater losses. But it is important to recognize that there were some dangerous aspects of this particular shift toward making riskier bets that doomed the entire economy, and for those that knew enough to look for them, there were plenty of red flags.[63]

For most of the 20th century, investment banks were separated by law from commercial banks to help protect depositors' money. The original separation of these two types of banks was a product of the Great Depression and was made formal when the Glass-Steagall Act was signed into law in 1933 by President Roosevelt. This changed when that law was repealed under President Clinton in 1999. The repeal of Glass-Steagall allowed banks to take on riskier bets in a way that now intersected with the money of depositors they were charged to protect.

For the first time since the Great Depression, banks were free to make risky investments that put depositors' assets at risk without their customers having an understanding or a voice in how the bank operated. In 2006, it would have been difficult to grasp exactly how one's savings account was tied to an abstract financial instrument like a collateralized debt obligation that existed on the balance sheet of the same bank.

By 2006, the banking sector had become so intertwined that counterparty risk existed everywhere. Counterparty risk is simply a fancy way of saying that if one bank were to experience financial trouble, it would affect other banks in ways that depositors had no way of understanding. Customers usually aren't aware of this, but it is not uncommon for banks to loan money to one another on a short-term basis – even for just 24 hours – to help cover needed liquidity. This is the way banks handle shorter-term fluctuations in the amount of cash they have on hand. Imagine at the end of the day Bank A looks at their balance sheet and they have an extra few million in cash that they don't want to leave lying around not earning yield. At the same time, Bank B looks at its balance sheet and notices that they are a few million dollars short on cash, but they still need to open its doors tomorrow morning. In this case Bank A might loan Bank B a few million dollars for a day to cover their shortfall, and the loans are usually collateralized by assets the borrowing bank has on hand.

This collection of banks offering these short-term and usually low-risk loans is referred to as the "Repo Market," as there is an agreement to repurchase the asset after a specified time when the liquidity is no longer needed. The entire banking system depends on the Repo Market to provide the needed liquidity so banks can open their doors each morning, and the Repo Market – which averages over $4 trillion in loans every day[64] – depends on banks trusting each other.

In 2008 we all got to see what happens when banks stop trusting each other. The assets being offered up for collateral – the complicated opaque financial instruments I mentioned above – were suddenly not so pristine, and banks started to refuse to loan to other institutions whose assets they thought posed too great a risk. In quick succession, this sort of attitude spreads, and illiquid banks are forced to sell their assets instead of taking out temporary loans against them. When many banks do this at the same time, the price of those assets starts to fall due to supply and demand. In this situation, stressed banks were forced to sell what they could, not what they wanted to. It became clear that some of these banks, whose balance sheets were propped up by the overvalued (i.e., "troubled") assets, were not just illiquid but in fact insolvent.

Reasonable people might easily conclude that insolvent banks should go out of business. If the bets it made don't pan out, it makes sense for the bank to go under. These banks took a risky chance by putting too much of their balance sheet in fancy financial instruments that most people couldn't understand. It's safe to say the banks didn't even fully understand what they were doing. A decision to let banks go out of business is made a little easier knowing that an individual depositor's funds were insured by the government through the Federal Deposit Insurance Corporation (FDIC).[65]

This is exactly what happened to Lehman Brothers and Bear Stearns, and it caused hardship for their customers, employees, and shareholders. But most of the rest of the banking sector was infamously bailed out by the US government, which purchased "troubled assets" from banks. The government stepped in to buy, at inflated prices, the complicated securities that other banks simply would not touch. The goal was to shore up the balance sheet for these banks and keep them from imploding. This constituted a government bailout for failing banks through what was known as the Troubled Asset Relief Program (TARP). The price tag was steep: $700 billion.[66]

Why did the government bailout some banks and not others? Why did they choose to bail out banks and not the ordinary citizens who were having trouble making their mortgage payments? Why did the government, instead of letting the free market decide winners and losers, choose to bail out anyone at all? You can fill a book with the answers to these questions, and many people have.[67] The very short answer is that banks have a very special relationship with the government and were allowed to grow so big and so interconnected that if dominos kept falling, it was clear they were all going to fall. The very lubricant of our economy – liquidity and easy credit – would dissipate overnight, and the gears of the entire country would grind to a halt. By letting more banks fail, the contagion would spread, and many more financial institutions would also become insolvent. In turn, the entire economy would have crashed.

Letting that happen would have been horrible; there would have been a terrible global recession and many millions of people would have struggled to make ends meet. On the other hand, it would have cleared out risky, nonprofitable banks and businesses and allowed responsible businesses to survive. In the end, we would have recovered and learned valuable lessons about risk, contagion, and implementing safeguards for the economy. But allowing that pain to occur is no way to get elected, so the government decided to pump money into an industry that systematically bent and manipulated the rules for their own profit.

One might be tempted to call such policies socialism for the banks, but it's actually much worse. The profits were privatized while only the losses were socialized. The $31 billion in risky, troubled assets now belonged on the government's balance sheet, while the banks – with their newly pristine balance sheets – were able to carry on as normal, including obscene bonuses for bank executives. To make matters worse, the fundamental reason for the bailouts was to provide liquidity to the system and encourage the banks to lend so the economy could function. Instead, the banks ended up using this money to issue dividends to shareholders and drive up their stock prices through a series of stock buybacks.[68]

There haven't been any fundamental changes since 2008. The relationship between big banks and the government is still quite cozy. The government is still willing to step in during other liquidity crises, like the one that quietly rattled the Repo Markets in 2019.[69] Traditional economists will say that there is no alternative to the government stepping in and stabilizing the system for the benefit of the same wealthy and reckless people that destabilized it in the first place. And it is no surprise to learn how quickly the government can mobilize and how effective its actions can be when wealthy people are in danger of losing money.

"Chancellor on the brink..." was the UK version of this story that Satoshi referenced in the genesis block. This is exactly the type of thing that gets people occupying Wall Street – and is exactly the type of thing that motivated a monetary revolution like Bitcoin.

The Former Monopoly on Money Creation

Understanding how banks control monetary policy in the United States and around the world is crucial for understanding crises like the Great Depression or the Great Financial Crisis. But it's also crucial for understanding ordinary financial matters. You may not think it affects your everyday life, but it does. Every day.

As we will soon see, Bitcoin's monetary policy is hard coded for the next 10,000 years or more. Unfortunately, the current system run by politicians and central banks is not so tidy. Around the world, countless currencies have collapsed and needed hard resets to the severe detriment of the citizens using that currency. In some cases, countries have been forced into becoming dollarized, completely giving up control of their monetary policies. The best of the bunch, America, hasn't done a great job either.

America's central bank is called the Federal Reserve and it is exclusively responsible for controlling the monetary policy of the United States. Despite its purposefully misleading name, the Federal Reserve is in fact a private bank. Though there is some oversight by elected officials, the Federal Reserve is not a part of the United States government. Proponents of the Federal Reserve system will argue that the dynamic nature of its monetary policy allows for flexibility. The monetary supply can be adjusted to react to realities on the ground and promote economic growth or counteract economic downturn. However, it is worth asking if this is actually what happens in practice. In my lifetime I have seen the monetary policy in the United States prop up speculative bubbles in the stock market, encourage risky behavior by banks, and set monetary policy that supports wealthy individuals over regular people. The entire system is entangled in politics which encourages short-term planning like avoiding downturns during an election year. This is no way to run a monetary policy in which people need to plan and make economic decisions.

So how does it work? In its privileged position as a central bank, the Federal Reserve sets interest rates that banks use to lend to one another. These interest rates propagate through the system and affect how much it costs to borrow money for any purpose. In essence, the Federal Reserve sets the cost of money. When interest rates are low, money is cheap, more borrowing occurs and economic activity picks up. In the current system, when money is borrowed, it is created. The entire economy is supercharged by debt and the Federal Reserve gets to decide how much that debt costs. It is a blunt instrument. The Federal Reserve understands by lowering interest rates, the money supply will generally increase, but it doesn't exactly know by how much, when, or where that increase will occur. The dynamic, flexible, and responsive Federal Reserve that is supposed to fine-tune our world's economic ups and downs is more like a surgeon operating while wearing oven mitts.

When the United States was on a gold standard, there was less of a need for a central bank to control the money supply, since the dollar was pegged to a scarce, hard commodity. Since the 1970s the Federal Reserve has been operating under a dual mandate: ensure price stability and protect full employment. In other words, the Federal Reserve is expected to keep inflation under control (price stability) and alleviate any economic downturns (full employment). Many people today think that the Federal Reserve acts with a third mandate, which is to protect the value of assets like equities in the stock market. This is evidenced by the fact that the Federal Reserve has quickly reversed decisions about monetary policy if the stock market goes down by too much.[70]

One of the arguments against having human beings in charge of monetary policy is the short-term pain avoidance of letting the economy reset or go through contractions as part of a normal and healthy business cycle. Economic growth is fueled by debt and tends to happen when money is cheap. By not allowing the economy to occasionally retract, we don't allow the mechanics of capitalism to pick winners and losers within the economy. An economic contraction forces unprofitable businesses to change their models or go out of business, making room for more valuable enterprises. This is generally known as creative destruction. Because the Federal Reserve's monetary policy is focused on short-term metrics and intertwined with politics, the Fed tends to make cheap money available for too long. Instead of normal business cycles expanding and contracting, it seems that the goal is to keep the foot on the accelerator until something breaks. This is pretty much the only thing we've seen the Fed do for the past 20 years.

The Complicated Game of Monetary Policy

Unsurprisingly, to fully implement this illusion of a forever booming economy, the Federal Reserve wasn't content to just dial interest rates up and down. So we have seen them develop some new arrows for their quiver. As a result of the 2008 financial crisis, the Federal Reserve cut short-term interest rates to zero, making it impossible to stimulate the economy with further cuts. To deal with this reality, the Fed pursued a new tool, opaquely called "Quantitative Easing," often referred to as "QE." QE was a decision by the Federal Reserve to purchase financial assets like government bonds, mortgage-backed securities, and even stocks.[71] The effect was the ability to introduce more money into the system and to exert control on the interest rates of longer-term debt instruments. Previously the Fed only had direct control over short-term interest rates. QE was a powerful new tool for the Federal Reserve that allowed them to spend into a crisis without limit. This includes the Fed directly purchasing government debt with no functional upper bound.

When QE was first implemented, it was described as a temporary emergency action to respond to a financial crisis.[72] But every attempt to taper or reduce QE since its inception has been met with turmoil in asset markets and a reversal by the Federal Reserve. Nor have the emergencies stopped coming: the financial crisis of 2008 resulted in the Federal Reserve using QE to grow its balance sheet by about $1 trillion. About a decade later, the economic crisis from Covid in 2020 resulted in the Fed's balance sheet increasing by about $5 trillion. In fact, since the new practice of QE was implemented in 2008, the total assets on the Federal Reserve balance sheet increased from $900 million to almost $8.9 trillion in 2022.[73] This represents an increase of almost 10,000% – without any reasonable plan to unwind those balances in a way that doesn't crash the entire economy. When the next crisis hits, how large will the QE have to be to meet it?

While QE gets a lot of attention, the Federal Reserve has other tools to affect the monetary policy of the United States. One tool the Federal Reserve has to affect monetary policy is to manipulate the reserve requirement ratio imposed on banks. This is the percentage of deposits that banks are required to secure, while the rest is free to be lent out or invested by the bank. Most adults understand that banks don't keep your actual physical money on the premises. They loan out a portion of it to make a profit. The reserve requirement ratio can be thought of as a balance between safety and stability (high ratio) and encouraging economic activity by providing more loans (low ratio). Traditionally the reserve requirement ratio in the United States was 10%, meaning that banks were free to loan out or invest 90 cents of every dollar depositors gave to them. Depending on your personal risk tolerance, this might seem like a dangerously low number. What if a bank reserved 10% of its deposits and one morning 11% of its depositors showed up expecting their money? That lack of liquidity can lead to some pretty disturbing things.

But in 2020 in the midst of the Covid-19 pandemic, the Federal Reserve changed the 10% reserve requirement ratio, dramatically dropping it to 0%, where it remains at the time of writing.[74] Banks are now free to loan out or invest 100% of the deposits they hold. This is essentially a free pass for banks, who have a track record of being blind toward risk when they see profits, to do things with other people's money without a safety net. A 0% reserve requirement ratio means that banks are encouraged to create as many loans as possible to keep the economy moving, which was the entire point of the Federal Reserve making the change in the first place. Our entire economy, and its rate of growth, is so deeply rooted in debt that a slowdown in lending will bring the entire enterprise grinding to a halt. For the Federal Reserve, an economic slowdown is a bigger risk than giving banks a blank check.

In order to keep the current system running, debt is required to fuel growth. Even a small slowdown could lead to a catastrophic unwinding of that debt. The Federal Reserve has had to engage extreme policies to keep the train going down the tracks. These include wiping out all short-term interest and setting the rates to essentially 0% for most of the time since the 2008 financial crisis. They have had to go to extreme efforts to perform large enough QE by adding to their balance sheet consistently for over a decade. They have completely eliminated the reserve requirement ratio and have not announced any plans to change it. Any one of these measures would have been considered impossible 20 years ago. Now, they are all necessary to keep the entire global economy from imploding. Most people have no idea any of this is going on.

There is one tool left in the toolbox that to date the Fed has resisted using – bringing interest rates into negative territory like the European Central Bank did starting in 2014.[75] A negative interest rate literally means that you must pay to keep your money in the bank. It is an intentional penalty on savings to urge people to consume more in an effort to prop up the economy.

In sum, to fully understand the monetary policy of the United States, professionals spend countless hours watching every move the

Federal Reserve makes and they parse out each syllable of each public statement. The slightest change in wording from one month to the next leads to dramatic reactions in the financial markets. The decisions that the Federal Reserve makes, and its ability to create new financial tools to achieve its goals, makes the entire system hard to predict. This leads to an inability to accurately predict and plan one's economic calculations. The system is hanging on for now, but our fates are tied to a central bank whose decisions are biased, hard to predict, benefit the wealthy, and are only partially effective.

By way of comparison, the monetary system of Bitcoin is easy to understand. When the Bitcoin network started, each block reward representing new money being introduced into the system was 50 bitcoin. That means that starting January 3, 2009, that block reward was produced and awarded every 10 minutes. These block rewards are built into the system and are the only way new bitcoin can be created. The only way to get this reward is to engage in proof of work to protect the entire network. The Bitcoin protocol also specifies that after every 210,000 blocks, or roughly 4 years, the block reward is halved, an event Bitcoiners call the "halvening." The first such halvening occurred in late 2012 when each block reward was reduced to 25 bitcoin. Today, the block reward sits at 6.25 bitcoin per block. These halvings will continue until about the year 2140, at which point all the bitcoin that will ever exist will have been issued. No amount of computer power or hacking expertise will ever be able to change this. The total supply of bitcoin will be 21 million forever.

This is a regular and predictable control of the money supply in the Bitcoin economic system. Those who use Bitcoin are able to make accurate economic calculations based on this issuance schedule indefinitely. There are no politicians or bankers involved. There is no human bias. There are no conflicts of interest to question why Bitcoin has a particular monetary policy. There is no way to game the system. An economic system built entirely on Bitcoin may have ups and downs, but the time, energy, and expertise devoted to predicting what central bankers and politicians will do with their monetary policy will be completely eliminated. It is a transparent, impartial system that has eliminated the short-term goals of politicians so people can decide how to invest, save, and spend their own money.

The various properties of Bitcoin allow ebbs and flows within our economy that do not spiral out of control but instead cyclically fix themselves. An economy based on Bitcoin would have less debt and would rely on markets, not central banks, to set fair interest rates on the cost of money. An economy based on Bitcoin would also not rely on credit and money creation to grow, but would instead grow or contract based on human progress and productivity. And an economy based on Bitcoin would allow for the deflationary effects of technology to increase a person's purchasing power over time instead of debasing the money supply for the illusion that the economy can grow endlessly.

Until 2009, central banks had a monopoly on money creation. The Federal Reserve in particular had a privileged position of controlling the creation of the US dollar, which as we will discuss in Chapter 7 is the global reserve asset. In order to keep the US dollar system afloat, they have needed to abuse that monopoly time and again. Thankfully, there is now an alternative. One day the economic house of cards will fall and the Federal Reserve will run out of tools to prop it up. When that day comes it is important to remember that Bitcoin didn't cause the old system to fail, it just provided us a lens through which to understand both the problem and the solution.

The Tale of Two Banking Systems

The cozy relationship between banks and the US government didn't always exist. The founding fathers were split on the issue and the debate between Thomas Jefferson (wary of powerful banks) and Alexander Hamilton (supporter of powerful banks) is well understood.[76] Jefferson was concerned that strong centralized banks would accumulate wealth and influence and, in turn, would destroy the principles of thrift and hard work by providing too much easy credit. Jefferson made his opinions clear by disparaging the banking industry as "more dangerous than standing armies."[77] Sadly, over the course of the next 200 years, Jefferson's view on banks has been proven correct on innumerable occasions.

The debate about banking's role in US society continued through most of the 19th century. Two attempts at establishing a central bank for the fledgling nation were made in 1791 and 1816. In both cases, the formation of these central banks followed wars (the American Revolution and the War of 1812) that jeopardized the fiscal state of the nation. In each case, the central bank's 20-year charter was allowed to expire as a result of political stalemate.[78]

In fact, for most of America's existence, our political leaders have been divided on the issue of banking, its role in commerce, and how it should intersect with a diverse population and competing constituencies. In Jefferson's mind, the issue of banking was categorized neatly as a conflict between powerful urban interests and those of rural farmers. In hindsight, we can add more nuance to that argument, but the flavor of Jefferson's concern still rings true today. For those that are paying attention, banks always seemed designed to serve the wealthy and connected at the expense of the "little guy." Whenever they are allowed to, banks seem to consolidate wealth and power and serve the people and communities from which they can profit the most.

Today the financial system in the United States underserves a shamefully large proportion of the population. 22% of people in the United States do not have a bank account or are considered underbanked.[79] Not surprisingly, these unbanked and underbanked Americans are disproportionately minorities and low-income individuals. Further, 42% of Americans have no exposure to the stock market.[80] Nor is this a uniquely American phenomenon – the systems in other rich Western countries reflect similar disparities. People without assets or access to banking and reasonable credit are continually at risk. Even a small financial disruption can debilitate their economic stability for life.

Those people who need to rely on cash checking or payday loan companies end up spending exorbitant amounts of money just to access the money they need. In the case of emergencies, those that need financial support the most will pay the highest possible interest rates on the money they borrow. In many cases, these desperate customers aren't paying market rates for their loans, but instead the maximum interest rate allowed by law. In some states the annual percentage rate (APR) is more than 600%.[81]

There is wise financial advice that says "borrow when you can, not when you have to." For people struggling to make ends meet, this advice isn't practical. Affluent individuals are able to make their money work for them, while the people at the lowest income levels end up paying extra just to use the money they have.[82] It is expensive being poor.

This inequity in access is not just a comparison between the poor and the obscenely rich. A lot of people don't realize that a substantial number of Americans struggle just to interact with the financial system every day. Although plenty of people struggle to pay their bills because they don't have enough money, few of us rarely think that struggle is because they don't have access to the financial infrastructure they need. But a quick survey of the financial landscape reveals a wealth of obstacles in their way: physical access to banks, credit scores, documentation, minimum balances, and overdraft fees, just to name a few. Most of the nickel and dime rent-seeking that buoys the bottom line for banks comes at the expense of those that cannot afford it, while the apps, websites, and automatic payment systems wealthier people use to make their financial life frictionless are only available to them because they have a preexisting relationship with a bank. If banks were expected to balance profits with providing a service to communities, this likely wouldn't be a problem, but we don't live in that world. The large national banks have been gradually deregulated over the last few decades and have no incentives to work with and for the people that need them.

Try to think about the most innovative developments brought to you by banks in the last 20 years. What new monetary technologies have the legacy institutions brought to the market? The answer I usually hear is that we are now able to "tap" our credit and debit cards instead of "swiping" them, which is not exactly a monetary innovation.

But there was a major innovation that has flown largely under the radar. Banks have developed and implemented a completely legal innovation called "debt resequencing."[83] There's a good chance you have never heard of debt resequencing, but it should not be surprising that this is the type of thing banks are spending their time coming up with. I'll illustrate the concept with a simplified example.

Suppose you start the day with a balance in your bank account of $100 and you perform the following transactions in this order: debit $20, debit $50, deposit $100, debit $70, debit $50. If these transactions are processed in order, there is enough money in your account to cover each one of these debits. Though you may not have a lot of money, you have acted responsibly and have not spent money you didn't have. But with debt resequencing, banks have a legal right, within some parameters, to process transactions in any order they like. With debt resequencing your original sequence of transactions could be turned into debit $70, debit $50, debit $50, debit $20, and deposit $100. When the transactions are processed in this order, your account will be hit with two separate overdraft fees, and these types of fees are typically about $30 each.[84] Instead of ending with a net $10 balance in the first scenario, now you're in debt by $50. Debt resequencing allows banks to reshuffle transactions to optimize the amount of revenue they receive from fees. About 40% of banks engage in this practice.[85] It is obvious that such practices hurt the people who can least afford it – and just as obvious that these policies intentionally affect those who are least likely to have the time, energy, and resources to understand the policy or fight back.

This type of predatory behavior by the banks targets the most vulnerable members of our society. To anyone who cares about treating human beings with dignity, this should be a disturbing call to action.

The Money in Your Bank Account Isn't Yours

Most Americans do have a bank account and for about a century have trusted their bank to custody their money and keep it safe for them until it is wanted or needed. This trust has been solidified since the Federal government insured deposits through the FDIC and this high level of trust has brought stability to the banking industry and global commerce. But it is important to understand that banks are not in the business of holding onto your money and keeping it safe. You don't even have to finish the movie *It's a Wonderful Life* to learn that lesson. Banks take your money and record it on their balance sheet as an asset. For the most part they are then free to do with that asset whatever they please. To complete the transaction, they record the balance in your account with them as a liability.

The result is that the money in your bank account – the numbers you see on a screen – is no longer yours and it isn't money. It is an IOU for the money you gave the bank. In America today, banks usually make good on those IOUs. But that hasn't always been the case and, unfortunately, there are plenty of places, even today, where the numbers people see on their screens aren't safe.

If you lived in Cyprus in March of 2013, you would have likely woken up one morning to learn your bank was working with your government to seize 6.75% of the money you had saved in your bank account. For any amount over 100,000 Euros, the amount seized would have been 9.9%.[86] This money grab was billed as a one-time tax, but it should be obvious that this is not how taxation works in functioning economies. As you might imagine, such news would normally cause a widespread bank run where individual depositors would rush to withdraw their money from the bank before it was seized. Unsurprisingly, for regular depositors, it wasn't possible to withdraw funds because this plan was announced on a Saturday during an extended three-day bank holiday. The banks were closed and there was little people could do to protect their money. ATM withdrawals were limited to 400 Euros, but even with that limit ATMs quickly ran out of cash.[87]

Banks in Cyprus would remain closed for 12 days and would end up reopening under strict capital controls, which would limit withdrawals and how much cash travelers were allowed to take out of the country.[88] By that time the original plan to take 6.75% of all deposits had been scrapped due to the ensuing political uproar. The original plan had been replaced with a different plan that would close Cyprus' second largest bank, protect all deposits under 100,000 Euros, but also freeze, and ultimately seize some deposits over that amount.[89]

There is no shortage of angles from which to analyze this episode in Cypriot banking. In some ways the problem began when banks in Cyprus used the assets from their depositors to make risky, profit-seeking investments in Greece. When these investments suffered from the contagion of the Greek economy collapsing, the banks in Cyprus needed help from the European Central Bank in the form of Emergency Liquidity Assistance. But Cyprus had become a tax haven for foreign savers. Because 37% of the country's deposits were from abroad – and those mostly came from wealthy Russian oligarchs[90] – there was no political will for the European Union to bail out Cypriot banks directly. The seizing of depositors' funds was an attempt to force Cyprus to pay its way, giving cover to European politicians while still trying to save the banking system in Cyprus.

The point in recounting this story here is simply to note that the deposits you have in a bank are not yours and they are not safe if the bank or government decides they will freeze or confiscate those funds. Real people in Cyprus were hurt by these actions and confidence in the entire financial sector suffered as a result. Nor is what happened in Cyprus an anomaly. Countries across the world, whether to address fiscal problems or tamp down political dissent, freeze funds, seize money and impose stifling capital controls. For example, in December 2001, Argentina froze bank accounts and eventually forced citizens to convert withdrawals of US dollars into Argentine pesos.[91] Such measures hurt ordinary people and invariably cause social unrest. That month the resulting riots in Buenos Aires were so violent that they contributed to the resignation of the Argentine president.

Some might say this could never happen in the United States, but that is both wrong and myopic. In fact we don't need to hypothesize whether in times of economic trouble the American government would be willing to confiscate its citizens' money to help ensure the "greater good" – it already did. That's exactly what happened when the Great Depression tightened its grip on both the United States and the world. On March 9, 1933, only 5 days after President Roosevelt's inauguration, the Emergency Banking Act was introduced in Congress during a week-long national bank holiday. The Act quickly passed both chambers and was signed into law by the new president that same day, giving the Federal Reserve the powers to supply unlimited currency to banks once they reopened on March 13, 1933.[92] There was only one problem – they didn't have the gold they needed to print more money.

Less than a month later, on April 5, President Roosevelt invoked the new Emergency Banking Act to justify Executive Order 6102.[93] Through it, President Roosevelt made it illegal for individuals or business entities to own physical gold. This prohibition included gold coins, bullion, and certificates. Apart from minor exceptions like rare collectible coins, American citizens were given less than one month to surrender all gold in their possession to their nearest member branch of the Federal Reserve system. When surrendering their gold, people were given paper dollars at the exchange rate, established by the 1900 Gold Standard Act, of $20.67 per ounce. Failure to exchange one's gold for paper money was punishable by a fine up to $10,000 and or prison time of up to ten years. It turns out that if times are hard enough, even in America the government is willing to seize a hard monetary asset like gold and give you paper in return.

At the time the American dollar was on a gold standard, and quite likely a lot of individuals didn't think much about this exchange despite it being forced upon them. The dollar's peg to gold was trusted and the exchange rate of $20.67 was well established, having been the exact dollar price for one ounce of gold for over 54 years.[94] For the greater good, millions of Americans surrendered their gold for paper money. As one might imagine, Executive Order 6102 had a tremendous effect in helping the US Treasury shore up its reserves of the precious metal. With these increased reserves, the government was able to increase the money supply to help ease the pain of the Depression.[95]

The rug pull didn't come until a few months later. On January 30, 1934, President Roosevelt, with overwhelming support from both chambers of Congress, signed into law the Gold Reserve Act. This new law changed the price of an ounce of gold from the historic $20.67 to a new value of $35 per ounce.[96] This was a deliberate devaluation of the dollar by the United States government. A citizen surrendering one ounce of gold for dollars in March of 1933 would theoretically only be able to purchase 0.59 ounces of gold the next January with the money they were given. This was over a 40% devaluation of the dollar that the government issued in exchange for gold in the first place. Even that theoretical exchange wasn't possible, as owning gold was expressly outlawed. It wasn't until 1975 that Americans could again freely own gold.[97]

Be Your Own Bank

Outlawing gold and forcing Americans to use dollars was helpful for a government desperate to ease the turmoil of an economic collapse. But these policies resulted in the debasement of the American dollar at the cost of folks trying to save using a hard monetary asset like gold. Indeed, it would have been hard to convince people to keep using dollars if the more stable alternative in gold had not been outlawed. This pattern of governments forcing citizens to use inferior money by law is found throughout history. During times of financial turmoil or political "necessity" even the government in America will force citizens to exchange real, hard money for paper money only to debase that paper shortly after.

Perhaps one might consider such an extreme policy impossible to implement today, but that's a prime example of January 5th thinking. Given the unfortunate trajectory of the political reality in America, it isn't at all inconceivable to think that a politician might get elected (or reelected) and declare your favorite charity or social cause an enemy of the state to justify your funds being frozen or seized. It's entirely possible that American banks might once again find themselves in a precarious fiscal situation that would lead them taking from deposits that you thought were yours. At the end of the day, the dollar bills you have in your bank account right now are not yours. They are simply IOUs that your bank is taking risks with that you aren't aware of.

Every single person should have access to money that can't be frozen, censored, or confiscated as a universal human right. Being able to save and spend your money however one wants is a critical component of free speech. Bitcoin is that money. It was designed to operate outside of the close-knit web that exists between governments and banks. At its very root, Bitcoin is freedom money.

An amazing reality is that when you use Bitcoin, you have the option to be your own bank. Through the examples we've examined above (and countless others), we can see that using banks requires trust in the institution and trust in the government not to lean on the bank to freeze or steal your funds. Banks exist to custody your money and help facilitate economic activity. The nature of Bitcoin as a trustless digital asset means that those services are no longer required from a third party.

It is fairly easy to take custody of your own bitcoin and keep it safe and protected. To be your own bank, you need two different types of "wallets" for your Bitcoin, each of which is perfectly designed to replace one of the services that your bank currently provides. A "cold" wallet is one in which you will secure the main bulk of your Bitcoin wealth.

Sometimes called a hardware wallet, this is a device, usually costing around $50, that secures the private keys needed to access your bitcoin. It is called "cold" because the device remains offline and cannot be accessed remotely. To be clear, your bitcoin do not exist on this device – they exist, fully protected, on the blockchain. Your hardware wallet simply secures the private keys needed to access your funds. Setting up and backing up your hardware wallet is not difficult, but must be done carefully.

A "hot" wallet is one that is connected to an internet-capable device. These are meant for your "walking around" money. These are usually applications on a phone or computer that allow you to secure a small amount of bitcoin that you might use on a daily basis for transactions and allow easy and frictionless payments directly from one device to another. People keep as much bitcoin funds in their hot wallet as they would be comfortable carrying around in cash in a physical wallet. Setting up a hot wallet on your phone is as easy as setting up any other app you currently use. By setting up these two wallets, you can protect and custody your own wealth and also allow for frictionless transactions.

Taking custody of your own bitcoin and securing the private keys needed to access it is a critical step for anyone serious about owning and using Bitcoin. This is in contrast to leaving your Bitcoin on an exchange where you bought it. The fact that such a step eliminates the need to trust a third party like an exchange is encapsulated by the ubiquitous Bitcoin phrase "not your keys, not your coins." The implication of this common warning is that without having secured your own private keys, you don't have bitcoin – you have an IOU just like the traditional banking system.

Being able to opt out of the banking system is an amazing benefit of Bitcoin, but requires additional responsibility. For most readers, this will require more learning that is outside the scope of this book. I have included some resources in Appendix to guide anyone interested in learning more. I passionately encourage you to do that learning. By taking custody of your bitcoin on a hardware wallet, you will see numbers on a screen that do not represent an IOU from a bank. Instead, for the first time, will see actual wealth that you own and control without the need to rely on or trust any other person or institution. Taking custody of my own bitcoin was a powerful moment that changed the way I think about money – and it's something that everyone should be able to experience.

But that's not the only benefit of being your own bank. With Bitcoin you can transfer bitcoin to any person directly without needing permission to do so. When you decide to send a friend $10 over Venmo (or any other popular payment app) to cover the cost of your avocado toast, it seems to both the sender and recipient that the money is magically transferred instantly. This works perfectly nearly every time and is a wildly convenient way to access and transfer funds. But this is a gimmick. Though it may seem that actual money frictionlessly traveled from one phone to another, what is actually happening is much more complicated and carries risks that most people in wealthy Western nations don't need to consider. Sending your friend $10 sets off a chain of events that, in the simplest possible terms, looks more like: phone to bank to bank to bank to phone. I will describe the various troubles with this system momentarily, but I want to highlight the fact that sending bitcoin to a friend removes the bank as an intermediary. It is actually every time simply phone to phone.

Asking Venmo to send $10 is the first step. Venmo then must communicate that information to your bank and ask it to adjust its private, centralized ledger to deduct $10 from your available funds. Your bank must then instruct your friend's bank to do the exact opposite by increasing their funds by $10 on their private, centralized ledger. But in order to do this, the two banks must adjust their own balance sheets of assets and liabilities, and this will necessitate using a third bank that has a relationship with both. This chain of at least three banks that is positioned between the two customers can take between 3 to 14 business days to actually complete the final transfer of money from the first account to the last. The instantaneousness of sending money to a friend through a payment app is simply an illusion.

Each link in the chain introduces the opportunity for the transaction to be denied or censured. In each link, both customers' personal information – including account numbers, full names, addresses, and more – are transmitted and saved in a way that must be secured, and too often isn't. In each link the nature of the transaction – who is sending what to whom – is recorded and preserved for possible future scrutiny. The things you buy or the charities you support today may seem fine, but how certain are you that they won't be used against you by an unscrupulous politician 20 years from now? It is a privilege not to have to worry about such things, and today in the United States most folks rarely do. But with bitcoin, these are not worries – and never will be. If being born into a stable democracy with functioning money and robust private property and free speech protections is a privilege, then owning and using Bitcoin is an improvement to that privilege and available to all 8 billion people on this planet.

For now, it doesn't make much sense for most Americans to opt out of the current system of facilitating transactions. It is still convenient and functional for everyday business. But it is important to have the option because the landscape of politics and finance can change quickly, and if nothing else Bitcoin can serve as a check on banks acting in dishonest ways. Because it is more secure, cheaper, and faster, Bitcoin will likely become the rails people use to transmit value. This may happen in your favorite app without you even realizing it – the same way most people can send an email quite easily but they have no idea how the system for doing so actually works under the hood.

America's sordid history with the banking system is sad and has often caught the attention of progressive politicians and voters who care about regular people. At many points it seemed that the only tool we had to combat the greed, influence, and misaligned incentives of banks was ineffective regulation. Now, for the first time, there is another option. Today we can provide ordinary people a way to check the power and influence of the entire banking industry. Bitcoin is the infrastructure that will allow people to take custody of their assets and be their own bank. And, as we will explore in the next chapter, people are starting to notice.

Chapter 5: How Bitcoin Helps Poor and Marginalized People

A Troubling Legacy of Racism

The spring of 2020 was a scary time. A deadly virus, about which we knew very little at the time, was spreading around the world. In addition to the worrying health implications, millions of people were facing economic hardship. Mandated shutdowns intended to slow the spread of the virus resulted in millions of people losing their jobs as people around the world stopped doing just about everything that involved being near other human beings. No industry was untouched, and working people were left vulnerable to the uncertainties the Coronavirus carried with it as it spread around the world.

Politicians from both sides of the aisle recognized the dire situation. Perhaps they recognized the threat to their elected positions or what the virus posed to the societal order in the broadest possible sense. With uncharacteristic speed and efficiency, the Federal Government sprang into action with well-meaning support for everyday people trying to survive both a health and economic crisis. The CARES Act, along with similar relief bills, totaled a staggering $3.4 trillion, which was intended to help small businesses and individuals weather the storm.[98] One of the most publicized components of these relief packages was known as the Paycheck Protection Program (PPP), which was aimed at helping working people by providing loans to small businesses that promised not to lay off wage earners in the aftermath of mandated shutdowns.

Concerns about the government printing money and injecting it directly into the economy aside, the PPP was a well-intentioned program that at least in spirit aimed to ease the burdens of millions of working folks that needed help. The loans provided through the PPP legislation were backed by the Small Business Administration (SBA) and were offered at low interest rates ranging between 1 and 4%. Additionally, as long as businesses were able to verify that they used 60% of the funds to pay wages, then the loans would be forgiven. And in fact, a vast majority were – over 91%.[99] The program was also a success from the perspective of how much and how fast money got to the people that needed it. In a dark, scary time, hundreds of billions of dollars, earmarked to help regular folks, flowed into the economy in a matter of weeks. Such efficient convergence of intention and execution from the Federal Government was unprecedented.

But there were very clear problems with the PPP and how it was administered, and whether the program achieved its stated goals is open to debate. This isn't surprising given its scope and how quickly it was implemented. It is also not surprising that the problems with how the PPP was rolled out manifested quite differently for some portions of the population than others. A close examination of the PPP, which was designed to help working folks, yields the very familiar truth that banks and the most affluent in our society benefited disproportionately from the program.

The PPP was meant to be administered by the SBA, but the agency itself was too small to efficiently provide loans and administer them in a timely way. So that job was handed over to banks. The overwhelming majority of PPP business went to the largest banks in the country. The largest three – JP Morgan Chase, Bank of America, and Wells Fargo – were all in the top five in the amount of PPP loans administered.[100] Unsurprisingly, these banks generally prioritized their existing customers by giving them quicker and easier applications for PPP loans and providing larger loans to those businesses they had a preexisting relationship with.[101] In the end, these large banks raked in profits of over $10 billion from fees for administering risk-free loans backed by the government.[102]

The large banks distributed PPP loans in a regressive way. Several large companies – including restaurant and hotel chains – were able to secure low-interest forgivable loans while money and support quickly dried up for smaller businesses.[103] Just two weeks after businesses were able to apply for loans, the funding had been used up.[104] In response, subsequent legislation augmented the program to secure more funding for loans until August of that year. Even then, analysis of the loans revealed only 25% of funds went to those individuals who would have otherwise lost their job.[105] Loans that were meant to bolster the working class tended to go to more affluent households that had the benefit of clever accountants and small businesses that existed only on paper. In the end, 72% of PPP funds were captured by households with incomes in the top 20% of the national distribution.[106]

It might make sense to some people that the deployment of PPP funds attempted a balance between speed and targeting. At the height of the pandemic, there was a sense of urgency that required various government agencies and their bank partners to act quickly. Ensuring loans went to the intended recipients and benefited vulnerable workers would have required time and oversight that would have slowed down the relief. It may be easy to criticize in hindsight, but at the time the number one priority was to rush money out the door. Keeping track of where it went or enforcing limits about who received it seemed like a distant second-place priority. That much was clear even for those of us watching in real time. It shouldn't be surprising that the urgency resulted in the big banks being able to profit and the big banks' customers getting preferential treatment that ordinary folks didn't get. That all seems to be the price of doing business in America today. So it shouldn't surprise anyone keeping score at home that the deployment of PPP loans meant to help regular people was not only unfair – it was objectively racist.

An analysis of PPP loans demonstrates that a disproportionate number of loans and funds went to predominantly white neighborhoods. These results aren't even close to being proportional. Nearly twice the number of loans were made to business owners that lived in neighborhoods that were in the top quintile of white residents.[107] Not surprisingly, white applicants had an easier time getting approved for loans. About 60% of all white applicants were approved for PPP loans, but the corresponding number for Black applicants was only 29%. Among those Black business owners who did not apply for a PPP loan, 65% claimed that they did not know their business qualified, and another 20% claimed they were unable to find a financial institution to process their loan.[108] These numbers constitute a stark difference from the experience white business owners had in receiving aid during the pandemic. Interestingly, Black business owners who applied for PPP loans through Fintech companies that use mostly automated systems had the best success in getting approved, whereas Black business owners that applied for loans through smaller community banks only had a meager 3.3% success rate.[109]

These results should not be surprising. By allowing banks to privilege existing customers during the PPP process, it was an almost certainty that those with resources and access to these financial institutions would benefit disproportionately. The disparity in PPP loans for white and non-white lenders isn't a new phenomenon. It is simply the latest chapter in the tale of institutionalized racism that is interwoven into our banking system. It is a problem that banks gave preferential treatment for loans meant to help working people to existing, affluent customers. But perhaps the bigger problem is that Black families and Black-owned businesses have placed in front of them systemic obstacles that prevent them from becoming the banks' existing customers in the first place. Banks have underserved and extorted Black and poor communities for decades.

It is well documented that the banking and real estate industries colluded to prevent Black customers from buying homes in white neighborhoods. This practice of limiting where Black families could own homes is known as "redlining" because the neighborhoods where Black customers were allowed to buy were literally shaded red on maps. Redlining was in effect in every major American metropolis in the years since the second world war, which amounted to legal segregation that straddled the years before and after the Civil Rights movement. In his book *The Color of Law*, Richard Rothstein explains in full detail how and why this legalized segregation kneecapped the ability of the Black community to build wealth over many decades.[110] Black families were not sold homes in the "wrong" neighborhoods by real estate agents and they weren't provided mortgages to buy homes in the "wrong" neighborhoods by banks. Even the Federal government promoted these injustices. The Federal Housing Administration refused to insure mortgages in Black neighborhoods while at the same time it subsidized the building of massive suburban housing tracts meant exclusively for white families. These federal subsidies were provided under the explicit condition that the suburban homes not be sold (or resold) to Black customers.[111]

A particularly poignant and humanizing description of redlining can be found in Ta-Nehisi Coates' famous article *The Case for Reparations,* in which he describes the impact decades of racist housing policy has had on real families.[112] The consequences of redlining are manifest. While public education in America became integrated after the Brown v. Board of Education decision by the Supreme Court in 1955, public education was, and is still today, funded through local property taxes. Schools in affluent white neighborhoods were both better funded and completely off limits to nearly all Black children regardless of the Supreme Court ruling. Nor were Black families allowed to purchase homes in neighborhoods where property values appreciated. For many white home owners, owning property was their first chance to achieve generational wealth.

This disparity between education and opportunity has had lasting effects. Today the median income of Black households is only about 60% of the median income of white households.[113] This is a devastating statistic, but pales in comparison to the fact that Black net wealth is on average only 10% of white families' wealth. These differences in income and wealth manifest most clearly in the difference in property values for both groups. For most Americans, their home is their most valuable asset, and Black Americans were expressly prohibited from buying homes in neighborhoods that gained value over time.

White families didn't only have these advantages over potential Black families when times were good and property values were on a decades-long rise. The Great Financial Crisis in 2008 also disproportionately affected Black communities when times were hard. In the years leading up to the housing collapse, Black borrowers were more likely to be given subprime adjustable loans even if they had excellent credit scores.[114] As a result, the market collapse and subsequent recession lead to white communities losing 16% of their wealth while Black communities lost about 53% of theirs.

In total, these injustices by both the government and by the real estate and banking industries have damaged the Black community's ability to gain and store wealth. What I've described in this chapter is only a small sample of a much larger problem, and even if most white folks aren't familiar with this history, it is well understood in the Black community. Not surprisingly there is a distrust of both government and banks in the Black community that would be hard for white people, even poorer white people, to truly appreciate.

Bitcoin in the Black Community

This history is why when Black communities have been given an opportunity to check out of the current financial system – complete with its institutionalized racism – they are doing so in droves. Bitcoin represents a new way to accumulate and store wealth that is open and permissionless. Anyone, including a person of color, can buy and hold bitcoin – even in small amounts – without a third party's approval. There is no need to go through a bank or the government. With Bitcoin there are no applications or credit checks. Everyone has the ability to participate.

Black Americans are flocking to Bitcoin because it is seen as a way out of the current financial system that excludes them. About 25% of Black Americans making over $50,000 own Bitcoin, as opposed to only 15% of corresponding white Americans.[115] This racial gap in

Bitcoin ownership also holds for younger investors. For a community that has been excluded from the main engines that drive wealth creation in our country for generations, Bitcoin represents a fresh start. After being shut out of land and home ownership since slavery was abolished, today the Black community seems eager to establish themselves at the center of the next financial transformation. By investing in a new form of stateless, censorship-resistant money, Black consumers are not just sending a message. They are trying to build generational wealth that will give their community a seat at the table as the new paradigm takes shape in the coming years and decades.

I shouldn't have been, but I was surprised to learn about the vibrant community that Black folks have built around Bitcoin. Unfortunately, I had to learn where to look for it. Most of the resources to learn and discuss Bitcoin with "like-minded" people are created and distributed by white people – at least the internet algorithms deciding what to recommend to me made it seem that way. I realized this wasn't really the case when I happened upon an interview that Lamar Wilson gave on the popular morning radio show *The Breakfast Club*.[116] The radio show has a mostly Black audience, and in the interview, Lamar described the basics of Bitcoin and how it would help the Black community step out of the very financial system that has oppressed them for generations. Lamar has been deeply involved in Bitcoin from almost the very beginning, and he patiently answered the hosts' questions and expertly diffused the very normal skepticism that most people have when they start grappling with Bitcoin in earnest for the first time. But it's clear his message struck a chord, and his interview on *The Breakfast Club* has been watched about one hundred thousand times since it aired in the spring of 2022.

It is hard to imagine just how many people Lamar has influenced through this single interview. Despite not necessarily being part of the target audience, the interview certainly changed my trajectory through Bitcoin. In the spring of 2022 I had been working on this book for a few months but was starting to lose steam, and was considering giving up on the project. Hearing Lamar speak to the Black community in ways that articulated Bitcoin's promise beyond simply turning a profit for those already with money revitalized my energies and I started working on the book in earnest.

I was lucky enough to tell Lamar how inspirational he was when I interviewed him for this book a few months later. He responded with his typical humility when I told him how that single radio interview re-energized my effort to write my book. By that time I understood that *The Breakfast Club* interview was simply a window into a more full and robust effort by Lamar and many others to educate the Black community about money and Bitcoin. A model of graciousness, Lamar took the opportunity to highlight other work that was happening in the Black community to bring Bitcoin to Americans that needed it the most. As founder of the Black Bitcoin Billionaires Club, Lamar spoke about that group's reach and influence within the Bitcoin community. In 2022 BBB organized the first Blackout Conference, an opportunity for Black folks to learn about Bitcoin and network within the community. BBB also sponsors the Bitcoin Classic basketball tournament in New York City where teams compete to win Bitcoin prizes and the packed crowd learns the basics of Bitcoin.

Perhaps most impressively, BBB has partnered with rapper Jay Z and Twitter founder Jack Dorsey to sponsor the Bitcoin Academy. The Academy is a 12-week series of free classes offered to residents of the Marcy Houses in Brooklyn, New York, where Jay Z grew up. Expert instructors provide a series of classes to help educate the community about Bitcoin. Both childcare and a meal are offered for free during the evening classes, and hundreds of individuals have taken advantage of the opportunity to learn about Bitcoin's ability to decouple the Black community from the legacy financial system. For those students that needed it, hardware and access to Wi-Fi were provided by the Academy. Students learned the basics of Bitcoin and general financial literacy. In discussing the program with Lamar, it is clear that the main focus is to encourage students to adopt a low time preference attitude toward money and wealth. Unbeknownst to them when signing up, at the conclusion of the program students were given $1000 worth of Bitcoin.[117]

The Bitcoin Academy is an inspiration for people who value educational opportunity and understand its capability to reshape the world. For many of the people in the Marcy Houses, Bitcoin represents the best way they have to pass down wealth to the next generation. That opportunity exists because Bitcoin provides a mechanism to circumvent both the banks and the government that have suppressed the Black community for generations.

Lamar's own origin story is humbling. He has no formal advanced education in either finance or computer science, and yet he has developed an impressive knowledge about both. He has started multiple companies and has developed a deep understanding of the fundamentals of Bitcoin at the "hands on keyboard" level. Learning about his path to becoming a well-known leader in the Bitcoin community and his strong advocacy for developing educational opportunities in the Black community has been fascinating for me personally.

What I've described about Lamar Wilson's influence on educating Black folks about Bitcoin is just the tip of the iceberg. But his story, like the story of how Bitcoin intersects with the Black community, is not really mine to tell. As inspired as I am about how Black Americans and other people of color have flocked to Satoshi's invention to sidestep the legacy institutions that have taken advantage of them for decades, I am not part of those communities. Any list provided would be incomplete, but it is important to give a sense of the size and scope of Bitcoin's impact on the Black community. I encourage interested readers to seek out more information to gain a fuller perspective on the vibrant, community-based movement that is bringing Bitcoin to Black Americans across the country, but for those interested in learning more, please consider the examples that follow a starting point.

Jon Logan is based in New York City and he is devoted to Bitcoin and creating more equitable and fair financial systems for the community in which he lives. Jon is a student of history and has a keen ability to articulate the systematic racism imposed on Black folks for generations. When I spoke to him about my progressive ideas about

Bitcoin, he immediately pointed out that the political label progressive is only useful if it is about making *progress*, adding that "you can't make progress unless you understand what the history is."[118] Jon is dedicated to bringing financial opportunity to the Black community and his work in developing the BankBlack[119] initiative is truly impressive. His work is focused on improving people's understanding of how institutionalized racism has affected the Black community and working to provide ways for that community to overcome very real obstacles.

Then there are impassioned educators like Najah Roberts who tour the country bringing Bitcoin education to Black neighborhoods. Her Digital Financial Revolution Tour will be run for the 3rd time in 2023 and visits dozens of cities across the United States.[120] Charles J. Kelly is a CPA who also teaches for the Bitcoin Academy. And then there is Justin Rhedrick (also known as the Bitcoin Vegan) who is the author of the book *From Bars to Bitcoin* that recounts his time being incarcerated and how he began his journey to Bitcoin. Justin now runs a nonprofit designed to help inmates use Bitcoin to improve their financial lives once they are released from prison – something he has firsthand experience of and an approach he used to great effect when he was incarcerated.

Isaiah Jackson is the well-known author of the book *Bitcoin and Black America*, which provides a full account of how and why the Black community can use Bitcoin to preserve wealth and participate in the future of world finance. The book is required reading for anyone who wishes to get a full understanding of how Bitcoin has the potential to improve the financial reality for millions of Black Americans that have been left out of the legacy system for decades. There are also new thought leaders in the space that I heartily recommend like Dawdu Amantanah, whose podcast *The Bitcoin Source* explores fundamental topics in Bitcoin with an eye toward the Black community.

I was dumbfounded and inspired by how integral thought leaders are bringing this lesson to the Black community in ways that simply aren't happening in other communities. It's often said that "Bitcoin is hope" and that is nowhere more true than a community that not only needs hope but needs the fair and transparent tools to make that hope a reality. I am excited to see what happens in this space in the coming years and I encourage you to tap into the resources I've summarized here to learn more and stay engaged.

Bitcoin Is for Everybody

Because Bitcoin in its fundamental conception was designed as a protest against the collusion between big banks and government during the wake of the 2008 Great Financial Crisis, in very real ways it was also tailored to the Black community that suffered the effects of that collusion for generations before most Americans were even aware it was a problem. The contrast Bitcoin provides compared to traditional banks is quite stark for the Black community, but in reality Bitcoin is poised to help everyone as it matures into an important financial tool on the global stage. Any person or group that has been left behind by the overly financialized and corporate partnership between large banks and the United States government will find something in Bitcoin. Its technology is poised to help a variety of marginalized groups both in America and beyond due to its censorship resistance, permissionless protocol, and privacy – the lack of which in the legacy financial system makes it hard or impossible to access for certain groups of people. Bitcoin may be the best chance there is to provide opportunity and financial security to some of the most vulnerable people in society. We will examine some potential use cases below.

Intimate partner violence affects millions of women, and a much smaller but still significant number of men, in the United States each day. Accurate statistics are difficult to obtain for obvious reasons, but we can assume that the numbers reported by the CDC are reasonable approximations. According to their most recent survey, over 23% of women nationwide experience severe physical violence in their lifetime.[121] This is a distressing fact that affects women across all income brackets, at all levels of education, and in all regions of the country. An obvious fact for most of these women may be surprising to most on the outside: The majority of victims of intimate partner violence are also victims of financial abuse. According to some research, as much as 99% of victims of physical violence reported being victims of financial abuse.[122] In fact, most women cite financial abuse as the number one reason they stay with an abusive partner.[123]

Common types of financial abuse include lying about or hiding joint assets and limiting access to funds. Abusers also often limit the victim's ability to know about or have a voice in the financial decisions of the household. These types of abuses in effect stifle a victim's ability to gain independence and leave an abusive situation. In some cases, abusers take out unauthorized debt and damage the victim's credit, which also limits a victim's ability to leave. The theme is consistent in that the victim becomes dependent on the abuser in every sense, including relying on another person for the basics of household budgets and financial literacy. Leaving an abusive relationship can be scary for many reasons beyond worrying about one's physical safety or that of children. Having the resources to secure a safe place to go along with employment and transportation is almost impossible if your abuser controls every financial detail of your life.

I want to be very clear that Bitcoin does not represent a panacea for victims of intimate partner violence. It certainly does not solve all problems nor does it make things easier to leave an abusive relationship by itself. But in some circumstances, education about and access to Bitcoin could mean the difference between being stuck in an abusive relationship and having the financial freedom and privacy needed to leave. Value can be stored in Bitcoin on the blockchain. The only thing one needs to gain access to that value are private keys. Victims of intimate partner violence, when it is time to leave, can do so with considerable funds by bringing a thumb drive or memorizing their passphrase. It is a horribly scary moment when you feel you have to leave with just the clothes on your back, but now there is an option to leave with the clothes on your back and as much bitcoin as you were able to save stored in your brain as a seed phrase. There is no chance the partner can freeze funds or drain accounts like in the legacy financial system. A partner cannot track purchases and determine your location. And there is no need to hide cash over time and then bring it with you. The funds you store in Bitcoin are safe, secure, and private, and will travel with you anywhere in the world.

This vision that victims of intimate partner abuse can use Bitcoin to help them leave abusive relationships isn't ready to roll out immediately. Nonprofit and government organizations designed to help these victims are underfunded and understaffed. Many have a hard time meeting the demand they have to help women in need right now.[124] Asking these women's support organizations to educate victims about Bitcoin and fund some of the infrastructure needed is a huge ask. But it is not impossible, and with more like-minded folks looking to make a difference, it is very likely in the coming years we will see Bitcoin emerge as a real option for distressed victims who need help and resources to leave an abusive partner.

What local and grassroots efforts can be made to help with this vision? If you've read this far into this book, perhaps you are one of the people interested in doing this work. Women's support organizations need experts to volunteer their time to teach about Bitcoin so victims storing their wealth with this technology can do so responsibly and with confidence. Donations of hardware wallets need to be made so these organizations can provide a secure and portable way to store wealth in Bitcoin without passing those costs onto the victims. Infrastructure needs to be implemented through women's support organizations so those who need fiat cash can easily trade in and out of Bitcoin when needed without having to access their legacy financial accounts. Financial support is needed to bootstrap women who don't have access to funds they can save in Bitcoin or who are unable to risk secretly saving over a period of time. There are many other ways to help. For those interested in pursuing such a path, it is worth reaching out to a local organization to see if they are willing to explore some of the options Bitcoin offers victims of abuse.

More generally, the concepts I've outlined to help women who are victims of violence leave abusive relationships applies to other groups too. There are millions of young people in the LGBTQ+ community who feel trapped in unsupportive households without the resources to leave. In much the same way support organizations might help victims of intimate partner violence with Bitcoin, the same can be done within this community too. A grassroots effort needs to be made to educate and provide access to an open monetary technology that can't be tracked, frozen, or drained. Across a variety of vulnerable communities, Bitcoin can be a way out for the people that need it the most.

It is difficult to fully appreciate the ways Bitcoin will shape our world to help vulnerable people. We are in the early days and the technology continually improves while adoption grows. Bitcoin will be easier to use and more normalized in 10 years than it is today. The change will be gradual, but with hindsight the difference will likely be as stark as comparing one's experience on the internet in 1995 and 2005. Just like the internet got a bad rap for its illicit uses in its early days, so did Bitcoin, but both are fundamentally a tool people can use to make the world a better place. This includes providing a level of privacy and financial security to vulnerable people around the world. In some ways, the true promise Bitcoin extends past America's borders and solves problems that most Americans never really have to think about. If Bitcoin represents an interesting potential to help vulnerable abuse victims in America, then it is an absolute necessity for billions of people today.

Bitcoin in Africa

Anita Posch is from Austria, but she spends quite a lot of time in Africa doing humanitarian work and educating people about Bitcoin. Anita straddles two worlds and has a direct perspective on the contrast between the very different financial systems available to the people in Europe and North America compared to the rest of the world. As much as anyone else, Anita lives within this contrast. I was able to speak with her about her work in between trips for her popular *Bitcoin for Fairness Series*, a collection of episodes of her podcast, *The Anita Posch Show*, that focus on the ways Bitcoin can directly help those on the African continent. Part of my conversation with Anita focused on the fact that those in developed countries have trouble seeing the value of Bitcoin because they live in stable political systems with financial infrastructure that usually works. The people that Anita works with in Africa must contend with just the opposite: unreliable payment networks, corrupt governments that freeze or seize funds, and rampant inflation that can ruin a typical person's savings in an alarmingly short time.

By following Anita's work, you quickly realize there is no need to explain to a person in Zambia (or Zimbabwe or South Africa) why they need Bitcoin, all you have to do is ask them about their financial experience and they will tell you themselves. Certainly that was Anita's experience. But she soon recognized that the needs that Bitcoin could meet ran deeper:

> *More and more I [recognized] the human rights aspect of Bitcoin as a tool that secures free speech, which is a human right, and also the freedom of transaction is basically the most important use case for me for Bitcoin... Giving fair financial global access for anyone, regardless of color, age, wealth, job, power, whatever – I think that's the baseline of everything Bitcoin is.*[125]

According to the Human Rights Foundation, 54% of the world's population lives under authoritarian rule, and that number is growing.[126] Over half of the world's population contends with the financial realities of insecure property rights, limited freedoms of speech, and weak rule of law. Most of the world could have their transactions monitored or censored, their savings in bank accounts seized, and the funds being sent to them from abroad stolen by their government. Most of the world needs to worry that the money they work for might not have the same purchasing power tomorrow as it does today. These types of financial oppression happen every day all around the world. Often just the suspicion of dissent against an authoritarian regime is enough to have a person's financial life wiped out with no due process or recourse.

Bitcoin represents hope for billions of people that are living this reality. Anita has made it her business to travel to Africa and put boots on the ground to bring that hope to real people. She has traveled to dozens of countries and has spoken to oppressed peoples about Bitcoin, providing workshops on the nuts and bolts of Bitcoin so the local population can understand not just the why but the how of using this new technology. She also devotes an incredible amount of energy to educating folks about how to avoid the scams that invariably infiltrate any new technology. By leveraging the support of the Bitcoin community, Anita has secured funding for African schools via private and censor-resistant bitcoin donations from all over the world. Unlike other forms of international aid, the local African governments are unable to seize, skim or freeze these funds. By working through the lens of Bitcoin, Anita has helped countless people overcome the once insurmountable surveillance, control, and oppression that is always a feature of government money under an authoritarian regime.

Bitcoin Is Freedom Money

Most Americans who only understand the bare outlines of Bitcoin approach it as an investment. For them, Bitcoin serves as an alternative to stocks or bonds that will provide them a yield for their savings. These people see Bitcoin as a vehicle to get more "real money" at some point in the future. This outlook betrays a tremendous privilege for people who live with a financial infrastructure that works and under a government that (mostly) respects the rule of law and free speech.

But for most of the rest of the world, Bitcoin isn't an investment – it is *the* real money. Bitcoin represents a way to transact privately and to secure the fruits of one's labor without having to worry about the government seizing it directly or debasing it through uncontrollable inflation. Most of the world doesn't have the luxury of thinking about Bitcoin as an investment when they don't even have access to secure bank accounts and aren't allowed to invest in Western stock markets in the first place.

While Anita Posch is famous in Bitcoin circles for helping people on the African continent understand and use Bitcoin, people well beyond Africa are adopting the technology because it helps them circumvent the broken and corrupt systems otherwise available to them. Nobody has done a better job of documenting that growing adoption among people living under oppressive authoritarian regimes than Alex Gladstein, Chief Strategy Officer at the Human Rights Foundation. Alex is a tremendous thought leader in the Bitcoin space and understands firsthand the difficulty helping the most disadvantaged folks in the world. His work for the Human Rights Foundation highlights the need for individuals and groups to be able to move funds in and out of totalitarian countries without fear of it being censored or seized at the borders. Fiat monetary systems don't allow this. According to some estimates, over 16% of aid flowing to oppressed people ends up in tax haven off-shore bank accounts.[127] The people in those countries are often not able to exercise free speech and criticize their governments in any way without the monetary system being weaponized against them. Personal funds of dissidents are frozen or confiscated and individual transactions are censored. Strict monetary controls are put in place prohibiting the population from buying or using other forms of currency that are less subject to debasement than the local fiat currency. Most people in the world do not even have reliable access to a bank account. From top to bottom, the financial system in most places in the world is designed to reinforce a corrupt, violent authoritarian government that is oppressing its people.

Alex chronicles these struggles and the subsequent successes people have using Bitcoin in his book *Check Your Financial Privilege.* The book is a tour de force that outlines rampant human rights violations and provides provocative vignettes of everyday people using Bitcoin to overcome the financial oppression supplied by the legacy financial system. Alex's book is a must-read for anyone who truly wishes to understand Bitcoin's impact on the world beyond an investment opportunity for those living in developed Western nations. I was lucky enough to interview Alex a few months after his book was released and it was a pleasure to hear his take on the ways Bitcoin intersects with politics in the United States and why he considers Bitcoin the premiere technology to level the playing field all over the world. In his view, a major promise of Bitcoin is it being "a tool to prevent fascist, racist or imperialist subjugation of people by using money as a political weapon... it's anti-colonialist, anti-jingoist and anti-imperialist."[128] In his view, Bitcoin doesn't just represent an opportunity to invest in a new asset to make money – it is a fundamentally important tool for freedom around the world.

As a response to the criticism that Bitcoin is useless, *Check Your Financial Privilege* chronicles the stories of people across the global south and beyond who, for a variety of reasons, actually need Bitcoin to survive. Alex does an impressive job relating how folks in Africa, Latin America, and the Middle East use Bitcoin to overcome the intentional obstacles that the legacy financial system imposes on them, and describes issues that Americans simply don't have to contend with. Hyperinflation and the fear of losing one's life savings due to improper monetary policy is one issue that regularly surfaces across the world. He also gives careful consideration to the billions of unbanked people across the globe and the many people who have bank accounts but can't be sure their funds won't be seized by corrupt governments. The book features the hardships created by the abuse of capital controls, laws that prohibit the use of a stable currency, or even how authoritarian regimes limit how much money a person can leave the country with.

Beyond the difficulties faced by individuals, Alex's book provides a thorough treatment of the economic hardship created when the people of one jurisdiction are forced to use money controlled by another jurisdiction. In almost all cases, and examples exist around the world, the more powerful country that controls the money is able to extract value from the less powerful country and suppress its economic capabilities. A dependency is established not just for the more powerful nation's currency, but for all financial infrastructure and economic output. The people of Palestine forced to use the Israeli Shekel is just one example. Several African countries that were once under French colonial rule still remain economic subjects of France through economic controls and oppressive policies. The dozen or so nations that use the American dollar[129] create a third category. In all of these cases, the people of one jurisdiction are forced to live under economic conditions created by and for the benefit of a system they have no voice in. For these countries and many more, the lack of monetary sovereignty is inimical to economic prosperity.

At the time of writing, two nations have made Bitcoin legal tender: El Salvador and The Central African Republic. It is no surprise that these two nations that adopted Bitcoin as legal tender had been operating under a lack of monetary sovereignty. El Salvador has been using the US dollar since 2001,[130] while the Central African Republic has been using the Communauté Financière Africaine (CFA) Franc since its inception in 1945. The effects of US dollar hegemony around the globe are documented in Chapter 7, but the effects of dollar hegemony on El Salvador are not surprising. Much ink has been spilt over El Salvador's adoption of Bitcoin.[131] On the other hand, the lesser-known monetary and financial history of the Central African Republic is equal parts fascinating and distressing.

The Central African Republic has a Human Development Index (HDI) of about 0.4, which ranks the nation 188 out of the 191 nations measured by the United Nations.[132] As the name suggests, its currency – the CFA Franc – is a holdover from the 18th and 19th centuries when most of the western and equatorial region in Africa was under direct French imperial control. In the 1960s France allowed nominal independence for these countries in western and central Africa, but maintains close political and monetary control over these nations to this day. Even today France still exerts an inordinate amount of control over countries in the CFA. All nations in the CFA are obligated to maintain 50% of their foreign monetary reserves in Paris in the French public treasury.[133] In exchange, the French government guarantees a stable peg for the CFA Franc to the Euro while maintaining control over all printing and distribution of money used in the CFA. Additionally, France has the "right of first refusal" for raw and natural resources sourced in its former colonies.[134] These types of arrangements are designed to extract value from the African continent for the sole benefit of France and have had disastrous effects on nations like the Central African Republic. The history and current details of this ugly neo-imperialist subjugation are explained beautifully in *Check Your Financial Privilege*.

Today, up and coming politicians in many CFA nations talk openly about this monetary repression and the need to reform monetary policy to a voting populace that is increasingly warming to these ideas. There is no surprise that Bitcoin might be viewed as the best hope for a more sovereign and brighter future for nations across the CFA. The Central African Republic may be the first of the former French colonies to experiment with a borderless money that can't be controlled from Paris, but it likely won't be the last.

For an American who lives in a nation that controls the global reserve currency and has access to both state-of-the-art financial infrastructure and the foundational rule of law, Bitcoin might not seem like a necessity right now. For most Americans, it might be an attractive investment opportunity or an interesting project that incorporates innovative new technology. But viewing Bitcoin through this lens is a luxury most of the world doesn't have. For most people, money doesn't work properly. The entire monetary system is designed to accrue value for those already at the top and any efforts to fight against the paradigm are stifled by the very autocrats that control the money. Bitcoin was designed with this in mind. The decentralized and open network can be used by anyone in the world for any reason. And no government or army, no matter their economic or military strength, is able to stop it.

Whether it's nations trying to escape the financial control exerted over them by another country or a desperate refugee trying to flee a war-torn homeland with their net worth safely intact, Bitcoin provides options to the people all over the world that need it most. In 2022 alone we saw many examples of Bitcoin in action – most prominently people fleeing their homes during the Russian invasion of Ukraine with the value of their digital assets intact. It would have been impossible to move cash or gold across borders on such short notice and in such chaos. Unsurprisingly, within days of the invasion ATMs were empty and banks were closed. Accessing money through the legacy financial system simply wasn't possible. Bitcoin filled a need for people who needed it the most. Because of its unique properties, we can expect to see more people in the future using Bitcoin to securely move value in their most desperate moments. Bitcoin will continue to provide the most vulnerable people in the world a resource to fight back and take control of their financial sovereignty.

Bitcoin isn't just a better version of money. It's an entirely new technology that allows nations to trustlessly deploy a hard currency that can't be inflated or controlled from continents away. At the same time, it allows individuals to remit their hard-earned money to family back home without risk of seizure or having to pay expensive intermediaries like Western Union. Bitcoin provides options for traditionally underserved communities to invest in digital property and take possession of their assets without needing to trust financial institutions that have exploited them for generations. It allows folks in the most vulnerable positions to take control of their financial situations without needing to trust a bank, government, or abusive partner. Bitcoin has the potential to make the whole world a better place.

Bitcoin represents something new – a tool to fight against power that ordinary people have never had. Until now.

Chapter 6: Inflation and Wealth Inequality

We Are Told We Need Inflation

The poster from Chapter 1 was hung in my office for about a week before I got someone to agree to my ubiquitous offers of "Let's grab lunch and talk about Bitcoin." This first lunch was with a friend and colleague who taught math but also taught economics. In some ways, he was the perfect person for me to talk to. He wasn't a Bitcoin expert, but he also wasn't starting at zero either. At this point in my journey, I was quite eager to learn from someone outside of the Bitcoin space because I really needed a "second opinion." After we found a quiet place to eat and talk, I started the conversation plainly. "I want you to convince me I'm wrong about Bitcoin. I have enough invested that I'd like to know now if I'm making a big mistake." We had a great conversation that was collegial and fun. Of course the fact that you're reading this book means he didn't convince me that I was wrong about Bitcoin, although to be fair that really wasn't his goal.

My colleague agreed with many of the points I made about Bitcoin being a sound monetary technology. But as an economics teacher he had one primary concern: Bitcoin was deflationary. The worry is easy to explain. Without an inflationary money supply, it is impossible for the economy to grow, and we risk a deflationary spiral with no ability for the government to save us by increasing the money supply when hard times hit. This matches perfectly with the classical Keynesian view of macroeconomics that is taught in schools, including by my colleague.

Keynesian economists support the idea of the government increasing spending during recessions or economic slowdowns, even if this requires deficit spending. They also believe when the economy is doing well the government should spend less and tax more to create a buffer for the next economic slowdown. Through coordination between the government and the central bank, Keynesians believe that fiscal and monetary policy intervention can effectively counteract problems with low employment or high inflation as they surface. They take a very logical approach to the economy that is meant to smooth the boom-bust business cycle and support economic growth during economic downturns while keeping inflation in check when the economy is growing.

But there is a flaw with this Keynesian view – a flaw that Bitcoin is able to fix. This flaw has nothing to do with charts, equations, specific target interest rates or how much the government spends, or even how they spend it. The flaw is simply that it relies on experts in power to decide when and how to adjust monetary policy. Those experts are operating with noisy data and have access to only blunt tools to affect the money supply. The Federal Reserve makes decisions by using data about unemployment and inflation that are often weeks old and inaccurate. In particular, data for both of these important economic categories are often adjusted after the fact. And when the Federal Reserve does act, it usually does so by adjusting interest rates (the cost to borrow money) which, even ideally, affects the economy over the course of weeks or months in hard-to-predict ways. It is often the case that the Federal Reserve must make decisions about monetary policy in real time while the information they need won't be available for weeks or months. Knowing if they made the correct decision likely takes even longer.

Complicating matters further is the unfortunate reality that there are incentives that encourage the experts to keep the spigot of money flowing as long as possible. In practice, the temptation of the money printer to keep a booming economy booming is just too hard to resist. I have seen no evidence that even the most fundamental precepts of Keynesian economics have been employed in practice. If anything, the recent boom-bust cycles have been dramatic and deficit spending by governments around the world has ballooned in good economic times as well as in bad. The classical notion that deficit spending by the government is tolerable during an economic downturn has morphed into the current precept that "deficits don't matter."[135]

In 2022, the US national debt hit $31 trillion.[136] Any attempt to put this $31 trillion in a context that humans can understand is futile, but I will try. If you were to stack $100 bills 10 feet high and position these stacks end to end, this debt would create a 10-foot high wall of money that extended more than 2,422 miles. For a more complete understanding, the US border with Mexico is less than 2,000 miles. Politicians from both sides help build that wall. What's worse is that by all measures this debt is growing at an increasing rate. The graph of the debt follows an exponential model that looks essentially flat until about 1971 and has since grown at an uninterrupted pace. The national debt isn't just going up, it's curving up steeper and steeper.

The debt hitting $31 trillion may seem like an immense number, and it is. But Keynesian economists seem to prefer to measure a nation's debt as a ratio to a nation's GDP. The common argument is that deficits don't matter if the economy is growing. Setting aside the fact that this runs counter to the Keynesian belief that in strong economies governments are meant to spend less and tax more, it's worth noting that even this cherry-picked measure by Keynesians doesn't hold up. Before the 2008 Great Financial Crisis, most economists considered a debt-to-GDP ratio of over 100% detrimental to the economy.[137] But the ratio of debt-to-GDP has skyrocketed in the last few years, currently standing at almost 140%[138], which is higher than it's ever been in history – even during the wild debt spree that was paying for World War II. We learn more about debt and the cost of war in Chapter 8.

Inflation: The Cost of Debt

In the past, I readily dismissed critiques of the national debt or deficit spending as the language of the right wing. As a progressive, I felt any attempt to curtail the debt was simply a cloaked attempt at dismantling the safety net the government provides for our society's most vulnerable. I assumed that complaining about how much the federal debt had grown was just a Republican proxy for arguing against "handouts" given to "freeloaders." I *still* think this is true, but learning about Bitcoin has caused me to change my view about the significance of our national debt for being able to sustain progressive programs in the long run.

It was a surprising moment when I realized this debt won't be paid off – and isn't intended to be. The system is structured in such a way that this debt, and the deficit spending that creates it, are designed to increase indefinitely. Politicians like to claim that we're taking on debt our children will have to pay. That isn't true. Under our current fiat system in which the government can create more money to spend, the debt will never be paid off. Instead, this level of debt makes inflation mathematically *necessary*. And as I explain in the rest of this chapter, inflation supports both public and private debt all over the world while disproportionately hurting poor and vulnerable people.

The fact that the US national debt will never be paid off definitely runs counter to one's intuition. As fundamental as learning right from wrong, we learn that debts need to be paid – period. But the reality is much different. As we will learn in detail in Chapter 7, the International Monetary Fund and World Bank provide loans to developing countries that they know cannot be paid back. This is done intentionally so that these nations are subject to the leverage that rich Western countries like America wish to impose on them. It is easier to extract resources and wealth from these countries if they are financially insecure and in debt, and international organizations, predominantly under American influence, understand this.

This is also why your credit card company would prefer you max out your credit card each month and pay the minimum payment. Paying off your credit card debt may be in your best interest, but the company would prefer you be indebted to them indefinitely. Debts don't always need to be paid, and depending on who is doing the lending and who is doing the paying, it may be surprising how rarely they actually are.

America, of course, is in a different position than other poor nations and certainly can't be compared to a recent college graduate with credit card debt. The United States has managed to make its debt a strength on which the entire world economy is directly dependent. While America will never reach the level of zero national debt, it will continue to print money to service (i.e., pay the interest on) the debt we have and print money to roll over the debt (i.e., pay off old debt with new debt) and continue to take on fresh debt with each new spending bill. Economists will tell you the mechanism by which this happens is continued nominal (i.e., not adjusted for inflation) economic growth which is fueled by inflation. They will say that every dollar that is borrowed by the American government today will eventually be paid back, on time and in full nominal terms. But the dollar used to pay back that debt will also be borrowed – and will be tragically debased. Every dollar borrowed in 2022 for a 10-year treasury note will be paid back in 2032 dollars, and today's dollars will not have the same purchasing power in 10 years. Inflation is the mechanism by which the government can pay back that debt with dollars that have been debased over time. This makes their payments easier and keeps the entire house of cards from crashing down.

All this plate spinning is still possible even if the growth of the economy slows in real terms (the nominal growth *adjusted* by the inflation rate) – so long as it grows in nominal terms. Inflation is needed to keep the economy growing so that debts, both public and private, can be paid off more easily. In a very real sense, the "deflationary spiral" that my economics teacher friend worried about is a fear based on the entire system being saturated in so much debt. Given the current reality, deflation is a valid concern, but without so much debt, deflation is a lot less scary. After all, the current fiat inflationary system encourages and incentivizes debt at all levels of society. Should the world transition to a more stable currency like Bitcoin, it would necessitate unwinding most of that debt which originated through cheap credit.

This would likely be a painful transition, but it could sow the seeds of a brighter future. When the world was on the gold standard, prices regularly increased for periods of time, but would also decrease. The natural ebb and flow of price signals, unadulterated from the "noise" created by printing money, resulted in price stability through the 19th century. Inflation rates in the United States also alternated between positive and negative throughout the century in a way that balanced around an equilibrium. The result is that a dollar from 1800 actually had slightly *more* purchasing power in 1899 – a fact that is surprising only through our modern lens that has normalized inflation.[139]

The concern about deflation may actually be overstated. All of the modern examples of currency collapse, and there are plenty, resulted from "inflationary spirals." Undisciplined central banks print too much money due to the incentives we've discussed. The currency is intentionally debased as a result and too much money chases too few goods. Without much warning, the money supply slips past the event horizon and an inflationary spiral ensues, causing the devastation of the entire economic structure of the country. Prices for goods and services are adjusted higher several times a day, leading to absurd examples like taking a wheelbarrow of money to buy a loaf of bread. Regular people – often forced to hold that currency by law – are left holding worthless paper.

The time between not being able to feed your family with money you worked hard for and civil unrest is really quite short. The transition can be quick and dramatic and the violence horrifying. Argentina[140], Zimbabwe, Kenya, Burkina Faso, Belgium, Peru, South Korea, and Sri Lanka[141] have all seen civil unrest in the form of protests or violence as a direct result of inflation. And this is just an incomplete list from 2022. For both individuals and nations, inflation is a clear danger that disproportionately affects poor nations and poor individuals.

The premise of Jeff Booth's book *Price of Tomorrow* (also mentioned in Chapter 3) is that technology makes the world deflationary. As technology builds more efficiencies into the economy, prices for goods and services should trend down. The reason we see the opposite is because the institutions that control the money supply are incentivized to keep prices going up to keep the economy from collapsing. Central banks around the world are fighting against the powerful tide of the natural deflation we should expect. The expansion of the money supply may look and feel good in the short term because it acts as an accelerant to a booming economy. But by controlling the price of capital and contributing to inflation by creating more money, central banks are causing the misallocation of capital because cheap debt makes it easier and more attractive to invest in unsound projects. Low interest rates mean individuals and institutions chase yield by going further out on the risk curve. This often means investing in companies or projects that don't ultimately produce economic value. While we are taught that inflation is a necessary and healthy part of a growing economy, it is far from it.

The Signal in the Noise

Changes in price can be important signals to consumers and investors. If supply chains are disrupted or there is a disequilibrium between supply and demand, one would expect the price for a good to change. These changes perform an important purpose in how people make economic decisions. Noticing a shift in prices may mean you'll buy apples this week instead of bananas. Or it might mean making a strategic investment in company A instead of company B. But when the supply of money is constantly growing, the aim is to have prices continually go up. The signal gets lost and people are unable to make sound decisions. In fact, the incentive is to buy as much as possible *before* prices increase. The value of frugality and saving is lost.

We usually think of inflation as changes in the price of consumer goods because this is what is reported in the news. Some economists are a bit more sophisticated and view inflation through the lens of a growing money supply. Like the national debt, the graph of the overall money supply shows exponential growth. The curve is flat until the early 1970s when it starts bending upwards at a steeper and steeper pace.[142] As governments around the world combatted the economic effects of Covid, there was a huge bump in the money supply in 2020, which resulted in a single-year increase in the United States of 27%.[143] This was the largest such increase in the nation's history.

This steady increase in the money supply is how sustained inflation in terms of consumer prices happens. As opposed to temporary price fluctuations, the purchasing power of a dollar goes steadily down over time. Each dollar added to the overall money supply makes the dollars you already have less valuable, with the net result of the currency being debased.

The government reports measures of inflation through the Consumer Price Index (CPI). The CPI measures the relative change in a basket of goods a typical American household buys: things like food, apparel, housing, transportation, and other goods and services. But there are deep flaws with the very concept of the CPI. Reporting inflation as a single number about a standard basket of goods and services makes no sense. Each individual purchases a unique basket of goods and services for which price changes are important but not reflected in that figure. Folks in the market for used cars care about different price changes from people shopping for groceries. The price of college tuition changes differently than that of insulin. Each of us has a unique basket of goods and services we care about and hence a unique inflation rate with which to contend.

The problem isn't simply that the inflation numbers reported by the government don't match your basket of goods and services. What's worse is that they don't even match the baskets of goods and services used in the past. The methodology to arrive at the number the government reports each month through the Bureau of Labor and

Statistics (BLS) has changed over time. For example, the 9.1% CPI inflation reported by the BLS in June 2022 was the largest since 1981.[144] But the definition of CPI has changed over time, and if the CPI in June 2022 was measured using the same methodology in place in 1980, the CPI would have been reported as even higher – well over 16%.[145] In fact, by the 1980 measure, the CPI has not dipped *below* 5% in over 35 years, despite nearly all of the official CPI reports hovering around the Federal Reserve's 2% target. By regularly changing the methodology and massaging the official numbers, the government "hides" in its reports most of the inflation that working folks feel in their lived experience.

For example, in 2009 a massive amount of money was pumped into the economy to help stave off the collapse promised by the Great Financial Crisis. The details of the Federal government's bailout of the banks were discussed in Chapter 4. At the time, there was concern among some economists that increasing the money supply that much would result in inflation, and the Federal Reserve smugly claimed victory in subsequent years when it didn't. The only problem is that the new money from 2009 actually did cause inflation – just not the specific price increases measured by the CPI. While the CPI hovered around the Federal Reserve's target of 2% each year after 2009, the price of assets like homes and stocks shot up. Since the lows of 2009, median home prices in America rose from $208k to over $440k in 2022 – an increase of over 100%.[146] The cost of stocks, as measured by the S&P 500, increased by over 400% during the same timeframe.[147] The Federal Reserve felt comfortable pumping money into the economy to save it from collapse precisely because there were no signs of the CPI increasing beyond what they considered acceptable limits. But the story was different for assets like homes and stocks that affluent Americans already owned. The result of this specific type of inflation was that the gains were all skewed toward the wealthiest in our society. While the price of ground beef may not have risen tremendously, working folks found it harder to invest in the stock market or buy single-family homes.

Scarce Resources and Asset Inflation

This is only a part of why inflation, which is mathematically necessary under the current financial structure, is an insidious penalty that disproportionately affects the poor and working class. When inflation is caused by an expansion of the money supply, the new money does not spread through the economy in an equitable way. As we have seen with housing and stock prices, that new money gets pumped into attractive, scarce assets that benefit the folks who already own them. The same is true for money that gets put into rare collectibles, expensive wines, fine art, and collectible cars. These items are out of reach by most people and their appreciating value benefits those that do not need the help. By the time the fresh dollars trickle down to the hands of the working poor, asset prices have already gone up. One might be able to overlook the fact that a hard-working middle-class person can't buy rare fine art. But if the price of housing is simply out of reach, this has damaging effects that ripple throughout society.

As we talked about in Chapter 2, one of the main functions of money is to serve as a store of value. By this measure, the United States dollar has done a poor job because inflation has eroded the purchasing power of saved dollars through the years. Everyone from Wall Street investors to regular people has to look elsewhere for a store of value, which usually means extending further out on the risk curve. A "safe" savings account is guaranteed to lose purchasing power over time when adjusted for inflation. While a small minority might be able to invest in rare collectibles, most working-class people aren't even in the stock market. For those making over $100,000 per year, about 89% own stocks, but among people making less than 100k, fewer than half own stocks.[148]

Of course, the answer to the store of value problem for working-class Americans has been baked into the "American Dream" in the form of home ownership. A single-family home is an aspiration for people because they want a safe, comfortable place to live and raise a family. But a house represents even more than that. People have increasingly viewed their home as a store of value – in other words buying a house has become an acceptable vehicle to store a large percentage of one's net worth. At least some of the increase in the price of homes is attributable to a monetary premium that society has placed on owning such property. People are paying more for houses because in addition to paying for a place to live they are investing in a store of value.

Regular folks competing with one another to bid up the price of a home is one thing. Unfortunately, today first-time home buyers are in competition with wealthy people looking to buy a second or third home because it is the "smart" thing to do with their extra money, since dollars by themselves are not a good store of value. The idea of a single-family home being a store of value or even an investment has caught the eye of Wall Street, too. In recent years investment firms like BlackRock, JP Morgan Chase, and Goldman Sachs have started buying a large number of single-family homes, which in effect drives up prices and takes homes off the market.[149] During the pandemic, entire neighborhoods were snatched up by investment firms.[150] With essentially unlimited access to capital and favorable loan rates, these large investment firms are able to outbid any regular family looking to buy a home.

The inability to buy single-family homes is just one of the ways inflation has hurt working people. After the Second World War, productivity and wages in America increased steadily and comparably, but by the 1970s productivity and wages decoupled. While productivity rose unabated, typical wages flatlined, creating a gap between the growth in what was produced and resources finding their way to the workers doing the producing. Today, that gap is as large as it has been in modern history.[151]

Once the world untethered from the gold standard in 1971, wages lagged inflation in harmful ways. The deflationary abundance that is the promise of innovation, increased productivity and technological efficiency has all flowed away from workers and toward the wealthy.

America currently suffers from the worst inequality in all G7 countries,[152] and the problem is getting worse. The Gini coefficient is the usual measurement of inequality within a nation, with a high number representing more inequality. In the United States, the Gini coefficient has been steadily increasing through recent decades.[153] In fact, according to the World Bank, the United States has more wealth inequality than both Haiti and Malaysia. [154]

The progressive people I talk to understand that wealth inequality is a serious problem. The United States now has more inequality than in the years leading to the Great Depression,[155] and the problem has gotten much worse during the recent pandemic.[156] It is not a Marxist cry for complete equality to say that this level of wealth accumulation and the disparity between the rich and the poor is dangerous. The fact that the top 1% in America owns more wealth than the bottom 90%[157] is a risk to a well-functioning economy and threatens social unrest. Inflation is not the only culprit to blame for wealth inequality, but it is an important factor that is rarely considered in serious conversations. The recent uptick in inflation that has occurred since 2020 has undoubtedly hurt the working poor in our country who struggle to put food on the table. There is no shortage of anecdotes about people deciding between necessities because they simply can't afford everything they need. As a criticism of inflation's effect on the poor, this is low-hanging fruit. The more surprising fact is that even low levels of inflation – like the Federal Reserve's target of 2% – still have a disproportionately damaging effect on the poor and middle class in America.

The Foundation for Research on Equal Opportunity (FREOPP) is an independent, nonprofit, non-partisan organization that seeks to expand economic opportunity to those who most need it.[158] FREOPP urges policymakers at all levels to better understand the issues that poor people face and to adopt policies that promote equal access to resources. It is common sense to observe that because wealthy families are able to more easily absorb price increases, they are not as affected by inflation as poorer families. But FREOPP's research takes matters a step further by examining the type of goods and services in a poor family's "basket of goods" and the percentage of income that must be devoted to necessities across several income brackets. For example, housing represents a much higher percentage of spending for poor people than for wealthy people, and the effect of inflation on rent alone causes disproportionate hardship for families in lower income brackets. These types of discrepancies result in poor families being much more harshly affected by inflation – even during times of "modest" inflation when the Federal Reserve is considered to have done a good job managing price stability. By examining the compounding effect of inflation, FREOPP found "that from 2004 to 2020, earners in the bottom decile experienced inflation that was 71 percentage points higher than for the top decile."[159]

Most people probably think the Federal Reserve's target of 2% is an acceptable or even desirable level for the rate of inflation, but the accumulated effects of even this amount of inflation are profound even if you are not poor. Regardless of your income level, it would take less than 35 years for $1 to lose half of its purchasing power at that rate. As a result, each dollar the average person saves when they start their working career is worth less than 50 cents before they retire. And as we have seen above, because every family's "basket of goods" is different, this loss of purchasing power is actually devastating to poor families. It takes no special analysis to conclude that higher inflation rates are even more damaging.

While the 2% target hurts poor folks, when inflation breaches 9% as it did in 2022, everyone is affected and the Federal Reserve takes notice.[160] Because the central bank has blunt tools to address runaway inflation, we see an unfortunate but reliable boom-bust pattern in response to business cycles. The Federal Reserve is happy to keep its foot on the accelerator as long as inflation, as measured in evolving ways, isn't extreme. In these boom times, the well-connected and rich add to their wealth.

When inflation is out of control, the solution is to raise interest rates as quickly as feasible to decrease demand. This seems like a good goal but is very difficult to accomplish without unintentionally starting a recession. Through most of 2021, the Federal Reserve and other government officials referred to the inflation regular people were feeling in their pocketbook as "transitory," meaning it would quickly pass and inflation *rates* (not the actual prices) would return to normal. It took until June 2022 for Treasury Secretary Janet Yellen to admit she and Jerome Powell were wrong about inflation being transitory.[161] By August of 2022, Jerome Powell was setting the narrative for both Wall Street and Main Street to expect economic hardship. During the annual policy speech in Jackson Hole, Wyoming, Powell warned that while the Federal Reserve's actions "will bring down inflation, they will also bring some pain to households and businesses."[162] This pain is sure to mean layoffs and reduced hours for working folks. When it comes to inflation, both the illness and the cure hurt poor folks the most.

Creating Fair Money

There are two main differences between dollars and Bitcoin with regard to inflation. The first, and most obvious, is that the monetary policy for Bitcoin is set now and into the future and is programmatically assured to be scarce. How much money is in the Bitcoin system does not depend on a small group of powerful bankers meeting in Washington each month. The amount of bitcoin that exists at any one time is known and will be known forever. Unlike dollars, there is no risk of a massive amount of bitcoin being pumped into the economy at the whim of politicians. Unlike dollars, there are no policymakers that get to debase the money supply and make the bitcoin you already own less valuable. The fact that the overall supply of bitcoin is fixed at 21 million makes it the scarcest asset in the world. In comparison the *supply* of dollars between March 2020 and December 2021 during the pandemic increased by 42%.[163] During the same time, the supply of bitcoin increased by the exact 3.3%[164] as it was programmed to do when the genesis block was mined in 2009.

Gold is known for having the highest stock-to-flow ratio among all assets within traditional markets. Put simply, this means that the gold in existence (stock) is many times higher than the gold produced each year (flow). The stock-to-flow ratio for gold is about 60, meaning at current rates it would take 60 years to mine the amount of gold that already exists.[165] By way of comparison, silver has a stock-to-flow ratio of 22.[166] Until 2024, Bitcoin will have a stock-to-flow ratio comparable to gold at 57. But in the spring of 2024, the amount of new bitcoin created in each block will be halved, and the stock-to-flow ratio will be more than double that of gold at 124.[167] No other commodity in human history has had a comparable stock-to-flow ratio. This is an important measure of scarcity and an assurance that prices denominated in bitcoin will not increase based on changes to the supply of money in the system. The 21 million cap on bitcoin is completely immutable, and the schedule for the release of that supply is known and fixed.

Bitcoin therefore provides a consistent frame of reference that allows all market participants to more easily interact with meaningful price signals. This means that changes in price in a system based on Bitcoin would actually reflect a signal that could inform the decisions of consumers and investors. Everyday people interacting with Bitcoin would not have to swim against a tide of the constant price increases needed by the fiat system. When prices for a particular good or service increase, they do so for a reason rooted in supply and demand. In all other cases, prices will remain the same or decrease in conjunction with increases in the efficiencies provided by technology and human innovation. The inflation that is baked into the current system would no longer be part of the calculus of saving, spending, or investing.

The second difference Bitcoin has with dollars in regard to inflation is more subtle and concerns how new money is created and who benefits from that creation. A defining characteristic of Bitcoin mining is that it requires work, or more formally an expenditure of energy. This expenditure of energy is precisely why the analogy with mining gold gained traction and has been used as a metaphor since Satoshi first incorporated it into the Bitcoin vernacular in the original Bitcoin whitepaper.[168] However, while the metaphor is useful, it is flawed in important ways. Unlike gold miners, Bitcoin miners are not just in search of bitcoin that already exist. The main work of Bitcoin miners is to secure the network. In return for that service, a miner is rewarded with freshly minted bitcoin. The fact that Bitcoin has both monetary value and cost tied to the real world provides the incentive for miners to expend the energy needed to secure the distributed network without the need for a centralized authority to control the system. But this is also the only way new bitcoin come into existence.

Anyone, anywhere in the world, can get a share of the new bitcoin if they do work to help secure the Bitcoin network. There is no requirement to be rich or well-connected. There is no requirement to own a bank or pull political strings. The network is a completely flat and open collection of peers working in concert to operate a monetary technology. Participating in the act of securing that network and reaping the reward for that work is an opportunity that is open to the entire world. Those who can't afford to contribute a lot of hash power to the mining effort can join pools with other people and are rewarded proportionately to the power they do provide. There is no theoretical minimum to join the process. In every meaningful sense, the process to gain newly created money in the Bitcoin system is fair, equitable, and transparent. There are no backroom deals, no surprises, and no inside information.

An optimist might argue that the same is true for the "creation" of new gold. After all, although mining gold does require a bit of luck, in principle it is fair and transparent. There is also no scenario where a person or company is able to reliably mine gold without putting in a massive amount of work and expending a lot of energy. This is what makes gold a "hard" money – it is hard to create more of it. Its hardness, coupled with its scarcity, is what made gold the best monetary technology humans had access to for the five thousand years leading up to 2009.

But in practice mining gold is quite different from mining bitcoin. The process to mine new gold is not open to everyone: you need land rights, capital for heavy machinery, access to a labor force, and access to refining equipment to mine gold and bring new money into existence. In addition, the market is saturated and gold stores are increasingly difficult to find, while the marginal cost to mine and refine an ounce of gold now hovers closely to the price it will fetch on the open market.[169]

As a result, the analogy does not hold in critically important ways. Bitcoin not only improves on the hardness of gold and its scarcity, but it also improves on its accessibility. If you're reading this sentence, you are allowed to mine Bitcoin and you can do so in proportion to the amount of energy you are able and willing to expend. Further, the act of mining gold does nothing to secure the place of gold as a monetary asset, but you can rest assured that the primary function of mining Bitcoin is to protect the entire monetary network. In short, there is no competition when you truly compare the systems designed to create new money in the form of Bitcoin and gold. For many millennia, gold represented the best way humans could create new money, but now Bitcoin is better.

Who Is Closest to the Spigot?

Needless to say, in comparison to Bitcoin, the process to create new fiat currency is an abject failure rooted in political gamesmanship, cronyism, greed, and perverted incentive structures. In the 18th century, in his book *An Essay on Economic Theory*,[170] Richard Cantillon explained why newly created money does not flow through an economy equitably. In the simplest terms, those closest, in a political or financial sense, to the source of the new money will benefit to a greater extent than those farther away. The premise, put in modern terms, is that those with privileged access to new money like large banks or well-connected companies are able to invest that money in hard assets that retain their value before the devalued money slowly spreads to the rest of the economy. Affluent folks with connections to banks, that have connections to the Federal Reserve, will buy houses, stocks, gold, or even Bitcoin with those dollars. By the time they reach a working-class person in the middle of America, the prices for goods and services that person needs or wants have gone up.

Consider the following simplified example to see what has come to be called the "Cantillon Effect" might work in practice. Imagine a small, isolated island economy with 10 participants. This economy is circular and has achieved an equilibrium with 1000 tokens that the 10 participants use as a monetary good in exchange for goods and services. In practical terms, plots of land on the island are scarce as there are a limited number for the community of 10. Foodstuffs are also limited, but much more elastic to demand because there are practical ways higher prices offered for fruit or fish could incentivize increased production. The small economy hums with some owning land and others renting. Some folks fish and some folks grow food. Some of the people in this system are objectively better off than others, but in a theoretical sense all 10 people have an opportunity to access a share of the 1000 money tokens by providing goods and services that their peers need or want.

One day, Person A finds a buried chest with 500 money tokens and decides to keep it a complete secret from the other nine people on the island. Not only does Person A have access to knowledge about a 50% increase in the money supply, but they also can use this "new" money. What happens?

Assuming Person A decides to use their newfound money to purchase scarce assets that will retain their value, buying plots of land would be the logical choice since there can't be any more produced. At first, the newfound money will allow Person A to buy parcels of land at normal market prices. If needed, the money he discovered will allow him to outbid others for a desirable property. The money for that land will then go to the previous owner (let's call them Person B). Person B will have more money to spend on rent or foodstuffs. Without any formal announcement, the laws of supply and demand kick in, and the island "intuits" that there is now more money chasing the same amount of goods. By the time Person C has money tokens flow to them by selling their wares to Person B, inflation has increased the cost of their needs and wants. Person C has more money, but things cost more too. This inflation helps Person A, whose new property has increased in value since they knocked over the first domino in this process. And while Person B benefited less than Person A, they will still end up better off than Person C. This is because Person B was able to do most of their purchasing with the previous less-inflated prices. By the time Person C makes a purchase, inflation has begun to raise prices. The further a person is from the buried chest, the less they benefit. By the time all 500 new tokens are distributed in the economy, there is net harm done by inflation to those "farthest" from the money in the chest. Person A and the few others who had early access to the new money will end up better off.

This is a simplified and imperfect example, but it does illustrate the point that folks with special access to new money are not only able to purchase scarce assets before the effects of the new money (i.e., inflation) trickle through an economy, but they are incentivized to do it. This Cantillon Effect is at work in the modern-day fiat system and has helped contribute to the widening wealth gap that seems to grow every year. By virtue of their wealth, the wealthy are able to position themselves at the front of the new money queue and gain access to dollars they know will be devalued by the introduction of the very money they get to hold first.

New money is introduced to the economy at practically zero cost and given to specific parties, usually banks, before others. Those closest to the points of money infusion hold a special arbitrage opportunity by being able to buy assets, goods, and services whose prices have not yet reflected the increase in the money supply. Bankers and asset holders who are positioned close to the Federal Reserve stand to benefit disproportionately compared to those that are farther away. This method to create money is inherently unfair and hurts the most vulnerable within our economy. The poorer a family is the more likely they are to be shut out of the banking system entirely. Over 5% of American households are unbanked and have no access to freshly printed money, while the percentage of Black households that are unbanked is closer to 14%.[171]

While the introduction of new money to support a 2% rate of inflation is widely considered by mainstream economists as healthy, the benefits of this system do not get distributed with any semblance of equity. The same 2% inflation that helps a banker or corporation actually hurts the working poor. We are told without the 2% inflation, the economy cannot grow. But you don't need to be a progressive to look around and see for whom the economy has really grown since 1971. From the vantage point of five decades, everyone can see that having a money supply not pegged to a hard commodity asset like gold allows for printed money to flow to the most affluent and well-connected in society.

Liberals and progressives often make a big show about fighting against wealth inequality, but the tacit assumption is that wealth inequality is simply a symptom of a larger problem – the pernicious structure that allows wealth inequality in the first place. Folks on the left are really fighting against the rigged mechanisms and opacity that promote wealth accumulation for the very few at the expense of everyone else. As this chapter makes clear, Bitcoin helps with this. Since the world was stripped of its hard money peg, we have seen wealth inequality explode to stratospheric levels. Most liberals would point to the regressive policies of Reagan and other Republican politicians to explain this phenomenon, and I wouldn't argue against them. But it is important to recognize that the underlying monetary structure that underpinned those policies is also to blame. The era of the fiat dollar has resulted in the most extreme wealth concentration seen in the United States since 1929, and there are no signs the trend will slow down. In fact, since the Great Financial Crisis[172] and the 2020 pandemic[173] things have only gotten worse.

There are two critical differences to a Bitcoin system as compared to fiat money. To be clear, one of those differences will not be that wealthy individuals, as measured by how many bitcoin they have, no longer exist. Of course there will always be some who have more than others. But one key difference is that those individuals who have a lot of bitcoin are not able to influence the protocol of money creation to obtain more. The creation of bitcoin is algorithmic as opposed to a political decision that benefits those closest to power and information. The creation of bitcoin is vastly more transparent and fair than fiat money and much more easily understood than the creation of new dollars.

The second key difference is that unlike fiat dollars, bitcoin has become more distributed over time. Despite what you may read in mainstream media about this topic, the measurements used by those claiming bitcoin is concentrated toward a very few are comically inept. Arguments like those seen in the *Wall Street Journal*[174] that claim alarming wealth concentration in bitcoin make fundamental errors in determining how many bitcoin are held by individuals versus exchanges, or even accounting for bitcoin that have previously been lost. A careful analysis of bitcoin distribution over time reveals a steady decrease in inequality since the network's inception. By some accounts, the Gini coefficient for Bitcoin (0.48)[175] is below that in the United States (0.49),[176] and it is certainly less than the global Gini coefficient, which hovers around 0.65.[177]

The key takeaway is not where the inequality stands right now, but instead the trend. The decreasing trend in inequality is exactly what we would expect to see from a new monetary medium as it gains adoption. As measured by the Gini coefficient, we have seen a steady decline in inequality over time when analysts properly factor in custodial and exchange wallets.[178] It is impossible to predict the future, but because increased adoption will require further dissemination of bitcoin to new users and because the fundamental structure of Bitcoin is open, transparent, and fair, I expect this trend to continue. Unlike the fiat money system, Bitcoin has the potential to make the world's economic systems operate more justly. It is hard to imagine a scenario where this is the case with dollars.

Staggering wealth inequality is a true marker for a society in trouble. And that is precisely where we are now in both America and globally. Politicians and voters on the left have good intentions to make the current system more fair, but these are simply attempts to turn the dials from within a system that is structurally unjust. Because they already have so much there is no way to change the incentives for those who create money and control the process.

But a new system is possible. Bitcoin provides a chance for a more fair and transparent monetary system. It does not promise equality, but true equity is possible. With progressive voices helping to guide policy and make decisions in a new political system, we can step away from a corrupt, opaque system that benefits the few at the expense of the many. Bitcoin is hope, and progressive voices are needed to help move us in a more just direction.

Chapter 7: The Untold Cost of US Dollar Hegemony

So You Want a Strong Dollar?

The World Economic Forum is a meeting of important politicians, policymakers, and economic leaders from around the globe. Once a year the Forum is held in Davos, Switzerland, and is a Who's Who of influential people. If you're a very important person, you will find yourself in Davos during the WEF. If you're not quite that important, but you care a great deal about global macroeconomic developments, then you will be paying very close attention to what is said in Davos. The WEF itself has gained attention as a metaphor for the oversized impact that billionaires and politicians have on global economic policy that affects every person in the world. Peter Goodman's book, *Davos Man: How Billionaires Devoured the World* sets the tone well:

> *"Davos Man" has grown into a catchall... as shorthand for those who occupy the stratosphere of the globe-trotting class, the billionaires – predominantly white and male – who wield unsurpassed influence over the political realm while promoting a notion that has captured decisive force across major economies: when the rules are organized around greater prosperity for those who already enjoy most of it, everyone's a winner.*[179]

In Davos, political and industrial leaders pontificate on every aspect of trade, finance, and economics. In 2018, while at the WEF in Davos, President Donald Trump gave an interview with CNBC in which he firmly claimed, "The dollar is going to get stronger and stronger, and ultimately I want to see a strong dollar."[180] On the surface, this seemed to be an appeal toward Trump's "America First" base. After all, if America is the best, strongest country, of course it is going to have the best, strongest currency.

Trump celebrated the strong dollar and took credit for it.[181] But Trump wasn't the first American president to applaud a strong US dollar. It's been happening for decades. It is a political trick for winning low-information voters and engendering a sense of pride and patriotism: Dollar strong = America strong. But the reality is much different, and the promise of a "strong" dollar has counterintuitive implications for Americans and the rest of the global community.

What does a strong dollar mean in reality? On the one hand, if you've ever traveled abroad, you've probably recognized that converting dollars to another currency does affect your purchasing power. Any American in Mexico will enjoy a higher purchasing power than they are used to once they convert their dollars to pesos.

But from a macroeconomic perspective, a strong US dollar means that goods and services produced in America, priced in dollars, are more expensive to the rest of the world. When the goods and services that the United States produces become very expensive, economic actors quickly realize they can get what they need for less money elsewhere. As a result, a strong US dollar leads to a trade deficit and undercuts America's ability to export actual products to other countries. All things being equal, the strong dollar makes things too expensive for businesses in other countries and they stop buying American. At the same time, American businesses are incentivized to import cheaper materials and products from abroad.

It's hard to categorize America's trade deficit as completely bad. In some ways, it has allowed for an increase in the standard of living for most Americans by providing them with cheap products they can buy that make them happy. But in part as a result of the strong dollar, America is also making less stuff because of the trade deficit. There are empty factories along the entire rust belt that tell sickening stories of financial hardship for everyday people trying to feed their families. In a very real sense, the "strong" dollar that politicians have used to rally their patriotic supporters these last 50 years has hollowed out this country's industrial base.

The cumulative shift these issues have caused in America's political and economic landscape has been astonishing, but not surprising. The connection between a strong US dollar and the subsequent trade deficit was easy to predict. These issues were well understood by politicians and most serious economic players as far back as the 1960s when economist Robert Triffin identified the risks that a strong US dollar – partially the result of using the dollar as the global reserve currency – would impose on the domestic economy.

In basic terms the "Triffin Dilemma," as it came to be known, identified that any national money used as a global reserve currency would drive up international demand for it, making it stronger. This trend would then play out in predictable ways as a conflict between maintaining the benefits of having a global reserve currency and the impacts such policy would have on trade deficits and domestic production.[182] The Triffin Dilemma correctly identified the tension the United States had to address between the US dollar maintaining hegemonic status around the globe and factory workers in Ohio trying to make ends meet.

The fact that Triffin identified this concept as a dilemma is apt. The United States is forced to make choices between providing the world with a liquid supply of the global reserve currency to keep the world economy running or supporting the jobs and industries underpinning the American people. We now see the results of those collective choices. There is no doubt we have seen a shift toward the financial sector and away from manufacturing in the United States over the last several decades.[183] There has been a lot of talk about the

Democratic Party abandoning white, working-class voters in America's heartland. What seems more obvious is the leaders of this country, regardless of political affiliation, have spent the last several decades defending a strong dollar and US dollar hegemony around the world.

At the same time manufacturing in America began its long decline, the financialization of the American economy has been on the steady rise – since the early 1970s when Nixon closed the gold window. This has disproportionately benefited those at the top of the economic ladder.[184] Despite technology making financial processes more efficient and less expensive, the cost of financial intermediation continues to grow, with large banks and their CEOs soaking up the difference. This has provided a boon to politicians and the American financial sector at the express detriment to working people in America and almost everyone else around the world.

There is no doubt that wealth concentration, as measured in America and internationally, is a serious problem. The hollowing out of the American manufacturing sector is one major reason for this decades-long shift toward inequality in the US. At the same time, banks have gotten bigger and profited more. As a general rule, we simply don't make things anymore. Instead, we move money around.

To be clear, the financial sector is important for a healthy economy. We need banks and insurance companies to provide liquidity and capital for our economy to thrive. But it is not healthy to have the financial sector be the largest portion of the economy because it harms real economic growth.[185] It is not healthy for banks to act as speculative investors while the working people of this country see factory doors being closed.

But wealth inequality is not just the result of a few rich, greedy CEOs. Throughout this chapter, we will see how wealth inequality in this country is a structural problem caused by how the dollar is created and how its hegemonic status is maintained. But to best understand that structural problem – and how Bitcoin can help – we need to understand how we got to this point in the first place.

How We Got Here

For about a century, the United States dollar has enjoyed an immense privilege as the world reserve currency. It wasn't always like this, and maybe more surprising, one day it will no longer be. It might be hard for most Americans to imagine the monetary system that has existed their entire life is simply a short blip in the history of money and is likely to transition to a new system within their lifetimes. The currency used for international commerce and as a reserve asset by nation-states changes roughly every 80 to 100 years. Since 1450 the currency of the following nations has served the role as the global reserve currency:[186]

Nation	**Years**	**Duration**
Portugal	1450 - 1530	80 years
Spain	1530 - 1640	90 years
Netherlands	1640 - 1720	80 years
France	1720 - 1815	95 years
Great Britain	1815 - 1920	105 years
United States	1921 - present	101 years +

The next reserve currency will likely establish itself this decade and for the first time in history a stateless, decentralized, natively digital option exists. We have no way of knowing if Bitcoin will take on the role of global reserve currency when the need arises, but we can say with certainty that whatever currency winds up serving that role will be shaped by both the monetary policy and the technology developed within Bitcoin since its inception.

It is worth considering how we arrived at this juncture. The dollar's ascent to the hegemonic monetary unit of the world followed a long and interesting path. Understanding it is important for grasping the current system that Bitcoin is aiming to replace. By studying the dollar's history, we also see how fiercely the United States has been willing to defend the dollar's privileged status.

In the aftermath of the first World War, the United States dollar was uniquely positioned to become the world reserve currency. America had a functioning industrial base that wasn't razed by the war and held abundant reserves of gold to back a stable money with a strong network effect. Since then, the definition of what a dollar is has changed, but the dollar has remained the dominant global monetary unit.

When the dollar stepped into the role of global reserve currency in 1921, it operated on a gold standard in which the dollar's value was directly pegged to the value of gold. The exchange rate was a fixed $20.67 per ounce of gold for many decades leading up to 1921 and for about a decade after. Most countries operated in this way, only occasionally suspending their currency's gold standard in times of war and crisis. These suspensions are discussed in more detail in Chapter 8. Proponents of the gold standard claim that using a hard currency like gold encouraged price stability, thrift, and economic planning.

But then another war arrived, even worse than its predecessor, destabilizing economies around the world as well as their financial systems. In the summer of 1944 war was still raging in both Europe and the Pacific. It would be another year before World War II would come to a close, but 730 representatives of 44 nations met in a remote hotel in Bretton Woods, New Hampshire to decide on what the world's monetary system would look like following the anticipated Allied victory.[187] The agreement that was made during this month-long conference became known as the Bretton Woods system and it would structure the global economy for over a quarter of a century.

Various options were considered at Bretton Woods for a global reserve currency, including a concept of an international "basket" of currencies (called the bancor).[188] However, this idea was not going to fly with the most powerful nation emerging from a devastating world war. The ultimate decision was made to peg the United States dollar to gold at the then-standard exchange rate of $35 per ounce, and all other national currencies pegged to the dollar at a fixed exchange rate. There is more information in Chapter 4 about how and why in the 1930s an ounce of gold changed from $20.67 to $35.00. This re-established the dollar in a privileged status and renewed its role as the global reserve currency in the postwar world. For obvious geopolitical reasons, Bretton Woods was an offer the other countries of the world could not refuse. The system necessitated nations around the world to trust America to be good stewards of the dollar by properly maintaining its peg to gold.

Throughout the rest of the 1940s and the 1950s, the Bretton Woods system mostly operated as designed. It wasn't until the 1960s that the system started showing signs of strain. The first bad omen for Bretton Woods came in 1961 when the London Gold Pool was created to defend the US dollar peg to gold at $35.[189] Later in the decade, due in part to increased expenditures by the US government for domestic initiatives and the Vietnam War along with a nascent but growing Euro-dollar system (i.e., dollar-denominated assets held in foreign banks[190]), it became clear that the United States was unwilling, and perhaps even unable to maintain the dollar peg to gold. Because too many dollars had been printed compared to the gold backing them, the US dollar had been debased beyond repair.

In August of 1971, facing increasing pressure from foreign governments to trade out debased dollars for gold reserves, President Nixon closed the "gold window" and ceased the direct convertibility of US dollars to gold.[191] This decision was a fundamental change in monetary policy that allowed the US government to stem the outflow of gold from its reserves. It also had the obvious effect of removing the entire world from the gold standard with a stroke of a pen. Moving forward, the only thing backing the dollar was people's trust in it.

Though it is rarely described in such harsh terms, by closing the convertibility of dollars into gold, the government of the United States effectively defaulted on its financial obligations.

Since that day the world has operated on a fiat standard, with no national currency being pegged to a hard asset like gold. As before, the US dollar would continue to be the world reserve currency, but after Nixon's action, the dollar and every other money in the world would be free to float in value against one another.

There was a clear danger in this. Not only was it likely that currencies would devalue without the gold standard, but the stable, predictable Bretton Woods system had been scrapped. International commerce would have increased friction from currency values continuously floating, and this would invite speculators and arbitrageurs to take advantage of the new system. Not surprisingly, the dollar cost for an ounce of gold, which had been artificially suppressed for years by the Bretton Woods agreement, increased by over 1,200% between 1971 and the end of the decade.[192] One may be tempted to think that the value of gold had increased, but the reality is that the value of the dollar had plummeted. A dollar bill from 1971 today only has the equivalent purchasing power of 13 cents.[193]

Of course, changes to what the dollar means are nothing new: because it existed in a different global environment, the dollar that existed under the Bretton Woods system was different from the dollar that existed prior to the Second World War. The same is true in 1971: the "dollar" as it was defined in August after President Nixon's actions was clearly different from the dollar that existed a month prior under the Bretton Woods system. Having money backed by nothing but the full faith and credit of a government is much different than having one backed by gold: the former means you can print money with impunity, while the latter places strict limits on currency manipulation. And while that system still exists today, it wasn't the last time the definition of a "dollar" changed.

That Thing in Your Wallet Is a Petrodollar

The United States unilaterally dismantling the Bretton Woods system that had been keeping the postwar economic world running for 26 years had long-lasting repercussions. Across the globe, nations held dollars as reserve assets that were suddenly backed by nothing. At the height of the Cold War with the Soviet Union, this posed a serious threat to US dollar hegemony. While it was unlikely that any single nation could have taken on the mantle of providing the world reserve currency at that time, the thought of a financial multipolar world in which a collection of currencies filled the role that the dollar had previously held was a distinct possibility. This threat had the potential to undermine America's dominance on the international stage, and Nixon knew that something had to be done.

In 1974 Nixon sent new Treasury Secretary William Simon to Saudi Arabia to try and implement a plan conceived by then Secretary of State and National Security Advisor Henry Kissinger.[194] Though certain aspects of the deal remained a state secret for many years, several steps of the plan were clear from the outset. The first was to convince the Saudis to price their oil exports in dollars. Dollars received by selling exported oil are now referred to as petrodollars. The second step of the plan was for Saudi Arabia to recycle their newfound petrodollar wealth by purchasing US treasuries to help finance America's growing public debt.

For many reasons this system was crucial for the United States to maintain global dominance through the rest of the 20th century. For one, there was an increase in the demand for dollars abroad, since any importer of oil would need access to dollars to purchase Saudi oil. Pricing oil in dollars quickly spread to the entire OPEC consortium,[195] further increasing the demand for dollars and ossifying the global reserve status of the currency. Secondly, this plan gave the United States the unique ability to print dollars with which they could buy oil. Other nations, particularly those hostile to US interests, either had to procure dollars for oil or dig it out of the ground on their own. This provided an obvious strategic advantage to the United States. Thirdly, America had found in Saudi Arabia a consistent and stable purchaser of their US Treasury debt. This allowed the US to accrue larger and larger deficits directly funded by oil money from the Middle East. Lastly, the consistent purchase of US treasuries helped suppress interest rates on that debt, making the US debt easier to service.

This was a complete win for the United States. The genius of Kissinger's concept was to get something very valuable (oil) to directly depend on something that was depreciating at a noticeable rate (dollars). We could accrue debt, print money, buy oil, have the Saudis buy more debt, print money, buy oil, and so on... Other nations, assuming they needed oil, were forced to play along also. Demand for dollars goes up. Confidence in the dollar then goes up. America has access to cheap energy. America is then able to finance its growing debt.

In his book *Super Imperialism*, Michael Hudson rightly identifies that the United States' ability to turn its debt into the basis of the international economic order was unprecedented in history.[196] With the aid of the petrodollar, the United States was able to shift the entire global economy away from asset money like gold to settle international payments and toward the debt money of American treasuries. At the height of the Cold War, America's status as a debtor nation went from being a potential weakness to an element of surprising strength. By monetizing American debt in this way, the United States was able to pursue both a robust (if inefficient) welfare state and unprecedented military expansion across the globe. Through the next few decades, the world would see American influence expand exponentially through the dual tracks of economic and military dominance – dominance fueled by deficits funded by weaker, poorer nations.

The obvious question is why would the Saudis agree to such a petrodollar deal in the first place? In 1974, the Kingdom of Saudi Arabia wasn't exactly a staunch US ally. In fact, a year earlier Saudi Arabia and the other OPEC nations, in response to America's military support of Israel, had both cut oil production to drive up prices and imposed an embargo on the United States. This embargo, which banned the export of oil to various countries sympathetic to Israel's effort in the Yom Kippur War, put an acute strain on the United States economy that (partially) manifested in the now infamous gas lines of the 1970s. The cost of a barrel of crude oil began the decade in 1970 at $3.35 and ended the decade more expensive by a factor of ten, priced at $32.50.[197] When Treasury Secretary William Simon arrived in Saudi Arabia in 1974, he was entering hostile territory, and it certainly seemed like he lacked the leverage needed to secure Kissinger's petrodollar framework. But striking the deal was crucial both to America's economic success and to stunting the Soviet Union's ability to influence the oil-rich Arab world.

But America had something that Saudi Arabia very much wanted. In exchange for Saudi Arabia reinvesting billions of petrodollars into American debt, the United States would provide military support and equipment to the Kingdom of Saudi Arabia. By 1975 Saudi Arabia imported over $5 billion worth of military equipment from the United States, representing a 16-fold increase from the amount they spent just 3 years prior. At the insistence of King Faisal bin Abdulaziz Al Saud, the connection between treasury purchases and the military alliance was kept completely secret at the time.[198] Much later the world learned that Saudi Arabia was able to purchase US treasuries outside the normal process at preferred rates.[199]

The petrodollar system may seem like a pretty clever accounting trick, but the long-term implications of this deal are massive. Often overshadowed by Watergate, it is reasonable to argue that both the abandonment of the gold standard and the creation of the petrodollar system deserve as much attention as the scandal that ended Nixon's presidency. The deal struck in 1974 to prop up the "worthless" US dollar began a decades-long relationship between the United States and Saudi Arabia that continues to have distressing ripple effects today.

Your Petrodollar Likes Dictators

It is beyond the scope of this book to recount the entire history of US-Saudi relations within the context of wider US involvement around the world since the petrodollar system began in 1974. It is valuable, though, to consider how the system that Kissinger and Nixon set into motion has generally influenced America's place in the world since then. Our focus here is examining just some of the ways in which a broken monetary system has invariably led to violence, manipulation, and suffering. Most of those negative externalities of broken money have been exported, through the decades, beyond the shores of the United States. This is a unique benefit afforded to the nation that controls the dominant monetary unit, as damaged as it may be. It is valid to ask if the world would be a better place if there was better money available simply because the lengths the United States has gone to preserve the dollar are truly striking.[200]

In 2016, Chris Murphy, a Democrat from Connecticut, joined Rand Paul, a Republican from Kentucky, to introduce in the Senate a bipartisan resolution to halt the sale of arms to Saudi Arabia.[201] This particular 2016 resolution was introduced in response to the Saudi involvement in the Civil War in Yemen. A growing chorus of human rights organizations had criticized the Saudi government and accused the country of war crimes that included targeting of civilians and children.[202] Senator Murphy made clear his view that the close relationship between the United States and the Kingdom of Saudi Arabia needs to be more carefully considered: "My first desire is for our relationship with Saudi Arabia to come with a greater degree of conditionality than it currently does." The resolution stalled following a procedural vote, but the sentiment behind the resolution lived on. Similar resolutions, each with bipartisan support, have been introduced in nearly each Congress since 2016. For example, Rand Paul and Bernie Sanders put a similar one forward in 2021.[203] In 2019 multiple resolutions prohibiting the sale of arms to Saudi Arabia managed to pass Congress with bipartisan support, only to be vetoed by President Trump.[204]

These perennial attempts by the Legislative Branch to reign in arms sales to Saudi Arabia and the corresponding push back from the Executive Branch are nothing new. Since 1974 Presidents from both parties have been consistent in their material support for Saudi Arabia regardless of the wider public sentiment or concerns about human rights violations. There exists a special relationship between the two nations, and it seems that billions of dollars' worth of arms sales is only one half of America's obligation to keep the petrodollar intact. The other half seems to be turning a blind eye to humanitarian atrocities committed by the Saudis. It is not an oversimplification to conclude that America's toleration of the Saudi's human rights record is a direct result of our global monetary system being based on American debt and Saudi Arabia owning a large share of it.

Over the decades we have been able to see how the Faustian bargain of the petrodollar has materialized, and the results have not been pretty. In March of 2016, Saudi officials threatened to sell over $750 billion in American debt and other assets.[205] Such a move would have been devastating to both countries and would clearly destabilize the US dollar, but is exactly the type of situation that could arise when the very fabric of a nation's economic structure depends on debt that other countries are expected and pressured to buy.

The threat was made as a direct protest to legislation being considered by Congress that would allow Saudi Arabia to be held responsible in American courts for their role in the 9/11 terrorist attacks. By this time the 9/11 commission had been able to conclude that they "... found no evidence that the Saudi government as an institution or senior Saudi officials individually funded the [terrorist] organization."[206] But the wording seemed vague and most noticeably did not rule out the possibility that government officials or members of the Saudi royal family knew about or supported the 9/11 terrorist plot. It is well known that 15 of the 19 hijackers were Saudis, as was the mastermind behind the plot, Osama bin Laden. It is not surprising that the Saudi government responded by putting its thumb on the economic scale. President Obama was quick to side with the Saudis, warning that the proposed legislation could have "potentially serious financial consequences for the United States," adding that the bill "threatens to create complications in our relationships with even our closest partners."[207]

In May 2016, the Justice Against Sponsors of Terrorism Act passed the Senate by a unanimous voice vote. A few months later, the bill unanimously passed again, this time in the House of Representatives.[208] But in a move that he thoroughly foreshadowed, President Obama vetoed the bill. Five days later Congress overrode Obama's presidential veto – the only time this happened during his presidency – and the bill became law.

Despite some consistent pushback from elected representatives in Congress, powerful people within the American bureaucracy and the Executive Branch always seem to toe the line in regard to Saudi Arabia. American capitulation to Saudi Arabia has been a decades-long, bipartisan phenomenon. It was evident for the entirety of George W. Bush's presidency,[209] particularly in the heartbreaking wake of the September 11 terrorist attacks. Obama vetoed legislation aimed at holding Saudi Arabia accountable. Trump vetoed legislation designed to limit billions of dollars of arms sales to Saudi Arabia. After some unfulfilled promises that seemed to break from his predecessors, Biden has tacitly approved of Saudi Arabian offensives in Yemen and a related blockade that is believed to have caused tens of thousands of Yemenis children to starve to death.[210] It turns out that Presidents of both political parties are consistently eager to support the Kingdom in ways that might be surprising without an understanding of how the international economic engine works.

Even political enemies like Presidents Biden and Trump seem to find common ground when it comes to Saudi Arabia. Biden's version of getting "tough" with Saudi Arabia was to offer a fist bump instead of a handshake to Saudi crown prince and de facto leader, Mohammed bin Salman during his visit to the Middle East in the summer of

2022.[211] Just four years earlier Trump had refused to repudiate Mohammed bin Salman for the torture and execution of dissident Saudi journalist Jamal Khashoggi.[212] Despite harsh rhetoric on the campaign trail, in 2022 the Biden administration reversed course and made moves to shield Mohamed bin Salman from a lawsuit filed against him for Khashoggi's killing.[213] At every turn, it seems, American leadership is willing to forgo American ideals to keep the hegemony of the US dollar intact.

It bears repeating that the point here isn't that America is bad and does bad things. The key point is to examine the incentives for doing so. Instead of asset money like gold, the world's monetary system has been based on American debt since 1971. This system has allowed the United States to spend its way into a high standard of living for its citizens while establishing the dominant military presence around the globe. But it also means that to keep the system running smoothly, the most powerful nation in the world is beholden to foreign interests at times and in ways that are harmful to the principles of liberal democracy and humanitarian justice.

Nor is this a uniquely Middle Eastern phenomenon. In recent decades the Chinese government decided to join Saudi Arabia with its purchase of US treasuries, using the dollars resulting from their trade surplus with America. Between 2000 and 2011, as Americans' appetite for cheap items made in China came into full bloom, and Chinese holdings of US debt increased from $73 billion to over $1.3 trillion.[214] Owing the Chinese government that much money has come with the same flavor of tolerating human rights violations and oppression that came with our indebtedness to Saudi Arabia. Recent examples of American capitulation to China despite grotesque abuses and humanitarian catastrophes abound.[215] The lyrics may be different, but they rhyme.

It is important to understand that America does not simply support these atrocities to get more money. American abides them to protect the idea of what money is in the first place. Consider the facts: the United States represents 4% of the world population, and our economic output as measured by GDP is about 15%.[216] In contrast, the US dollar, and debt it is pegged to, represents nearly 60% of the reserve currency used around the world.[217] Almost 90% of all international transactions involve the US dollar,[218] even when neither of the parties is American.

Maintaining US Dollar Hegemony

The United States has not wasted the opportunity to wield influence all over the globe to both capitalize on and preserve the hegemonic role of the dollar. For decades the US has leaned heavily on international organizations like the World Bank and the International Monetary Fund (IMF) to deploy policies that benefit America, usually to the detriment of developing nations. Both were institutions created within the Bretton Woods system in the wake of World War II. The IMF was established to help maintain the exchange rates between national currencies as outlined by the Bretton Woods version of the gold standard. The World Bank was originally called the International Bank for Reconstruction and Development. Its primary purpose was to provide credit to nations trying to rebuild after the war. The two institutions work closely together in synergistic ways and often hold joint meetings. The headquarters for both institutions are quite literally across the street from one another and are a short walk from the White House. Indeed, any nation wishing to join the World Bank was required to also be a member of the IMF.

At face value, these organizations made sense at the time. If the Bretton Woods system was to thrive, there had to be a way to ensure stable exchange rates that pegged the dollar to gold and all other fiat currencies to the dollar. The IMF filled that purpose. Likewise, the World Bank was an attempt to avoid the mistakes the victorious countries made after World War I. Instead of forcing Germany to pay punitive war reparations that lead to inflation and economic collapse, the global community would help to rebuild all of Europe through the World Bank. The effort was a huge success. Countries receiving aid from the World Bank, in concert with the United States' Marshall Plan, were able to exceed their pre-war industrial output by 1951.[219]

But instead of folding up shop after having completed their stated aim, both organizations went looking for new goals. Certainly by 1971 the need for both of these organizations, as defined by their original charters, had completely evaporated. To understand what happened since 1971, it is important to understand that from their very inception, the United States has maintained crucial control over both of these international institutions – from how they operate to what priorities they promote. Their leadership has been led almost exclusively American,[220] and the people holding these positions come from the top tier of American investment banks and have held influential political positions within the United States government. In the World Bank's original charter, the United States was given so many voting rights that it effectively constituted a unilateral veto power.[221] Today, the United States and its allies still enjoy an effective veto power on its decisions.[222] The voting powers in the IMF are even more skewed toward the United States.[223] From the original drafting and ratification of the Articles of Agreement through today, it is easy to see that nothing happens within the World Bank or the IMF unless it is in America's best interest. As Hudson puts it in *Super Imperialism*, both the IMF and the World Bank were effective in "establishing the postwar order for most of the world on extractive and increasingly militarized laissez-faire principles under US leadership and domination."[224]

In 1971 when President Nixon severed the gold peg of the dollar, the President of the World Bank was former Secretary of Defense Robert McNamara. McNamara is most famous for escalating American involvement in Vietnam under Presidents Kennedy and Johnson. But his legacy as President of the World Bank had lasting implications that still affect the world today. Under McNamara's leadership, the World Bank deftly shifted its focus from rebuilding worn-torn Europe to fighting global poverty.[225] It's hard to know for sure if McNamara truly believed in this new mission for the World Bank, but there is no doubt he leveraged that mission to great effect in order to promote American interests all over the world. What is more obvious is that the World Bank, working in concert with the IMF, has since used the framework of fighting global poverty to impose strict requirements on developing nations in exchange for much-needed loans. These requirements had the effect of forcing developing nations to export commodities and other natural resources, dampened investment in internal infrastructure and education, while forcing countries to import finished items and consumables from the United States.[226] Stringent and harmful austerity measures are placed on nations needing loans from the World Bank, which is an ironic double standard considering the United States has been able thrive by monetizing its debt. As a result, the internal capital of these poor nations suffered and they became more, not less, reliant on the United States and international agencies like the World Bank and the IMF. Nations indebted in this way exposed themselves to leverage from the United States for a variety of geopolitical ends, and throughout the Cold War, this leverage was used to great effect to ensure these developing countries were dependent on Western nations and disincentivized to fall under the communist umbrella of the USSR. This type of debt-trap diplomacy provided the United States plenty of leverage and incentive to shape the world order.

There are numerous examples one could cite of the influence of the World Bank on world affairs, but certainly one of the most notorious was its dealings with Chile. Under McNamara, the World Bank refused to do business with the democratically elected President of Chile, Salvador Allende. Despite the politically neutral mission of the World Bank, this was strictly a decision based on the United States' fear that Allende would push Chile closer to socialism. The World Bank suspended all loans to Chile in response to President Nixon's worries that Chile would become "another Cuba."[227] It was never proven that America had any direct involvement in the military coup that deposed Allende and instated Augusto Pinochet as the de facto dictator of Chile. But America did support Pinochet in material ways once he came to power. Despite widespread and well-documented human rights violations by Pinochet's regime,[228] it did not take long for McNamara and the World Bank to warm to Chile once again. In 1974, the year after the military coup that brought Pinochet to power, McNamara flew to Santiago to meet the Chilean leader. Shortly after that meeting, Chile began receiving loans from the World Bank again.[229]

There are other instances of McNamara leveraging the power of the World Bank in exploitative and harmful ways. For example, at the 1968 joint meeting of the IMF and World Bank, McNamara declared that developing nations that promoted birth control practices would receive preferential access to resources.[230] Instead of working to increase the amount of food these nations needed to sustain their populations, it was the World Bank's policy to not merely advocate population control but hold countries in the poor global south hostage until they adopted its policies. Of course, rich Western nations were not held to any population control measures. Astonishingly, McNamara would later speak favorably about the practice of forced sterilizations in nations like India that received loans and other aid from the World Bank and the IMF.[231]

The policies of the World Bank under McNamara became a template that gained wide use through the subsequent decades. In his book *Confession of An Economic Hitman*, John Perkins elaborates in great detail the lengths taken to extract value and resources from developing countries around the world under the guise of fighting poverty and providing aid. Perkins officially worked as an economist at an international consulting firm where he advised the World Bank, United Nations, IMF, and the US Treasury Department. As a general rule, infrastructure development in poor countries was paid for by loans from international organizations like the World Bank and IMF. Not only were these loans provided with onerous guidelines, but they were marketed with the full knowledge that the borrowing nation would be unable to pay off the debt as prescribed. False data was constructed and presented to the, often authoritarian, leaders of these countries that overstated the financial benefit of projects like building out an electrical grid or providing running water or sewage treatment to an area. The result by design was to saddle the borrowing nation in debt to keep them beholden to American interests.[232] Subsequently, the nation could become a pawn in whatever geopolitical chess match the United States decided to venture into.

Meanwhile, the lucrative contracts to do the planning and building all went directly to American companies by design. As a result, the actual money from these loans effectively never left American shores. In Perkins' telling, no expense was spared when it came to bribing officials (with money, sex, and drugs) in various developing countries around the world. Gigantic sums flowed to opaque consulting, contracting, and building companies involved in these schemes while leaders who decided not to take loans under the terms offered were often "unlucky" and were quickly replaced by new leadership willing to play ball. To those with an intuitive sense that the global system is corrupt, rigged, and unfair, *Confessions of An Economic Hitman* is filled with moments that shock but not surprise. But through the lens of dollar hegemony, one is able to make sense of the corruption, violence, and extortion in a clearer, if not still depressing, way.

These are just a few examples of how America has comported itself abroad since the end of World War II. These policies and actions can be traced, at least in part, to dollar hegemony and the need to perpetuate the system based on cheap paper dollars and US debt. Whether from Saudi or Chilean human rights violations, military coups, debt-trap diplomacy, or forced sterilizations, the US petrodollar system combined with the dollar serving as the global reserve currency depends on and perpetuates suffering all over the world.

Today, the outsized control America exercises over money – a country with 4% of the world's population controlling a currency that represents 80% of global trade – manifest in how America imposes sanctions that tend to hurt the populations of countries rather than dissuade bad actors on the international stage. In recent years, the United States has limited certain countries from the SWIFT program, essentially cutting those countries off from the flow of international dollars.[233] Such geopolitical and financial moves are devastating. To be sure, the dominance of the dollar has benefited some Americans, especially those who control the levers of the military-industrial complex or the financial industry. And despite some of the creature comforts we have come to enjoy as a result of a strong dollar, many Americans and the rest of the world seem to be worse off since the world abruptly transitioned to paper money about 50 years ago.

Bitcoin: A Better Global Reserve Currency

To date, all global reserve currencies have been tied to a specific nation-state. If it wasn't the Americans committing and condoning atrocities in the 20th century, it was the Britons in the 19th, and the French before them. It is difficult to imagine, especially if you're American, that the world can be different than the way it has been your entire life. But global reserve currencies do not last forever and the world is changing. It took until 2022 for the IMF to approve other suitable reserve currencies like the Euro and the Pound Sterling – but they did. The justification for this dramatic policy shift was that "it is important that the dollar has competitors as an international reserve currency because it creates a theoretical alternative for the rest of the world in case American policymakers lead the dollar down a damaging path."[234] This may be just the first crack in the dam toward Bitcoin becoming the world's reserve currency. If this seems impossible, it's not because it can't happen. After all, precisely because it is neutral, Bitcoin is an obvious competitor to the US dollar.

It is worth thinking about what would happen with a truly neutral reserve currency that no nation controlled for the first time in history. How would the incentives to exploit and dominate change? How might the world look after a century with Bitcoin serving the function of an international unit of account and a reserve currency that operates on a level playing field across all nations?

We might first note that the Triffin Dilemma would no longer be a concern if Bitcoin were used as an international reserve currency. Demand for one nation's money would not unduly favor that nation, nor would that demand undercut the working folks in that country by artificially strengthening its currency. The world would be able to engage in economic activity supported by a stable base layer of money that could not be contorted or manipulated by any one powerful interest. Trade between nations could be truly free because the money is truly neutral. The idea may seem too good to be true, but we may have the chance to see such a world.

It should also be clear that the global adoption of Bitcoin would represent an improvement over both the Bretton Woods system and the subsequent system of the petrodollar. Bitcoin is a hard money asset like gold. But it is also a fast transaction layer like paper money. A Bretton Woods system, in which the world trusts a single country to maintain a peg to a hard asset, is now decidedly antiquated. Individuals now have the ability to hold base layer money themselves which serves as a check on every government on the planet. Further, unlike the treasury bonds propping up the petrodollar, Bitcoin does not represent a liability to any other nation or entity. It is not debt that one country owes to another like the American debt that China and Saudi Arabia hold. And unlike the US dollar, Bitcoin does not require guns or war to protect it. No single nation – whether they are the "good guys" or "bad guys" – can simply print more Bitcoin or manipulate the protocol to exert control over other nations and other peoples. Bitcoin is immune from political, economic, and military power.

Wider adoption of Bitcoin would also strip power and influence away from the IMF and the World Bank. Nations, especially poorer ones, will be able to invest directly into a hard monetary asset that isn't built upon debt. The monopoly that the World Bank and IMF share in dealing out loans to poor nations allow them to impose devastating conditions on the loans that cripple both the nation and its poorest citizens. Bitcoin offers a way out of that system. And some nations are already seizing the opportunity. When El Salvador adopted Bitcoin as legal tender, the response from the IMF was cold but predictable. The IMF immediately threatened that El Salvador's adoption of Bitcoin would be a hurdle for the nation to receive a loan from the institution.[235] This may seem like the response of a well-meaning international organization encouraging El Salvador to be more prudent. But it could also be interpreted as the IMF recognizing the threat Bitcoin presents and pulling the usual levers to protect itself.

In the end, El Salvador was able to successfully issue its own bonds without the need to take out a loan from the IMF. These so-called "volcano bonds" are backed by both the country's Bitcoin reserve and the mined Bitcoin from sustainable hydrothermal energy near volcanos.[236] Even in its own report published in February 2023, over 16 months after El Salvador adopted Bitcoin, the IMF concluded that Bitcoin's "risks have not materialized."[237] Bitcoin provides an exciting opportunity to return financial sovereignty back to the global south by reigning in these international organizations that have a devastating legacy of oppression.

For decades both the United States and the international organizations it influences have been able to leverage the dollar's status as the global reserve currency to bully and exploit the poorest nations of the world. Bitcoin offers a completely new, more fair system. It is a progressive ideal to fight against bullies taking advantage of the vulnerable, especially when the bully is able to game the rules to their benefit. Bitcoin is progressive in exactly this way.

Chapter 8: Bitcoin and Peace

France Has a Problem

Imagine you were in charge of the French government in the summer of 1914. War has embroiled much of Europe and it is clear that France will not escape what will be eventually known as World War I. All summer long, declarations of war are announced between your allies and foes. Knowing it's only a matter of time before the Germans declare war, you must mobilize, strategize, and prepare. You don't need the benefit of historical hindsight to know that millions of French soldiers will die, and even more will be injured. Major swaths of your countryside will eventually fall under German control. Even if you end up winning this war, you are facing years of merciless, bloody, and horrific trench warfare that will surely reshape the continent and the world. And you have a problem: France operates on a gold standard.

France's gold standard means that every franc the government prints must be backed by a reserve of gold set to a fixed redemption rate. This is a problem because gold is *hard* money and acts as a natural limitation on the government. In this case, the adjective "hard" means difficult, as in gold is difficult to produce. It takes work to find it, dig it out of the ground, process it, etc. A country's membership to the gold standard would be considered a commitment to responsible fiscal and monetary policies. By having the franc pegged to a real-world scarce resource like gold, France was signaling that it would not print money to devalue its currency. A devalued currency is sometimes tempting because it would have the benefits of making debts easier to pay and improving the country's international trade prospects by making exports cheaper.

France is about to take part in the most costly war in the history of mankind to that point. There are guns and boots and tanks and ammunition and food to buy for a standing army of almost 9 million men. France's direct expenses for WWI will come out to be about $24 billion[238] or about half a trillion dollars measured in 2022 dollars. But since the French government is bound to the gold standard and also needs to pay for a war, it must do so by taxing its citizens, borrowing money, or using the resources it already has. Or it can find a way to get more gold. But finding more gold was *hard* in the summer of 1914.

The first option is a non-starter; in 1916 less than 2% of French households paid an income tax.[239] The other options of borrowing money or using the resources France possessed were much more politically inconvenient compared to the only other option France had.

That last option available to France was to abandon the gold standard and just start *printing* money. Germany declared war on France on August 3, 1914. How long do you think it took the French government to suspend the gold standard and start printing money – backed by nothing – to pay for the war? The answer is two days.[240]

That answer may surprise you, but we shouldn't judge the French government of 1914 too harshly. The Germans also suspended the gold standard in 1914 to pay for the war. So did the British. So did Russia. Austria-Hungary too. On both sides, a majority of World War I expenditures were paid for simply by printing money.[241]

This practice didn't start with World War I. Countries that were otherwise able to maintain a fiscally responsible gold standard and sound monetary policies for decades would routinely deviate from them when they were at war. An incomplete list of such instances includes the Roman Empire (especially toward the end), William the Conqueror's invasion of England, America during the Revolution, both the North and the South during the Civil War, and England and France fighting one another in the 1800s. It seems that whenever there is a desire for war, governments around the globe and through time quickly turn to printing money to pay for it.

Everyone Has a Problem

Beyond the inflation caused by printing money, there are other reasons that suspending a government's commitment to sound monetary policy during times of war is problematic. I will explain those reasons below, but first I want to provide the "brave" opinion that war is bad. I generally don't like war and think it should be avoided whenever possible. Some would argue that there is no such thing as a just war. I don't think you have to go that far in order to say simply that, all things being equal, peace is better than war. It doesn't matter if you're the kind of progressive that thinks we should never fight a war or the kind of progressive that thinks we should only fight the *really* important ones. In either case, reality (both historically and presently) is on the other end of the spectrum from where you are. And *money* has even more to do with it than you think.

Of course, one might ask if both the good guys and bad guys are printing money for war, and countries have been doing since time eternal, what's the big deal? Who cares if every government is ditching the gold standard and printing money to fund war? One answer – the textbook answer – is that printing money causes inflation, or the loss of the purchasing power of money. This has certainly been the case each and every time a country has printed money to fund a war, sometimes with disastrous consequences.

We have already studied in Chapter 6 the general negative impacts of inflation on vulnerable peoples. But the money printing that happened during World War I was so immense that it resulted in *crippling* inflation. In particular, the inflation suffered by the losing countries in the "War to End All Wars" had a direct causal effect on *starting* the next World War. To be fair, *some* of the inflation in these countries was due to printing money to pay for war reparations, which may charitably be considered an indirect cost of war. Nevertheless, the causes and effects of the hyperinflation suffered by Weimar Germany after WWI are devastating and well documented.[242]

Glyn Davis explained the following general trend regarding war's contribution to inflation and the tendency for governments to print money to fund war in his book *A History of Money*:

> *The military ratchet was the most important single influence in raising prices and reducing the value of money in the past 1,000 years, and for most of that time debasement was the most common... way of strengthening the 'sinews of war'.*[243]

The imagery of a "ratchet" is apropos. We are dealing with a machine that easily clicks in one direction but is designed to never reverse. This one-way increase seems to be the way with money printing and inflation.

A government having access to easily printed money to fund a war effort makes it possible to obfuscate the true cost of war to its citizens. Without being asked to pay more in taxes or to directly loan the government money by buying war bonds, the average person does not explicitly feel the cost of warfare, since the effects of inflation are always delayed compared to the printing of money. This obfuscation is facilitated even more easily in cases when the war is being fought somewhere else. If the population does not explicitly comprehend the true cost of war, it is easier to gain support for the war effort.

If a country had to fund a war by using real-world hard assets and directly taxing its population, it could still choose to do so. A particularly urgent geopolitical crisis would give the government the chance to convince the population of the importance of the war effort and justify its costs. Forcing a government to act according to these principles would set an appropriately high bar for starting a war. It would also ensure public sentiment about the war was based on a fuller and more accurate picture of the costs of the war effort. In the most general sense, the scope, intensity, and length of wars would be limited by two different but interconnected factors: the government's willingness to expend real-world hard assets and the citizenry's willingness for the government to do so.

All of this of course is just a sidelight to the real and true costs of war. In particular, we are avoiding a difficult discussion about who it is that fights and dies in these wars and who are the first in line to receive all that freshly printed money. It is well understood that the ones fighting and dying are disproportionately poor and/or undereducated and/or persons of color. The people profiting from the war expenditures but not fighting it are well-connected and wealthy cogs in the military-industrial complex. These are realities that are woven into the systems that lead a nation to war, and their full causes and effects are beyond the scope of this book. But it should be clear that money printing serves as the grease that keeps the machine of war moving, and that the poor and marginalized suffer again as a result. But as explained in Chapter 3, under a Bitcoin system printing money is simply impossible. Wars could not be fought so easily if Bitcoin was a nation's currency – certainly not wars that didn't have the support and financial backing of the entire populace instead of just those who stand to benefit most from such unfunded expenditures.

The Hidden Change in War

On December 8, 1941, the United States Congress voted to declare war on Japan, bringing the United States into World War II. The vote was 82 - 0 in the Senate[244] and 388 - 1 in the House, with Republican Jeannette Rankin the sole dissenter.[245] This was the last time Congress voted to declare war on any nation. Technically speaking, World War II was the last war America participated in.

In the common understanding, World War II was a necessary and justified war, and the American people supported the effort both in popular opinion and deed. Funding for the war was derived from the selling of war bonds, which were fairly popular among the populace, and an increase in federal taxes. War bonds constituted new government debt that was owed, for the most part, to ordinary citizens.

The appetite to support the war effort by offering the government this debt was large. For context, America's debt rose from the new programs offered under FDR's New Deal which was designed to alleviate the plight of the Great Depression. By 1939, that debt had reached an unprecedented $33 billion before the start of the war. This was an astonishing number at the time. When World War II ended, the federal debt had ballooned to $285 billion,[246] representing an 864% increase in just 6 years. Outside of very minor and temporary dips, the debt has risen each year since.

Federal income taxes were also used to fund the United States' effort in World War II. Before the war fewer than 8 million people paid individual income tax returns. By the end of the war that number had increased to about 50 million.[247] This represented an increase in individuals paying federal income tax from 6.1% of the American population to 35.7%. For the first time, non-wealthy people were being asked to pay income taxes, and for the first time those tax payments were being taken directly out of workers' paychecks.[248] Through both the war bonds and new taxation, the financial cost of the war was being passed on to a mostly willing American populace. Additionally, over 10 million men were drafted into the United States military during the course of the war, with many other men and women serving voluntarily.[249] Common sacrifices were made across the country, including rationing and wage/price controls. In an effort to reduce the use of gasoline, the government imposed a new speed limit for motorists – which turned out to be the least popular measure taken to support the war effort. United by a shared purpose, Americans in a very real way felt the cost of the war in both blood and treasure.

Roughly 40% of the United States cost for World War II was funded from current revenue. The rest came mostly from debt incurred through war bonds. There was also some debasement of the currency, which was mostly justified by the need to conserve industrial metals like copper, zinc, and tin for the war effort. For example, the mint changed the composition of the penny from mostly copper to mostly steel. This saved enough copper to manufacture 1.25 million artillery shells[250] and reduced the actual value of the coin while maintaining its face value. After the war, the net result of rationing, increased economic activity, and monetary debasement was serious (if short-lived) inflation. Inflation peaked in 1947 at over 14% before reverting to more normal levels by 1949.

The American effort in the Second World War is a remarkable story about how very involved the population of the United States was in the effort to fund and fight the war. The average American was tethered to the war in real ways: by buying war bonds, paying new and higher taxes, being willingly drafted to do the fighting, making sacrifices to ration needed supplies at home, and by electing representatives that voted to declare war.

Viewed through a 2023 lens, such direct connections between a voting populace of a democracy and an expensive, sustained, and bloody war seem pretty quaint and old fashioned. Like other things, the ways in which the United States justifies, executes, and pays for war has really gone downhill since the good ol' days.

In the 1960s, under the leadership of Lyndon Johnson, America embarked on a series of policy initiatives that came to be known as "guns and butter" programs. This is a reference to the country's increased spending in both domestic and defense-related priorities. Johnson's "Great Society" legislative programs hold a place of honor for any self-respecting liberal. These include programs to help reduce poverty, promote home ownership, provide healthcare to the elderly and poor people, and strengthen early childhood education. Johnson also famously oversaw legislation that protected the environment and secured voting rights for Black folks across the country. Each of these issues should be a top priority for any progressive person. But the significant cost of such programs was coupled with an increase in military expenditures from the country's growing involvement in the Vietnam conflict. Dating back to the 1930s, politicians and commentators had usually made a reference to a choice *between* guns or butter,[251] which framed government spending as a choice between domestic expenditures and funding efforts for war and defense. For the first time, Johnson was attempting to have both – with devastating consequences.

The United States first sent ground troops to Vietnam in 1965.[252] Unlike WWII, Congress did not vote to declare war this time around. Throughout this conflict, the typical American wasn't asked to sacrifice material comfort or ration supplies needed for the war effort. The speed limit wasn't even reduced during the Vietnam War. War bonds weren't offered by the American government, nor were citizens expected to pay new or higher taxes. Famously, young men across the country were being drafted against their will[253] to participate in the violence. These changes between 1945 and 1965 regarding how the citizenry was connected to the war effort are manifest. But one of the most important differences between the two wars, how the Vietnam conflict led to the dismantling of the last shreds of an international gold standard, usually gets less attention.

As the war intensified, so did its costs. The war, along with increased domestic spending, represented a problem – and the solution was destined to be government debt and money printing. As we describe more fully in Chapter 7, throughout the 1960s other governments began to suspect that the US dollar peg to gold, established under the 1944 Bretton Woods agreement, was beginning to unravel. Foreign countries holding US dollars understood that the US government would have trouble exchanging its debased currency for $35 per ounce of gold. Simply put, the creation of dollars to pay for domestic programs and war had outpaced the accumulation of gold. Given the choice between holding printed, paper money and a hard asset like gold, many countries started to choose gold.

Remarkably, unlike the wars that came before, the Vietnam War didn't just result in some inflation to contend with. It resulted in a complete unraveling of the international monetary system. This is a fact that most people don't fully realize even in hindsight. The situation came to a head in 1971 when France sent a warship to New York to collect and return its gold from the New York Federal Reserve Bank. A few days later, on August 15, 1971, President Richard Nixon closed the "gold window," refusing to exchange dollars for gold. In effect this constituted a default of the Federal government on its financial obligations and was the final death knell for the international gold standard that had existed to that point. This decision to abandon Bretton Woods also changed – forever – how wars are fought, justified, and paid for.

The Emergence of Forever Wars

In February 2003, an article appeared in The Guardian[254] describing the impact of Saddam Hussein's decision to sell Iraq's oil for euros instead of dollars. We have already learned enough to know that Saddam's decision was an afront to the petrodollar system established between Saudi Arabia and the United States since the 1970s. The Guardian article clearly described the ways that Iraq (read: Saddam) benefited from the oil-for-Euro arrangement, including earning a preferred interest rate on all Euro reserves. It was very likely that most people didn't fully grasp the significance of a Middle Eastern country selling oil for euros instead of dollars. But they couldn't miss the fact that the very next month America launched a full-scale invasion of Iraq. To be clear, the timing of the article was a coincidence in relation to the invasion. Saddam had been stating his intentions to sell oil for euros since 2000, and George W Bush had been stating his intentions to invade Iraq since 2001.

To this day nobody really knows with certainty why the United States invaded Iraq in 2003. We do know it was not because of weapons of mass destruction or terrorism. The study to determine conclusively that Iraq had no weapons of mass destruction cost the United Nations over $1 billion,[255] but most people were already convinced WMD was just a pretext to go to war. By most people I mean me and the hundreds of thousands of people in New York, Washington, DC, and other cities around the globe that protested the war before it even started.

Before learning about the petrodollar system and Saddam's move to an oil-for-Euro arrangement, I assumed the war was an opportunity for George W. Bush to avenge his father's legacy after the Persian Gulf War in the early 1990s failed to oust Saddam from power. I'm now doubtful that is the real reason, if only because it doesn't explain why an unpopular war and occupation built on a lie has lasted as long as it did. America has been at war for more than a generation. The young men and women currently deployed in Iraq (and until recently Afghanistan) were not even born when the Twin Towers fell. Our government has spent our nation's blood and treasure on these conflicts with little or nothing to show for it. And our nation's engagement in these wars has been deeply unpopular for over a decade and a half. So why did these "forever wars" last so long? The only explanation that actually makes sense is a little-understood one – that it is due in large part to America's fiat monetary system.

In 2003, the Bush Administration claimed the war in Iraq would cost $50-60 billion[256], which woefully "misunderestimated" the total cost. A subsequent study published in 2013 more accurately projected the cost of the Iraq and Afghanistan wars to be closer to $5–6 trillion.[257] More recent studies point to an estimate of $8 trillion.[258] Of this $8 trillion, over $1 trillion will go to interest payments because the war is being funded through deficit spending. How is it possible for a country to spend that much money on a war that most people don't support?

The answer is a simple one, but novel to most people. These wars last so long because the money they are using to pay for them is just printed, paper money. The American people are not expected to loan the government money through war bonds. The American people have seen no tax increases to pay for the wars. They have seen tax cuts. There have been no calls for common sacrifice by rationing important material goods to aid the war effort. In fact, our consumption has reached embarrassing levels. There hasn't even been a legitimate push to reduce our dependence on foreign oil in the 20 years we've been at war. The elected representatives of the people never voted on a declaration of war in either Iraq or Afghanistan. There is no draft that obligates the population to fight and die in these wars. In every conceivable way, the American population is segregated from the consequences of war.

Perhaps the most important difference between the recent forever wars and World War I is that there was no need to suspend or eliminate the gold standard in order to pay for the conflict. By the time America marched to war in 2001 and 2003, the gold standard had been dead for 30 years. Indeed, these wars are only possible because the war is funded through deficit spending and money printing. Such a situation, in a case as extreme as this, is only possible after 1971 and the dismantling of the Bretton Woods agreement. Wars like these are only possible when money is not tied to a real-life scarce resource. But a world in which Bitcoin serves as that real-life scarce resource completely eliminates this avenue for warmongering. In just such a scenario, Bitcoin would serve as the world reserve currency, eliminating the need for military conflict to protect the hegemony of a single nation's currency.

Bitcoin for a More Peaceful World

Any intellectually honest economist would admit that the gold standard has benefits and drawbacks. The main benefits are obvious: long-term, sustained, well-documented price stability and facilitating trade with less friction. In other words, things that *money* is supposed to be good at. The drawback, as explained by conventional economists, is that a gold standard does not afford the government enough control over the monetary supply and is overly limiting for a government that needs to respond to crises. This is usually explained as if the reader would naturally agree that the government should, indeed, be unlimited in its ability to manipulate the money supply. The assumption must be that government intervention in monetary policy is a net positive for the economy. We have already established that while such government intervention is beneficial to a small handful of well-positioned people, it is mostly responsible for the boom-bust business cycle, devastating wealth inequality, and longer, more common wars.

Using a hard money standard will not end war. No matter what economic principles are in place, there will still be conflict between nations, or between groups of people however they are defined or are assembled. There will always be tank factories making tanks. But a commitment to using hard money – and being unable to suspend that commitment – could be one important factor in making wars less common, shorter, less costly, and ultimately less deadly. If a nation is obligated to pay for war by using real life and scarce resources, the decisions to start a war or the ability to prolong one are made very differently.

The obligation to pay for war instead of printing money forces governments to be more transparent with their citizenry about why a war is necessary and how it will be paid for. In our current system, central banks obfuscate the true cost of the war by printing money. This keeps the population in the dark about the price tag for war, but it also makes it easier for the government to lie about why war is needed in the first place. In an important sense, printing money pulls many of the decisions about war away from the voting public and places those decisions in the hands of unelected officials in the central bank.

If the world were on a Bitcoin standard, this would all be mitigated. Bitcoin is a real world, scarce resource. Central banks can't print more of it. If a nation using Bitcoin wishes to engage in an armed conflict, they would have fewer options to pay for it than they have now. They can tax their population or they can borrow bitcoin. And to be clear, borrowing bitcoin is a different proposition than borrowing money you can just print to pay back. You are obligated to pay back that loan with something real. In either case, governments will be obligated to decide carefully how, when, and why they justify war, and the populations of those countries would have more leverage to end wars unless they were truly necessary.

Of course, the same might be said about gold and returning to the gold standard. So why is Bitcoin different from gold? Countries were able to drop the gold standard whenever it was convenient and/or they needed to march off to war. Why can't they do the same with Bitcoin? The answer is part of the reason many people say Bitcoin is like gold, but better. The physical nature of gold makes it difficult to use for transactions. It's heavy and hard to instantly verify. The physical nature of gold also makes it easy, over time, for banks to centralize reserves of gold from around the world – sometimes through force or confiscation. Even though gold had been the best form of money for thousands of years, its physicalness – the fact you can hold it in your hand – turns out to be a deficit and not an advantage.

The fact that gold is heavy essentially gave rise to paper money – which is lighter and easier to transact with. The fact that gold is confiscatable gave rise to central banks holding staggering reserves of this scarce resource. This ultimately led to central banks having a monopoly on money creation and printing. It's obvious that bitcoin is neither heavy nor confiscatable, and that Bitcoin will remain decentralized because the network supporting it is decentralized and open. It is easy for an average person to custody their share of bitcoin by themselves – no banks are needed. Government may be used to having the power to print more fiat money, but even if they wanted to, banks or governments can't create more bitcoin.

A Bitcoin standard, like a gold standard, would peg the world's economy to a scarce real world resource. Such a standard will have all of the same positive impacts as gold that we've outlined above. But amazingly, with a Bitcoin standard, there is no need for printed money to facilitate transactions. Bitcoin is the "heavy" hard money at the base of the system. It is also the "light" fast money that exists on the transaction layer. This is one reason why people have such a hard time defining Bitcoin. It isn't a replacement for one part of the system. It is a new system. In part, this means there is no need for governments to print money or for us to trust them to do so responsibly. There is no opportunity for governments to abuse that trust to fund a war, which they have been doing for hundreds of years.

Chapter 9: Bitcoin and Governance

Layer 1: The Constitution and Bitcoin

The Constitution of the United States is the foundational legal document that establishes the framework for the rule of law in America. By any reasonable measure, the 4,400 words are fairly simple compared to most legal documents and contracts. Yet despite its simplicity, the Constitution has proven to be fertile soil from which a complex system of local, state, and federal laws has grown. That complex system governs how citizens interact with the government and with one another. The most important characteristic of the Constitution is that it can be changed, allowing the living document to adapt to changes in society over time. This allows the legal framework of the nation to evolve as needed at the most foundational level. This is how, in the years since the Constitution's ratification, slavery has been abolished and women have secured the right to vote. To date, the Constitution has been amended 27 times.[259]

The second most important characteristic of the Constitution is that it is hard to change. An amendment to the Constitution requires the approval of two-thirds of both houses of Congress in addition to three-fourths of the States to be ratified. It is a cumbersome process outlined in the document itself and can take years to complete. For example, the most recent amendment was proposed 202 years before it was ratified.[260] But once an amendment has been ratified, it becomes part of the Constitution with all of the authority as the words originally written in the 18th century – and in some cases overriding them.

The difficulty in adjusting the Constitution is intentional. The system is designed to allow change to the foundational layer of law within the United States while maintaining a stable legal environment in which the government and citizens can feel secure in knowing what is legal and what isn't. It is practically impossible that a single political party or faction would be able to make flippant changes to the Constitution even after a landslide election win.

This ability of the Constitution to adapt to changing circumstances but only do so when it is essential is one of the main reasons that the United States continues to exist. If there were no ability to change the Constitution, it would have needed replacing almost immediately – after all, the Bill of Rights was added shortly after ratification to remedy the absence of key protections. At the same time, if it was easy to change based on the whims of the latest political party to secure power, it's likely the legal foundation of the United States would feel more like shifting sand. It is hard to imagine the United States maturing into a global power without a stable and reliable legal foundation to support the complex system of local, state, and federal laws that govern our society.

Perhaps unsurprisingly, Bitcoin's protocol has a lot in common with this approach. The Bitcoin protocol is a stable monetary base layer from which a robust and complex system of additional monetary layers, like the Lightning Network, can be built. There is a strong analogy with using a stable base layer of money like gold but needing a faster transaction layer of paper money.

One of the reasons that Bitcoin doesn't need to change that often is because it is the solid and stable base monetary layer on which transactions in the bearer instrument are settled with finality. You might think of this layer as the now defunct "gold layer" under a gold standard monetary policy. On top of that layer were built the layer of dollars which were backed by gold – and on top of that were deposit claims from a bank. Each layer provides an abstraction of the concept of value represented in the layer below it. In the case of a gold standard, the layers built on top of the base layer make transactions faster and more efficient, given that gold is heavy, hard to transport, and difficult to verify.

Under a Bitcoin standard, Bitcoin is the base layer. It's better than gold because Bitcoin transactions settle much faster than gold; 10-minute block times are pretty fast compared to shipping gold across an ocean. But waiting 10 minutes to buy a cup of coffee isn't feasible. That's not to say that there's not something valuable happening in those 10 minutes – that's the time needed to complete the proof of work that makes Bitcoin a "hard" currency. But your coffee would be cold after 10 minutes. So even faster and more efficient protocols like the Lightning Network are built on top of the Bitcoin protocol. In much the same way a local municipality might pass an ordinance that serves a very specific purpose without changing the foundation legal layer of the Constitution, layers can be built on top of the Bitcoin layer that could serve specific purposes. The Lightning Network makes transacting in Bitcoin faster than doing so on the base layer while maintaining the privacy Bitcoin users have come to expect.

A full treatment of the Lightning Network is beyond the scope of this book, but it's easy to get an intuitive understanding. The basic premise behind the Lightning Network is that bitcoin transactions are securely routed through channels created by users and the final settlement on the blockchain is required less often. It is important to note that most venders that accept Bitcoin today do so through the Lightning Network because it is practically instant and has practically zero cost to use. With the Lightning Network, you may pay a fraction of a cent to facilitate the transaction to purchase an item – and this fee isn't a percentage of the amount of money being sent. It is a highly effective Layer 2 solution to using Bitcoin for everyday purchases. In comparison to paying credit card companies a percentage of every retail transaction, the Lightning Network provides an attractive alternative. Because these improvements are possible with Bitcoin on higher layers, just like other monetary systems, there is less of a need to change Bitcoin's protocol itself.

It is usually a surprise when I describe to a person just starting their journey that Bitcoin isn't run by any individual or company. Nobody is in charge of it. That very concept is foreign to most people. Indeed, Bitcoin's governance is distributed to a decentralized network of peer nodes that validate transactions and blocks as they are added to the blockchain. Nobody is in charge. The design is crucial for several reasons. Decentralization makes it impossible for powerful entities to fight against Bitcoin in any meaningful way; there is no target, no mailing address, and no boss.

Another benefit of decentralization is it assures that change, when it happens, is consensus driven. This mirrors the balance that is struck in the US Constitution. Bitcoin can change or adjust in response to a previously unseen threat, but doing so requires cooperation across all users of the protocol. It is impossible to change Bitcoin without a consensus of node operators, miners, and developers all vetting the change, agreeing to it, and choosing to implement it. Changes to Bitcoin's core protocol are vanishingly rare and implementing one is a slow methodical process outlined in the Bitcoin Improvement Proposal process. Most people think of technology as fast and rapidly changing. Indeed, the standing ethos in most Silicon Valley companies is to "move fast and break things." Bitcoin is programmable money, but unlike most programming approaches the methodology and the ethos behind it is "go slow – don't break things."

The architecture of Bitcoin is fundamentally important to its success and how it should be viewed through a progressive lens. Decentralization is important for the reasons described above. In particular, we cannot expect to create and use a new monetary technology without pushback from banks or the government. Indeed, the structure of Bitcoin makes any such attack impossible and instead actually incentivizes all actors to interact with Bitcoin as honest participants. Of course, powerful entities will still try to attack Bitcoin the same way that phone companies attacked the internet, the Postmaster General attacked email, and candle makers attacked electricity. These attacks, whether it be misrepresenting energy use or claiming Bitcoin is only for criminals, are happening already and they are likely to continue for a while. But while they might be rhetorically effective, they simply are cover for the fact that these actors don't want Bitcoin to become the standard because its decentralized infrastructure and the incentives of Bitcoin are impossible to manipulate. A common concern among people learning about Bitcoin is "what if the government just shuts it down?" The beautiful truth is that they cannot – even if the government has a powerful military or control over the legacy financial system.

In addition to being decentralized, Bitcoin's architecture is open and flat. This is key to understanding the opportunity that exists for the people of the world to participate in a monetary system on a level playing field for the first time. All participants are peers; everyone is equal. There are no important people that get to change the rules or block access. Because Bitcoin is an open network, the powerful Wall Street CEO and a villager in Africa have the same access to the same rules and protocols. The same can be said about the issuance of new bitcoin – it's fair and transparent. Nobody is positioned closer to the spigot of fresh money by virtue of their previous status. Everyone is allowed to participate on equal footing. From the perspective of a typical ESG narrative, the governance of Bitcoin is outstanding. There are no 51% shareholders, no CEO, and no discriminatory policy. Each person who chooses to use Bitcoin does so as an equal peer.

The Way Bitcoin Reprioritizes Governance

The very first cypherpunks who adopted Bitcoin recognized that the new technology had the powerful potential to change how people interacted with money. They knew in the early 1990s that the new digital age was a general threat to privacy and specifically the loss of cash to carry out anonymous transactions was a key concern. In 1993 most people didn't know what the internet was and they certainly never considered the option of making a "real life" purchase on a computer. Luckily, there was a prescient group of privacy-focused coders that were devoting some serious energy thinking about what future life would be like in cyberspace. According to the Cypherpunk Manifesto, asking governments, corporations, and faceless organizations to grant privacy wasn't an option – it had to be coded. Cryptography was going to be a key tool in that code,[261] but private digital cash was a difficult problem to solve, even for the motivated geniuses that called themselves cypherpunks. The journey to solve that problem had several false starts and setbacks, but I doubt anyone in this small group would have predicted it would have taken so long to solve. It wasn't until 2008 when Satoshi Nakamoto distributed their whitepaper describing Bitcoin that the quest for private digital cash was finally complete. And yet despite privacy being a major motivator for its development, we now know the implications of Satoshi's invention extend well beyond the privacy of digital cash.

Outside of the very small and privacy-focused group of cypherpunks, it was libertarians who first truly appreciated Satoshi's invention for its potential to impact the way citizens and the government interact with money. I don't agree with the general libertarian view of the world, but even a progressive like myself doesn't disagree with their initial assessment. In our current polarized political environment, we can't seem to agree on much, but there is no doubt that most people would like to see a change in the way the government interacts with money, spending, and taxing. While there are still many unknowns, I believe Bitcoin will help bring about this change. Bitcoin is now it is a powerful economic force that is worth consideration by heads of state, heads of central banks, and heads of corporations. My hope is that by the time the really hard decisions get made, there is a critical mass of progressive people that understand Bitcoin and participate in the conversations that will affect change. I hope that is why you're still reading this book.

A monetary peg to hard money, like gold or Bitcoin, limits a government's ability to print and spend money ad infinitum. This has always been viewed as a key benefit of the gold standard. If each dollar you create needs to be backed by a reserve of gold, you have to be very careful about how you print dollars and what kind of resources you devote to acquiring more gold. All of this is also true for a currency backed by Bitcoin, or Bitcoin itself. For many centuries this limit on printing money was viewed as an important feature of hard money because it puts a real-world limit on the government, which already has tremendous power and resources. As we know all too well, politicians from both sides of the political aisle love to spend a lot of borrowed money on what *they* think is important. Unfortunately, we have all agreed to label this addiction to spending borrowed money as "tax and spend" when Democrats do it and "fiscal responsibility" when Republicans do it. The reality is that both parties are guilty of doing the exact same thing to try and achieve their separate goals. Governments must choose between taxing their citizens more, spending less, or taking on debt denominated in the currency they have the power to print. The evidence is obvious that increasing the debt is the easiest of these choices for a politician. In the United States, our public debt has grown from 35% of GDP in 1980 to over 130% today, bringing our public debt to a whopping $31 trillion.[262] Debt is the easier choice because it adds a layer of obfuscation between the citizens and the effects of spending, but spending borrowed money seems painless at the moment. Voters tend to notice tax increases and cutbacks in services. Public debt and the inflation it causes are a more subtle way for a government to get the money it needs.

There is a nuanced and important argument to be had here about fiscal responsibility. I'm not using the term as part of a conservative talking point, and I'm not even saying the government needs to spend less. But a government bound to reality by having a hard money peg must spend thoughtfully and efficiently to achieve its goals. This is technically possible under a gold standard, but the limitations of gold made it possible for governments to abandon the gold standard anytime it strained their ability to print and spend unchecked amounts of money. As discussed in Chapter 8, times of war are a good example of governments suspending the gold standard so they can print money to spend on emergent priorities. At issue here isn't how much the government spends, but instead how they fund that spending.

Progressives have been trained to instinctively push back against any claim from conservatives that the government should spend less money. This is because those claims from conservatives are disingenuous; their argument is actually the government needs to spend less money on the things liberals value while conservatives can spend whatever they want on their priorities. It's right to push back on this disingenuousness, but it is easy to see how the larger political narrative has been lost. At issue is how the spending is funded. Having a hard money peg limits the government's ability to print and borrow money, so in normal times they must tax the population for the money they want to spend. This isn't as much about reducing spending as it is about increasing transparency. When the government is forced to tax its citizens to pay for what it prioritizes, the voting populace of the country can make better decisions about how *their* priorities line up with those of their elected officials. This removes the layer of obfuscation that exists between the voter and policymaker.

As things currently stand, the government can take out increasingly large debts and use inflation to make paying that debt easier. This comes at the cost of working people who feel that inflation most acutely. Lawmakers can spend obscene amounts of money that will eventually get inflated away without the voting population immediately feeling any effect. The continuous loop of taking on more government debt and rolling that debt over so the citizens don't have to feel the pain immediately cannot happen if the government is forced to use Bitcoin or peg their currency to Bitcoin.

What We Want From Government

While some talk as if Bitcoin is the iceberg that undoes the fiat money system, in truth it's more like a lifeboat come to rescue us. As we have alluded to throughout this book, the continuous loop of debt and money printing can't really happen forever. This cycle of debt that causes financial instability, sends inaccurate price signals, produces crippling inflation, encourages boom-bust business cycles, funds wars, incentivizes businesses to take on large amounts of risk, motivates high time preference spending, disincentivizes saving, requires the United

States to ally with dictators and ruins the environment. This system – the one you were born into and have probably never questioned – is not sustainable. Bitcoin didn't cause any of these problems, politicians and the policies they enacted did. But Bitcoin does offer a solution.

Ray Dalio does an excellent job of contextualizing the rise and fall of empires in his book *Principles for Dealing with a Changing World Order*. Among the main theses that Dalio spells out in his book is that the long-term debt cycle we are currently in will soon reset, which will be both surprising and painful for those that aren't prepared.[263] While the geopolitical stature of the United States makes it possible for this cycle to extend beyond its normal lifespan, it can't last forever. In most of the world, the idea of a currency collapsing without much warning or an economic system being forced into crisis as a direct result of monetary policy is all too real. But as an alternative, in Bitcoin we have for the first time ever a stateless alternative to money creation that can put a check on the institution of government that already has tremendous power and resources.

A Bitcoin standard or a dollar peg to Bitcoin would make government spending, at least in democracies, more transparent and directly tied to the will of the people. Without the ability to endlessly create debt, the government's choices would be reduced to taxation, austerity, and borrowing within its means. This reestablishes the tie between voters who pay taxes and the policy makers. Politicians from both parties are guilty of spending borrowed, printed money and doing so with impunity – making the issue a bipartisan one. Because it eliminates the possibility of endless borrowing, a hard money peg would necessarily trim the government's size. But as macroeconomist Lyn Alden told me in an interview for this book, "the government will get smaller in order of what the population hates the most."[264] Things like wars on foreign soil would probably be the first to go. Other cuts to government spending would require strong progressive voices to advocate for policies that prioritize the will of the voters.

Sometimes critics in the Bitcoin community claim that as hard money, Bitcoin is hopelessly inconsistent with progressive values. The primary conceit in this argument is the notion that liberals simply want the government to spend as much money as possible. This is a convenient caricature to argue against, but it isn't based in reality. Both parties spend obscene amounts of money on what they think is important, and both do so with borrowed money because operating in this manner is more politically convenient from start to finish. The idea that Democrats are the "tax and spend" party is a complete fallacy.

In truth liberals don't simply want the government to blindly spend more – the hope is that the government will spend what is needed to protect progressive priorities. There is no doubt room for the government to be more transparent and efficient in that pursuit, but the reason liberals so vehemently push back against budget cuts proposed by conservatives is because the things on the chopping block are always progressive priorities. Perhaps a Bitcoin peg will allow us to step away from tribal mentalities and admit there is room for the government to be more transparent and efficient with how it spends money and what it prioritizes. That way both progressives and conservatives can discover whether their policies are in fact what the public wants to spend money on.

Public infrastructure, education, a safety net for vulnerable people, securing society's values through just laws, enforcing just laws, and protecting national security – these are all important things the government should be doing as a base case. As a liberal voter, I expect the government to invest resources in things that promote public welfare and to participate in markets where the profit motive fails to serve the population or creates perverse incentives. With a large dose of political will, these things can happen through a reasonable progressive tax, efficient spending, and transparently recentering the voter's priorities.

Nor does the adoption of a Bitcoin standard mean that the government can't borrow money. If the government needs more bitcoin, it can take a loan just like anyone else. Government borrowing, when it is necessary for an unforeseen emergency, can be done at market rates and can be paid back through transparent taxes, or defaulted on with the usual market dynamics that would affect any other borrower of money. There is no rule that says a developed Western country must be allowed to take on debt denominated in a currency it can control while poor countries around the world, to their great detriment, are forced to borrow in a currency that is controlled in Washington, DC.

Bitcoin could serve as a hard money peg that would be impossible for a government to break. Unlike gold, Bitcoin is easy and cheap for regular people to validate, secure, and use. As such, the populace could not be forced to use paper notes provided by the government in tough times – which is precisely what happened each time a government broke its promise by suspending its gold standard. A Bitcoin peg could also increase transparency and efficiency by making government intervention less necessary. There is hope that a system rooted in Bitcoin will be more transparent, reduce inequality and lessen the incentives for war.

This new world will hopefully be shaped by progressive Bitcoiners. But what's interesting to contemplate is that such a world may require *less* government intervention to create a fair and equitable playing field for society. Liberal voters currently turn to liberal politicians to turn the dial from within the fiat system to make things less atrociously unfair. A new system built on Bitcoin could be an opportunity to reshape society's relationship with money and the government's relationship with society without sacrificing any progressive values. This new system would lower the time preference so voters and politicians can focus on and start tackling problems that exist on a scale beyond the next election cycle. This new system would reduce the need for the government to protect vulnerable people because the incentives and ability of wealthy powerful people to extort and manipulate poor people will all be reduced. This new system is likely to change what we expect from and value in future politicians – so much so that those currently in office are starting to take notice.

The So-Far Bipartisan Approach to Bitcoin

Cynthia Lummis is a Republican that represents Wyoming in the US Senate. As a matter of record, there is scant little that Cynthia Lummis and I would agree about politically. She voted to acquit President Trump in his second impeachment trial[265] and she co-sponsored the State Marriage Defense Act.[266] Cynthia Lummis and I would probably not choose to have a beer together, but I do think that she acts in good faith from within a broken system to represent her Wyoming constituency. Of interest for this book is the fact that Cynthia Lummis was the first known United States Senator to own bitcoin and has consistently advocated for politicians to have a better understanding of how this new technology will shape the future. For this, she should be celebrated. Unlike some of her other political views, Cynthia Lummis is looking to the future with Bitcoin and is able to see past the system as it is. And, at the same time, she understood that Bitcoin can't run the risk of becoming another in a long list of partisan wedge issues. When Senator Lummis looked to draft legislation about Bitcoin and other cryptocurrencies, she looked for a co-sponsor across the aisle. She found an unlikely partner in the junior Senator from New York – Democrat Kirsten Gillibrand.

Kirsten Gillibrand was first elected to the House of Representatives in 2006 and represented me and many others like me in New York's 20th district. Shortly after that election, Gillibrand was appointed by the governor of New York in 2008 to fill Hillary Clinton's seat in the US Senate and has represented the state as a Senator since. Gillibrand came to the House as a pragmatic centrist and has worked to establish her liberal bona fides throughout her tenure in the Senate. She supports same-sex marriage[267] and voted to convict Donald Trump in both impeachment trials. On the surface, it would seem that Lummis and Gillibrand would have little common ground to stand on. Both Senators represent vastly different constituencies and do so by upholding vastly different political positions. But despite these differences, both Senators were willing to work together to draft positive Bitcoin legislation and promote it to their colleagues and constituents.

Known as the Lummis-Gillibrand Responsible Financial Innovation Act, the proposed bill is meant to bring digital assets within the regulatory perimeter. The bill was the result of months of hard work and an honest effort of going to the experts in the field to better understand Bitcoin and other cryptocurrencies. The fact that such a bill exists is a phenomenal milestone in the lifespan of Bitcoin, which has typically been treated as a built-in punchline for those in the legacy financial and political systems. The tide is turning.

The Lummis-Gillibrand bill is the first cohesive attempt to codify the rules and regulations the government will use to treat digital assets. This is critically important legislation. Because Bitcoin is such an innovative technology, it truly doesn't fit into any of the categories people, including lawmakers, typically use to understand money, commodities, or investments. Important highlights of the bill include language that officially treats Bitcoin as a commodity while almost all other cryptocurrencies are considered securities. This is important clarity that has been missing in the current regulations imposed on Bitcoin. Such clarity would allow investors and entrepreneurs to more fully understand the government's relationship with Bitcoin. The bill also provides a de minimis tax exemption, allowing people to spend up to $200 of bitcoin (adjusted for inflation) without needing to consider capital gains ramifications.[268] Such an exemption would make it easier to use bitcoin in the ways we discuss throughout this book.

The bill has been welcomed by most of the pragmatists in the Bitcoin community who want to see a common sense approach to the way the US government interacts with this new technology. The Lummis-Gillibrand bill also marks a distinct turn away from the sloppy and rushed 2021 Infrastructure Bill that misapplied even basic definitions from within the space.[269] Senators Lummis and Gillibrand not only understand Bitcoin better than most of their colleagues but also made strides to learn more and engage the community while writing their bill.[270]

Unfortunately, the Lummis-Gillibrand bill is unlikely to pass into law in its original form. That is the reality of our current political system. But the fact that the bill exists and provides a serious avenue for politicians to consider Bitcoin from within the legal and political landscape is important, as is the fact that the bill has bipartisan sponsorship – the ultimate hope and aspiration behind the book you're holding.

Bitcoin provides the same kind of potential to reshape the world that the internet did in the 1990s, and it is in America's best interest to lead the way on that innovation. By providing an accommodating regulatory environment for Bitcoin adoption, politicians have an opportunity to bring the best minds to the United States to work in a blossoming industry that has the potential to shape the world for decades if not centuries. If it is to be done well, that work should be bipartisan. It would be a shame if Bitcoin were to become the next political football that is used to divide voters into narrow categories so politicians can score easy points. In its essence, Bitcoin transcends political conventions as much as it transcends legacy financial decisions. The partnership that Cynthia Lummis and Kirsten Gillibrand have formed through their bill is critical for both Bitcoin and the role America will play in the next century. If we allow Bitcoin to be another hyperpolarized partisan issue, the innovation, jobs, and technology it represents will simply go someplace else. The results would be tragic. Imagine if in 1994 the internet became a wedge issue the political class manipulated to leverage their base and gain votes. How might the world, and America's place in it, look different?

The good news is that Bitcoin has not yet ossified into a neatly defined political category that appeals to only one political party. But as a progressive who tends to support Democrats, it is distressing to see so many elected liberals rail against the dangers of Bitcoin while conservatives like Kevin McCarthy encourage the responsible innovation Bitcoin offers. Bitcoin truly isn't any more conservative than it is liberal. It is distressing to contemplate that the supporters of these politicians are likely to follow their lead – unless they are offered a better and more complete narrative about the promise Bitcoin has to make the future better.

In February 2022 Ted Cruz tried to use Bitcoin as a political wedge during his speech at the CPAC conference. "Liberals don't like Bitcoin because it can't be controlled."[271] The truth is that liberals need to embrace Bitcoin. If the United States is to truly be a leader on the world stage in the coming decades, it is important that we don't allow members of the political class like Senators Warren or Cruz to make Bitcoin into a partisan issue. This book is an attempt to bolster the voice of the political left in the Bitcoin community because there is a real danger that, if we allow Ted Cruz and Elizabeth Warren to control the narrative, Bitcoin will become hyper-partisan. This will not destroy Bitcoin, but it could destroy America's chance to be a leader in an innovation that, with or without American input, will shape the world to come. The Lummis-Gillibrand approach seems better.

At the state level, the potential for Bitcoin to reshape money, push energy toward renewables and create high-paying jobs seems to be attracting attention from red states who tend to vote Republican. States like Texas with abundant solar and wind infrastructure seem to be taking advantage of the innovations that Bitcoin has to offer. Similar trends in increased Bitcoin mining can be seen in Georgia and Kentucky. In contrast, New York state recently passed a moratorium on new Bitcoin mining operations that use fossil fuels.[272] Although I firmly believe that Bitcoin mining will continue to trend toward renewables, I also believe that trend will happen because of incentives and market conditions, not through bans or regulation. It seems likely that New York imposing a moratorium will provide an opportunity for regulatory arbitrage which will unfortunately push miners toward other states that, at least for the short term, use *less* green energy.

At the state and local level, there is a real chance to impact policy and lawmakers from both parties have an opportunity to attract a business that will promote renewables, stabilize the grid, and provide jobs. Just as America is competing against every other nation to secure the infrastructure and power to mine Bitcoin and allow Bitcoin to thrive as a prominent industry, the states are competing against one another as well. It would be a shame if blue states with green energy like Washington, Oregon, and New York miss the boat as a result of political stubbornness.

When Dennis Porter founded the Satoshi Action Fund with Mandy Gunasekara in 2022, his primary goal was to educate policymakers and regulators about the benefits of Bitcoin mining.[273] The Satoshi Action Fund works with lawmakers at all levels of the US government from local politicians to sitting Senators. The group helps policymakers understand that Bitcoin mining is a potent tool to support their other public policy goals like employment and green energy.

Dennis and I had a chance to talk about his work and I was impressed by his ability to see the big picture and pitch Bitcoin as a tool that would interest both sides of the political aisle. Because he believes in the importance of Bitcoin for our future and operates from an assumption that the technology transcends our current political labels, Dennis is able to nimbly adjust his pitch to his audience. As he put it, "When I'm promoting Bitcoin to politicians it's easy to find things that either side agrees with. Bitcoin is truly one of those things that move us past the old political categories."[274] He travels the country to promote Bitcoin-friendly policy to sitting politicians and helps them navigate a novel, complicated industry. In our conversation he mentioned seeing the need for a more vocal group of progressive politicians to join the conversation. Although he considers himself a centrist, Dennis has probably done more behind the scenes to intentionally onboard elected Democrats to the benefits of Bitcoin mining than anyone else in the industry. If Bitcoin ends up being a non-partisan issue in the future, because of his work with the Satoshi Action Fund, Dennis will be at the top of the list of people to thank.

Separation of Money and State

It has not been that long in the arc of human history since most governments ceded control of religion within their borders. Of course, in many regions of the world, state-sponsored religion and theocracies are still common. But the norm in Western democracies is that religion plays no role in the fundamental workings of the government. This is widely viewed as *progress*.

Of course, separating the church and the state happened at different speeds in different contexts. The beginnings of religious freedom can be traced back to the Thirty Years War that began in 1618, but arguably found its first full expression in the separation of church and state that was fundamental to the founding of America and codified by the first amendment in 1791. France flirted with religious liberty during the French Revolution but it wasn't until a law passed in 1905 that the state and religion were separated.[275] Of course, England is technically still a monarchy and theocracy, with the monarch always serving as the Supreme Governor of the Church of England.[276] But in practice, the government in England is secular. A secular government is critical for the rights of the people and the protection of religious minorities. For most Americans and citizens of other liberal democracies, it seems hard to imagine a different system. On the other hand, a few hundred years ago it would have seemed unimaginable for almost anyone in the world for the government not to control the people's religion or for religion not to control the government. It was simply the water everyone swam in.

Because the powerful institutions of government and religion were so closely intertwined for so long, it was difficult for regular people to monitor and address grievances to authority figures. Those in charge were able to leverage their power to silence and control a populace that was forced to agree to conditions that weren't in their interest. It was nearly impossible to imagine a more free and just world. But then in the 15th century, an innovative new technology started to slowly turn the tide. The invention of the printing press in Europe was as impactful of an invention as could be imagined. In many ways it was a first domino that eventually toppled the connection between church and state.

The parallel is obvious. It may seem to most people that the connection between the state and the money we use is too strong to sever. In fact, much like religion centuries ago, many people believe that money is only valid when it comes from the state. We can see today in the case of religion that it was critical to freedom and prosperity for the powerful institution of government to be severed from the institution of religion. In much the same way, it is critical that we separate money from the state to ensure true freedom and long-lasting prosperity. The two institutions are too important and too powerful to be intertwined.

We now have the tools to imagine a world in which the government you're born into does not control the money you use the same way it doesn't control the religion you practice. This vision of the world cannot be unimagined. If you're just starting on your Bitcoin journey, this idea may seem heretical if not impossible. But thanks to an innovative new technology, money is able to be democratized, and we can rebalance the power that comes from controlling money. Bitcoin allows people the opportunity to take control of something governments have had sole ownership over for the last few centuries. In doing so, it becomes easier for regular people to monitor their leaders and hold them accountable. This is all not just imaginable but realizable.

History is replete with moments when government and religion were so intermixed that it was often impossible to determine which was controlling the other. But the same is true today when looking at government and money. Our experience tells us that the government controls our money, but at the same time most people will admit that money plays too large a role in determining government policy. Which is the dog and which is the tail?

A perennial rallying cry across the political spectrum is to "get money out of politics." In response, politicians compete to see who can earn the support of what they call "small donors" and even brag when they don't receive funding from certain companies, groups, or political organizations. Most voters understand all this posturing is smoke and mirrors and that it's almost impossible to tell how money actually influences politicians, regardless of their party. They only know that it does.

Like most people, I support the idea of "getting money out of politics," but it seems much more practical and efficient to get the politics out of money. Bitcoin allows this. With a Bitcoin standard, monetary policy isn't decided by politicians or those they appoint. Policy is set and isn't corruptible. And most importantly, the balance of power in politics tilts back toward citizens who will be able to check their elected representatives and hold them accountable in a more transparent way.

Separating money and the state is a monumental shift, and it is genuinely difficult to imagine all the consequences of such a foundational change. But one thing does appear likely – that it is ultimately going to happen. A favorite quote of President Obama's was this observation by Dr. Martin Luther King: "The arc of the moral universe is long, but it bends toward justice."[277] How soon just monetary policy will arrive in the form of Bitcoin is hard to predict – but all signs point to Bitcoin becoming that standard.

As a tool Bitcoin transcends the political categories we try to apply to it. In much the same way, it will reshape what governments look like and how they intersect with money and monetary policy. I have no way to guarantee that transition will be smooth. My strong belief is that the change will be a net positive to the world, though I can't promise this either. What I do know is that the history of governments unilaterally controlling money has resulted in extreme wealth concentration, policies that favor the well-connected, war, and violence. Because the bell of Bitcoin cannot be unrung, it is time to start imagining what a world looks like when money is independent from the state. It is time for progressives to start working toward the vision of the world they want to see.

Chapter 10: A Call to Action

100 Hours of Research

Several months after I hung up my Bitcoin poster in my office, a different colleague approached me, motioned to my poster, and asked if I invested in Bitcoin. The question was earnest and sincere, and she showed an actual interest in the topic. I found this surprising, because less than a year earlier (pre-poster), this same colleague had assumed it was a joke when I explained that I would be doing some extra work and devoting that money to buying Bitcoin. She laughed out loud and looked a little surprised when I didn't join her laughter with my own. To her, the idea of Bitcoin was just a punchline that didn't need a setup. Nine months later, she stood in my office looking to get some information about Bitcoin, or at the very least a validation that it was a real thing that she should consider.

I confirmed that I did invest in Bitcoin and that I would be happy to talk to her about it. I warned her that I could talk to her about Bitcoin for as long as she wanted – probably more than she wanted. And then I made the following claim: "You don't know any intelligent person who has studied Bitcoin for 100 hours and thinks it's a bad idea." Her response was off the mark but predictable. "So you're saying that I should invest in Bitcoin?" I quickly clarified. "No. I'm saying you should study Bitcoin for 100 hours."

I offer the same advice to you. Study Bitcoin for 100 hours. You've probably logged about 10 hours studying Bitcoin by reading this book. You only have 90 hours left to go. And there is plenty more to learn. To make this book accessible, we have glossed over almost all of the deep technical aspects of Bitcoin. But now that you have a solid basis with which to start, you may be inclined to dig a little deeper and learn more about the underlying technology. You should. Of particular importance is learning as much as you can about the best ways to buy Bitcoin and the best practices for storing your bitcoin so it can't be lost or stolen. You will have to learn at least a little bit about securing your seed phrase safely and you will have to develop a plan of succession so a loved one knows how to take control of your bitcoin should something happen to you. You will want to spend more time learning about exciting new developments like the Lightning Network, which is a fast transaction layer that operates on top of the Bitcoin network. If you have the interest and capacity to learn more about the proof of work consensus mechanism along with the difficulty adjustment, you should. It is among the most important and interesting developments of our lifetime, and understanding it is critically important for progressives because it is the focus of most of the criticism about Bitcoin. It is essential that people understand proof of work and why it is an advantage and not a problem in the Bitcoin system.

You can and should dive deeper into the inner workings of our current financial system as well. Bitcoin has offered me a new lens through which to view the many problems that society faces. There are social problems that exist and will persist, regardless of our financial system. It is important to concede that Bitcoin does not fix everything. Despite this, I have appreciated being able to re-explore some fundamental problems that, as a progressive, have always concerned me. Bitcoin has helped me understand those problems differently by allowing me to view our legacy financial system from the outside. It is fundamentally impossible to measure how broken the system is when you only take stock from within that system. It is like the fish trying to understand what water is. Bitcoin allows us to step outside of the system.

No doubt you will disagree with some of the ideas I've compiled in this book. That is okay. But take time to reflect on your disagreements, and see where they lead you. Even if your vision of the future is not the same as my vision, can you envision a different and better world? Can you see an opportunity for a more fair and transparent system? Can you imagine changing to a new system instead of tweaking the dials of the old one?

Each of the topics addressed in the chapters of this book can and should be explored more deeply. There is no shortage of books, podcasts, and videos available for you to learn from. I have compiled a list of resources for you in the Appendix. I encourage you to dive in and explore these things because I truly believe that Bitcoin is our world's best hope to change for the better, and we need everyone – including progressives – working with us.

Get Off Zero

You may have noticed that you are almost done reading this book and at no point have I referenced the price of bitcoin. Nor have I appealed to the common view, at least among Bitcoiners, that the dollar price will go up over time to support any of the arguments I have made. I think Bitcoin can make the world a better place even if it stays at its current price forever. This may surprise you if your only prior exposure to Bitcoin is through popular news articles that frantically track every rise and fall of the price. Friends sometimes approach me with updates on what they consider volatile the price swings of Bitcoin before I'm even aware of them. Those price changes can be exciting and dramatic, but I don't check the price regularly. I care about the *value* of Bitcoin, not its price, and the value that Bitcoin can offer the world has very little to do with its price on any given day.

But Bitcoin does have a price, and that price is worth considering if you are interested in making your first investment in Bitcoin. I won't give financial advice, but I can say that for most people most of the time, the only wrong allocation of Bitcoin is zero. So if you've done your 100 hours of research, or are on the way, and you think you should own some, I would probably agree with you. Please research various exchanges that operate within your jurisdiction and see if you can set up a low/no fee Dollar Cost Average (DCA) in which you buy a small amount of Bitcoin in regular intervals over time. There is no need to time the market or buy the dip or sell the top. Making small, fixed purchases over time without worrying about price is a low-stress way to grow your allocation to Bitcoin and stay within your personal risk tolerance. If dramatic price changes worry you, then allocate only an amount that will not cause stress.

Think of Bitcoin as your savings account and put whatever small amount of money you don't currently need toward a brighter future. Do not borrow money to buy Bitcoin and only invest money that you don't anticipate needing for the next few years. The beauty of Bitcoin is that you can easily buy $100,000 or $0.50 worth within minutes of reading this sentence. If you can only comfortably afford 50 cents worth of bitcoin, that's what you should buy. Just get off zero.

No matter what else happens, you can be sure that there will only ever be 21 million bitcoin in existence. There are no exceptions to this rule. If the technology continues to gain adoption at its current rate, sooner or later most people will have exposure. Believe it or not, you're still one of the early ones. Or you can think of it this way: there are about 8 billion people on this planet. 21 million bitcoin divided evenly among them is roughly 0.002625 (or 262,500 Satoshis). At the time of writing, that amount of bitcoin would cost you less than $60.

When it comes to investing in Bitcoin, the most common excuse I hear is that the person feels they are too late and that the real opportunity to buy Bitcoin was 10 years ago. I felt that way before I started. The person who you will convince to buy Bitcoin next year will feel the same way. You're not too late. You're right on time.

Find Bitcoin Politicians and Support Them

It is usually easy to convince a politician that they should support good-paying jobs, promote green energy, foster innovation, and protect vulnerable people from economic exploitation. It may be surprising for most politicians to learn that Bitcoin is the best possible way to do those things. Luckily, there are people out there doing the work of convincing them. We already learned in Chapter 9 that the Satoshi Action Fund is doing just that. We need your voice to join in that work. By encouraging politicians to enact pro-Bitcoin policies, we can usher in a new era of clean energy, economic stability, and peace. It is our best hope to combat the problems we face as a society.

When given the chance, talk to your local representatives about the promise of Bitcoin. Ask them to support policies that encourage mining Bitcoin with renewable energy in their jurisdictions. Ask them to support policies that encourage innovation in this maturing space so that innovation isn't exported elsewhere. Ask them to engage with the Bitcoin community so that well-intentioned regulations like consumer protections make sense and are coherent within the Bitcoin framework. Ask them to support policies that promote education about financial literacy that includes information about Bitcoin. Expect your political representatives to learn about Bitcoin and engage with it in good faith. I also wouldn't mind if you decided to hand your political representative a copy of this book.

We need more politicians that support progressive ideals without feeling the need to score cheap political points by railing against Bitcoin. We need politicians on the right, like Ted Cruz, to understand they can't paint Bitcoin as a right-only technology. We need you to support progressive politicians who want to use Bitcoin to make the world a better place. Please go and find them and support them. And if you can't find them, maybe consider becoming one.

Get Involved in the Community

The main reason I wrote this book is because I want there to be more liberal voices in the Bitcoin space. When I say that, I mean your voice, not mine. I could have given this book the title *The Progressive Case for Bitcoin*, but I didn't. What I have written here is just my perspective on a variety of very important topics. This book is *my* case for Bitcoin, but it is just the beginning of important work that I hope you will continue.

It has been my experience that wherever you turn in the Bitcoin community you will find positive, happy, and optimistic people. This is not because the world is on the right track – it's not. We can see in America that the social, political, and economic structures are under enormous stress and are in danger of breaking in ways most of us have never experienced. Along every axis, society seems to be on a knife's edge. It is unnerving – and things are much worse in most other places in the world. Despite this, Bitcoiners are optimistic because they can see a brighter future. There is danger in failing to opt into that vision of a brighter future. You are officially invited to join us.

We Need Your Voice

In a recent conversation, Peter McCormack explained to me the risks he sees in letting Bitcoin become a hyper-partisan topic. Allowing Bitcoin to become polarized could create a "wealth gap between the left and the right that would create a power gap and resentment."[278] While we can't foresee exactly how, we can be certain Bitcoin will reshape the world. We need principled and enthusiastic liberal voices adding to the dialogue about how Bitcoin should make the world a better place. There is a thriving community built around Bitcoin, but its loudest participants are currently right-leaning and libertarian. Let's lend our voice to the competition of ideas about how Bitcoin can be used to make the world more just, fair, and peaceful. Bitcoin isn't going away, and if progressives choose to fight it, the new systems will be crafted by those on the political right and liberals will be left behind.

Talk to your friends and loved ones about Bitcoin. Not just because it is a potential investment or a way to make money, but because it has the potential to reframe both the problems our society faces and their solutions. Write to your political representatives about why you support Bitcoin. Start your own podcast, create educational videos, or even write your own book. Make your voice heard at local Bitcoin meetups, and speak in person to the people who appreciate Bitcoin in your hometown.

Bitcoin needs your voice for two very important reasons: having liberals and progressives in the Bitcoin space will make the Bitcoin community better, and it will also make the world better. We need you to be involved in the Bitcoin community because many of the ideas discussed in this book are aspirational and require work. In considering everything from green energy to aiding marginalized individuals, progressive people have a place in the Bitcoin discussion and need to engage in the work that needs to be done.

But Bitcoin doesn't fix everything. It is exactly *for* this reason you should be involved in the Bitcoin community. Issues like structural racism, gay rights, abortion, early childhood education, health care and many others won't be solved because we have a new, better form of money to use. We will still need progressives to keep fighting for what is right within all of those issues. It is hard to imagine a world where liberals and progressives give up their voice when it comes to these important social issues. But it seems increasingly likely that people investing in Bitcoin now will have the resources and connections to make a lasting change in the world of the future. By ignoring Bitcoin now, progressives could seriously handicap their ability to effect the changes they want to see in the world.

As a progressive person, I believe Bitcoin represents the best opportunity there is to see the brighter future I have worked toward my entire adult life. I am excited to be able to share that opportunity with you and I hope that you will be motivated to share it with others. As a dedicated and informed community of progressives, Bitcoin can give us the tools needed to reshape the world we want to see. I encourage you to stay engaged and always keep learning about Bitcoin.

About the Author

C. Jason Maier lives in Connecticut with his family and dog, Toshi. For the last decade and a half, Jason has been living out his childhood dream by being a math teacher. He originally studied Bitcoin through a mathematical lens, but quickly developed a conviction about the way this new technology would reshape the world. Jason is committed to educating people about Bitcoin and making it as accessible as possible to everyone in the world – including you.

Appendix
A List of Resources for Continued Bitcoin Education

Videos (available on YouTube)
How Does Bitcoin Actually Work by 3Blue1Brown
Beginner's Guide Playlist by What Bitcoin Did
Bitcoin Technology Tutorials by BTC Sessions

Podcasts
The Progressive Bitcoiner
What Bitcoin Did
The Anita Posch Show
Bitcoin Fundamentals, The Investor's Podcast Network

Books
*Bitcoin: Hard Money You Can't F*ck With* by Jason A. Williams
The Internet of Money by Andreas Antonopoulos
Debt: The First 5,000 years by David Graeber
Layered Money by Nik Bhatia
The Price of Tomorrow by Jeff Booth
The Bullish Case for Bitcoin by Vijay Boyapati
Check Your Financial Privilege by Alex Gladstein
(L)earn Bitcoin by Anita Posch

Other
Bitcoin: A Peer-to-Peer Electronic Cash System
[Bitcoin whitepaper] by Satoshi Nakamoto
Bitcoin Magazine

Visit Jason's website (www.BitcoinProgressive.com) to contact the author and for a list of updated resources for those wishing to learn more about Bitcoin.

Endnotes

[1] Jackson Mejia and Jon Hartley, "Inflation's Compounding Impact on the Poor," FREOPP, last modified April 25, 2022, https://freopp.org/inflations-compounding-impact-on-the-poor-f82ea4d61d9b.
[2] https://www.iea.org/commentaries/for-the-first-time-in-decades-the-number-of-people-without-access-to-electricity-is-set-to-increase-in-2022
[3] Vanessa A. Boese et al., *Autocratization Changing Nature? Democracy Report 2022*, 6, accessed November 28, 2022, https://v-dem.net/media/publications/dr_2022.pdf.
[4] "Jeff Booth: Buying Bitcoin Is Not Enough," YouTube video, May 22, 2022, https://youtu.be/fYTWaqewC74.
[5] "The Truth Is Out: Money Is Just Created, and the Banks Are Rolling in It," Underground Network, accessed November 29, 2022, https://underground.net/money/the-truth-is-out-and-the-banks-are-rolling-in-it/.
[6] Committee on Banking, Housing, and Urban Affairs, Statement by Janet L. Yellen Secretary United States Department of the Treasury, S. Doc. No. 117, 1st Sess. (Sept. 28, 2021), accessed November 29, 2022, https://www.banking.senate.gov/imo/media/doc/Yellen%20Testimony%209-28-21.pdf.
[7] Federal Reserve, "Transcript of Chair Powell's Press Conference," September 22, 2021, https://www.federalreserve.gov/mediacenter/files/FOMCpresconf20210922.pdf.
[8] 31 U.S.C. § 5111 (Sept. 13, 1982), accessed November 29, 2022, https://www.govinfo.gov/content/pkg/STATUTE-96/pdf/STATUTE-96-Pg877.pdf.
[9] Paul Krugman, "Wonking Out: Biden Should Ignore the Debt Limit and Mint a $1 Trillion Coin," *New York Times*, October 1, 2021, https://www.nytimes.com/2021/10/01/opinion/biden-coin-democrat-republican-debt-limit.html.
[10] Federal Reserve Bank of St. Louis, "M2 (M2SL)," FRED Economic Data, accessed November 29, 2022, https://fred.stlouisfed.org/series/M2SL.
[11] Aïda Amer, "An Illustration of a $1 Trillion Coin," Axios, October 5, 2021, https://images.axios.com/YOF4BvNjM06906e4lhBBS6At2do=/0x0:1920x1080/1920x1080/2021/10/05/1633434245808.jpg?w=1920.

[12] Federal Reserve Bank of St. Louis, "Functions of Money," Economic Lowdown Podcast, https://www.stlouisfed.org/education/economic-lowdown-podcast-series/episode-9-functions-of-money.
[13] Jörg Guido Hülsmann, *The Ethics of Money Production* (Auburn, Ala.: Ludwig von Mises Institute, 2008), 197.
[14] Hülsmann, *Ethics*, 33.
[15] Because Bitcoin is programmable, if there were ever a need for more than 8 decimal places, that could easily be accomplished.
[16] R. E. C. Stearns, "Shell-Money," *The American Naturalist* 3, no. 1 (March 1869): 3, https://doi.org/10.1086/270343.
[17] "Stock-To-Flow Ratio," Swiss Gold Safe, accessed November 28, 2022, https://swissgoldsafe.ch/en/additional-information/fundamentals-precious-metals/stock-to-flow-ratio/.
[18] Fred Imbert, "JPMorgan CEO Jamie Dimon Says Bitcoin Is a 'Fraud' That Will Eventually Blow Up," Delivering Alpha, last modified September 12, 2017, https://www.cnbc.com/2017/09/12/jpmorgan-ceo-jamie-dimon-raises-flag-on-trading-revenue-sees-20-percent-fall-for-the-third-quarter.html.
[19] "Dig More Coal – the PCs Are Coming," *Forbes*, last modified May 31, 1999, https://www.forbes.com/forbes/1999/0531/6311070a.html?sh=552dc4d32580.
[20] Matt McGrath, "Climate Change: Biggest Global Poll Supports 'Global Emergency,'" BBC News, last modified January 27, 2021, https://www.bbc.com/news/science-environment-55802902.
[21] Alcoa Corporation, "Alcoa Sells Former Rockdale Industrial Site for $240 Million," November 1, 2021, https://investors.alcoa.com/news-releases/news-release-details/2021/Alcoa-Sells-Former-Rockdale-Industrial-Site-for-240-Million/default.aspx.
[22] Andy Uhler, "Central Texas: famous for barbecue, boots and … bitcoin?," Marketplace, last modified March 18, 2022, https://www.marketplace.org/2022/03/18/central-texas-town-hopes-crypto-mining-replaces-lost-jobs/.
[23] "Riot Blockchain Number of Employees," Macrotrends, accessed December 6, 2022, https://www.macrotrends.net/stocks/charts/RIOT/riot-blockchain/number-of-employees.
[24] Pierre Sama, Feroz Sanaulla, and Christine Vaughan, "How Crypto Mining Will Transform the Energy Industry," Roland Berger, last modified April 4, 2022, https://www.rolandberger.com/en/Insights/Publications/How-crypto-mining-will-transform-the-energy-industry.html.

[25] "Green Power Partnership Fortune 500 Partners List," Environmental Protection Agency, last modified October 24, 2022, https://www.epa.gov/greenpower/green-power-partnership-fortune-500r-partners-list.
[26] REN21, *Renewables 2021 Global Status Report*, accessed November 28, 2022, https://www.ren21.net/wp-content/uploads/2019/05/GSR2021_Full_Report.pdf.
[27] International Renewable Energy Agency, "Majority of New Renewables Undercut Cheapest Fossil Fuel on Cost," June 22, 2021, https://www.irena.org/newsroom/pressreleases/2021/Jun/Majority-of-New-Renewables-Undercut-Cheapest-Fossil-Fuel-on-Cost.
[28] World Economic Forum, "Renewable Energy Is Cheaper than Previously Thought," last modified October 18, 2021, https://www.weforum.org/agenda/2021/10/how-cheap-can-renewable-energy-get.
[29] "Average Costs of Fossil Fuels for the Electric Power Industry in The United States from 2005 to 2021," Statistia, accessed December 1, 2022, https://www.statista.com/statistics/183992/average-costs-of-fossil-fuels-for-us-electricity-generation-from-2005/.
[30] Marshall Brain, "How Power Grids Work," Sciences at Smith College, accessed December 1, 2022, https://www.science.smith.edu/~jcardell/Courses/EGR220/ElecPwr_HSW.html.
[31] Joachim Seel et al., "Plentiful Electricity Turns Wholesale Prices Negative," *Advances in Applied Energy* 4, no. 100073 (November 2021), https://doi.org/10.1016/j.adapen.2021.100073.
[32] David Pan, "Bitcoin Miners Shut as Texas Power Grid Nears Brink," *Bloomberg*, July 11, 2022, https://www.bloomberg.com/news/articles/2022-07-11/bitcoin-miners-shut-off-rigs-as-texas-power-grid-nears-brink#xj4y7vzkg.
[33] "How Much Energy Does a House Use?," *Constellation* (blog), October 24, 2022, https://blog.constellation.com/2021/02/25/average-home-power-usage/.
[34] "Bitcoin Mining Uses Less Energy than Christmas Lights," Mawson, last modified December 13, 2021, https://mawsoninc.com/bitcoin-mining-uses-less-energy-than-christmas-lights/.
[35] "The Story Behind the ASIC Evolution," *Bitmain* (blog), April 19, 2020, https://blog.bitmain.com/en/tag/antminer-s1.
[36] "Mining Hardware Comparison," The Bitcoin Wiki, accessed December 1, 2022, https://en.bitcoin.it/wiki/Mining_hardware_comparison.

---

[37] "Non-specialized Hardware Comparison," The Bitcoin Wiki, accessed December 1, 2022, https://en.bitcoin.it/wiki/Non-specialized_hardware_comparison.
[38] "Bitmain Antminer S19 XP (140Th)," ASIC Miner Value, accessed December 3, 2022, https://www.asicminervalue.com/miners/bitmain/antminer-s19-xp-140th.
[39] "Q3 Bitcoin Mining Council Survey," Bitcoin Mining Council, accessed December 3, 2022, https://bitcoinminingcouncil.com/bitcoin-mining-council-survey-confirms-year-on-year-improvements-in-sustainable-power-mix-and-technological-efficiency-in-q3-2022/.
[40] Sarah Cairoli, "Effects of Gold Mining on the Environment," Sciencing.com, last modified October 20, 2021, https://sciencing.com/facts-5218981-effects-gold-mining-environment.html.
[41] Anne Marie Green, "Who Doesn't Want the Right to Repair? Companies worth over $10 Trillion," PIRG.com, last modified May 3, 2021, https://pirg.org/articles/who-doesnt-want-the-right-to-repair-companies-worth-over-10-trillion/.
[42] U.S. National Debt Clock, accessed December 3, 2022, https://www.usdebtclock.org/.
[43] Jack Hersch, "Deep Dive: US National Debt Hits 100% of GDP. Should the Credit Markets Care?," S&P Global, last modified February 22, 2021, https://www.spglobal.com/marketintelligence/en/news-insights/latest-news-headlines/deep-dive-us-national-debt-hits-100-of-gdp-should-the-credit-markets-care-62691039.
[44] "Is the Fed Buying Our New Debt?," CRFB.org, last modified May 11, 2020, https://www.crfb.org/blogs/fed-buying-our-new-debt.
[45] "Value of $1 from 1913 to 2022," In2013Dollars.com, accessed December 3, 2022, https://www.in2013dollars.com/us/inflation/1913?amount=1.
[46] Jeff Booth, *The Price of Tomorrow: Why Deflation Is the Key to an Abundant Future* (Place of publication not identified: Stanley Press, 2020).
[47] Roman Krznaric, *The Good Ancestor: How to Think Long-term in a Short-term World* (New York: Experiment, 2020), 97.
[48] James Hunt, "Congo National Park's Bitcoin Mining Bet Saved It from Going Bust: MIT Tech Review," The Block, last modified January 13, 2023, accessed February 11, 2023, https://www.theblock.co/post/202302/congo-national-parks-bitcoin-mining-bet-saved-it-from-going-bust-mit-tech-review.
[49] Shawn Amick, "Kenya's Largest Power Provider to Offer Geothermal Energy to Bitcoin Miners," *Bitcoin Magazine*, last modified June 2, 2022,

https://bitcoinmagazine.com/business/kengen-to-provide-geothermal-energy-to-bitcoin-miners-in-kenya.

[50] Alvaro Murillo, "Costa Rica Hydro Plant Gets New Lease on Life from Crypto Mining," Reuters, last modified January 11, 2022, https://www.reuters.com/technology/costa-rica-hydro-plant-gets-new-lease-life-crypto-mining-2022-01-11/.

[51] Terence Zimwara, "Kenyan Firm Using Wasted Energy to Mine Bitcoin – Business Model Said to Potentially Help Decentralize Mining," Bitcoin.com, last modified October 11, 2022, https://news.bitcoin.com/kenyan-firm-using-wasted-energy-to-mine-bitcoin-business-model-said-to-potentially-help-decentralize-mining/.

[52] Tom Mitchelhill, "Bengal Energy to Mine Bitcoin Using Stranded Gas Wells in Australian Outback," CoinTelegraph, last modified March 31, 2022, https://cointelegraph.com/news/bengal-energy-to-mine-bitcoin-using-stranded-wells-in-aussie-outback.

[53] MacKenzie Sigalos, "Exxon Is Mining Bitcoin in North Dakota as Part of Its Plan to Slash Emissions," CNBC, last modified March 26, 2022, https://www.cnbc.com/2022/03/26/exxon-mining-bitcoin-with-crusoe-energy-in-north-dakota-bakken-region.html.

[54] "Global Gas Flaring Reduction Partnership," The World Bank, accessed December 3, 2022, https://www.worldbank.org/en/programs/gasflaringreduction/gas-flaring-explained.

[55] Jeff Benson, "Bitcoin Firm Crusoe Energy Raises $505 Million to Grow Flare-Gas Mining Business," Decrypt, last modified April 21, 2021, https://decrypt.co/98424/bitcoin-firm-crusoe-energy-raises-505-million-grow-flare-gas-mining-business.

[56] Lisa Martine Jenkins, "Exxon Is Dealing with Greenhouse Gas Emissions by … Mining Crypto?," Protocol, last modified March 24, 2022, https://www.protocol.com/bulletins/exxon-bitcoin-mining-gas-flaring.

[57] "Vespene Energy," Vespene, accessed December 3, 2022, https://vespene.energy/.

[58] White House Office of Science and Technology Policy, *Climate And Energy Implications of Crypto-assets in The United States*, 24, September 2022, http://whitehouse.gov/wp-content/uploads/2022/09/09-2022-Crypto-Assets-and-Climate-Report.pdf.

[59] Troy Cross, interview with the author, July 12, 2022.

[60] "Human Microphone," Wikipedia, accessed December 6, 2022, https://en.wikipedia.org/wiki/Human_microphone.

---

[61] "Timeline of Occupy Wall Street," Wikipedia, accessed December 6, 2022, https://en.wikipedia.org/wiki/Timeline_of_Occupy_Wall_Street.
[62] Simon Ashby, "Risk Management and the Global Banking Crisis: Lessons for Insurance Solvency Regulation," The Geneva Papers on Risk and Insurance, *Issues and Practice* 36, no. 3 (2011): 330–47, http://www.jstor.org/stable/41953142.
[63] Michael Lewis, *The Big Short: Inside the Doomsday Machine* (New York: Norton, 2011).
[64] Katie Kolchin, Justyna Podziemska, and Ali Mostafa, *The US Repo Markets: A Chart Book*, Securities Industry and Financial Markets Association, February 6, 2022, https://www.sifma.org/wp-content/uploads/2022/02/SIFMA-Research-US-Repo-Markets-Chart-Book-2022.pdf.
[65] "Deposit Insurance FAQs," Federal Deposit Insurance Corporation, last modified December 8, 2021, https://www.fdic.gov/resources/deposit-insurance/faq/.
[66] Emergency Economic Stabilization Act of 2008, H.R. 343, 110th Cong., 2d Sess. § 115 (Oct. 3, 2008), accessed February 11, 2023, https://www.govinfo.gov/content/pkg/PLAW-110publ343/pdf/PLAW-110publ343.pdf.
[67] Andrew Ross Sorkin, *Too Big to Fail: The Inside Story of How Wall Street and Washington Fought to Save the Financial System – and Themselves* (New York: Penguin Books, 2018).
[68] Mehrsa Baradaran, *How the Other Half Banks: Exclusion, Exploitation, and the Threat to Democracy* (Cambridge, MA: Chautauqua Institution, 2016), 16.
[69] "What Happened in Money Markets in September 2019?," *Federal Reserve*, last modified February 27, 2020, https://www.federalreserve.gov/econres/notes/feds-notes/what-happened-in-money-markets-in-september-2019-20200227.html.
[70] Heather Long, "2019: The Year the Federal Reserve Admitted It Was Wrong," *The Washington Post*, last modified December 11, 2019, https://www.washingtonpost.com/business/2019/12/11/year-federal-reserve-admitted-it-was-wrong/.
[71] Anna-Louise Jackson, "Quantitative Easing Explained," ed. Benjamin Curry, Forbes.com, last modified January 19, 2022, https://www.forbes.com/advisor/investing/quantitative-easing-qe/.
[72] Valerio Cerretano, "Quantitative Easing Now Looks Permanent – and Has Turned Central Banks into Pseudo Governments," The Conversation, last modified January 23, 2020, https://theconversation.com/quantitative-easing-

now-looks-permanent-and-has-turned-central-banks-into-pseudo-governments-130098.
[73] "Credit and Liquidity Programs and the Balance Sheet," Federal Reserve, accessed December 6, 2022, https://www.federalreserve.gov/monetarypolicy/bst_recenttrends.htm.
[74] "US Reserve Requirement Ratio," CEIC, accessed December 6, 2022, https://www.ceicdata.com/en/indicator/united-states/reserve-requirement-ratio.
[75] Lily Jamali, "European Central Bank Likely to End Its Negative Interest Rate Experiment," Marketplace, last modified May 23, 2022, https://www.marketplace.org/2022/05/23/european-central-bank-likely-to-end-its-negative-interest-rate-experiment/.
[76] "Hamilton v. Jefferson: The Central Bank Debate," YouTube video, January 28, 2020, https://www.youtube.com/watch?v=f-If7tU7lkE.
[77] Thomas Jefferson to John Taylor, May 28, 1816, accessed December 6, 2022, https://founders.archives.gov/documents/Jefferson/03-10-02-0053.
[78] Baradaran, *How the Other Half Banks*, 31.
[79] "Report on the Economic Well-Being of U.S. Households in 2018," Federal Reserve, last modified May 2019, https://www.federalreserve.gov/publications/2019-economic-well-being-of-us-households-in-2018-banking-and-credit.htm.
[80] Lydia Saad and Jeffrey M. Jones, "What Percentage of Americans Owns Stock?," Gallup, last modified May 12, 2022, https://news.gallup.com/poll/266807/percentage-americans-owns-stock.aspx.
[81] Megan Leonhardt, "This Map Shows the States Where Payday Loans Charge Nearly 700 Percent Interest," CNBC, last modified August 3, 2018, https://www.cnbc.com/2018/08/03/states-with-the-highest-payday-loan-rates.html.
[82] Baradaran, *How the Other Half Banks*.
[83] "Debt Resequencing - Is it Legal?," Shamis & Gentile, P.A., last modified September 21, 2020, https://sflinjuryattorneys.com/debit-resequencing-is-it-legal/.
[84] *Your Guide to Preventing and Managing Overdraft Fees* (FDIC, n.d.), 1, accessed December 6, 2022, https://www.fdic.gov/consumers/overdraft/overdraft-hi-rez.pdf.
[85] "Debt Resequencing," Shamis & Gentile, P.A.
[86] Matthew O'Brien, "Everything You Need to Know About the Cyprus Bank Disaster," *The Atlantic*, last modified March 18, 2013,

https://www.theatlantic.com/business/archive/2013/03/everything-you-need-to-know-about-the-cyprus-bank-disaster/274096/.
[87] Liz Alderman, "Facing Bailout Tax, Cypriots Try to Get Cash Out of Banks," *New York Times*, March 16, 2013, https://www.nytimes.com/2013/03/17/business/global/facing-bailout-tax-cypriots-try-to-get-cash-out-of-banks.html?hp.
[88] Max Ehrenfreund, "Cypriot Banks to Reopen Amid Criticism of Bailout," *The Washington Post*, last modified March 27, 2013, https://www.washingtonpost.com/business/cypriot-banks-to-reopen-amid-criticism-of-bailout/2013/03/27/dd56757c-96e1-11e2-b68f-dc5c4b47e519_story.html.
[89] Michele Kambas, "Cyprus Banks Remain Closed to Avert Run on Deposits," Reuters, last modified March 24, 2013, https://www.reuters.com/article/us-cyprus-parliament-idUSBRE92G03I20130325.
[90] O'Brien, "Everything You Need to Know," *The Atlantic*.
[91] "Corralito," Wikipedia, accessed December 6, 2022, https://en.wikipedia.org/wiki/Corralito.
[92] An Act to Provide Relief in the Existing National Emergency in Banking, and for Other Purposes, H.R. 73, 73d Cong., 1st Sess. (Mar. 9, 1933), accessed February 11, 2023, https://govtrackus.s3.amazonaws.com/legislink/pdf/stat/48/STATUTE-48-Pg1.pdf.
[93] Exec. Order No. 6102, 3 C.F.R. (1933), accessed December 6, 2022, https://www.presidency.ucsb.edu/documents/executive-order-6102-requiring-gold-coin-gold-bullion-and-gold-certificates-be-delivered.
[94] "Historical Gold Prices," Only Gold, accessed December 6, 2022, https://onlygold.com/gold-prices/historical-gold-prices/.
[95] AN ACT To protect the currency system of the United States, to provide for the better use of the monetary gold stock of the United States, and for other purposes, H.R. 87, 73d Cong., 2d Sess. (Jan. 30, 1934), accessed February 11, 2023, https://govtrackus.s3.amazonaws.com/legislink/pdf/stat/48/STATUTE-48-Pg337a.pdf.
[96] AN ACT To protect the currency system, H.R. 87.
[97] AN ACT To protect the currency system, H.R. 87.
[98] "Breaking Down $3.4 Trillion in COVID Relief," Committee for a Responsible Federal Budget, last modified January 7, 2021, https://www.crfb.org/blogs/breaking-down-34-trillion-covid-relief.

[99] Sascha Pfeiffer, "Virtually All PPP Loans Have Been Forgiven with Limited Scrutiny," NPR, last modified October 12, 2022, https://www.npr.org/2022/10/12/1128207464/ppp-loans-loan-forgiveness-small-business.
[100] U.S. Small Business Association, *Paycheck Protection Program (PPP) Report*, August 8, 2020, https://home.treasury.gov/system/files/136/SBA-Paycheck-Protection-Program-Loan-Report-Round2.pdf.
[101] Julia Lurie, "How PPP Loan Distribution Became the New Redlining," *Mother Jones*, last modified May 1, 2021, https://www.motherjones.com/politics/2021/05/how-ppp-loans-new-redlining-covid-relief-racial-disparities-reveal/.
[102] Laura Sullivan et al., "Small Business Rescue Earned Banks $10 Billion In Fees," NPR, last modified April 22, 2020, https://www.npr.org/2020/04/22/840678984/small-business-rescue-earned-banks-10-billion-in-fees.
[103] Jonathan O'Connell, "White House, GOP Face Heat after Hotel and Restaurant Chains Helped Run Small Business Program Dry," *The Washington Post*, last modified April 20, 2020, https://www.washingtonpost.com/business/2020/04/20/white-house-gop-face-heat-after-hotel-restaurant-chains-helped-run-small-business-program-dry/.
[104] Lucas Kwan Peterson, "Column: The PPP Is Letting Our Small Restaurants and Businesses Die," *The Los Angeles Times*, last modified April 18, 2020, https://www.latimes.com/food/story/2020-04-18/ppp-cares-act-small-business-loan-relief-failure.
[105] David Autor et al., "The $800 Billion Paycheck Protection Program: Where Did the Money Go and Why Did It Go There?," *Journal of Economic Perspectives* 36, no. 2 (May 1, 2022): 60, https://doi.org/10.1257/jep.36.2.55.
[106] William R. Emmons and Drew Dahl, "Was the Paycheck Protection Program Effective?," Federal Reserve Bank of St. Louis, last modified July 6, 2022, https://www.stlouisfed.org/publications/regional-economist/2022/jul/was-paycheck-protection-program-effective.
[107] Alicia Plerhoples, "Correcting Past Mistakes: PPP Loans and Black-Owned Small Businesses," American Constitution Society, last modified February 25, 2021, https://www.acslaw.org/expertforum/correcting-past-mistakes-ppp-loans-and-black-owned-small-businesses/.
[108] Public Private Strategies, *Business Owners of Color and COVID-19*, December 10, 2020, https://irp-

cdn.multiscreensite.com/45d2c930/files/uploaded/Distribution%20Version%20%2812.10.2020%29%20for%20RMS%20Poll%20Launch%20v1.pdf.

[109] "Disparities in PPP Lending to Black-Owned Small Businesses," National Bureau of Economic Research, December, 2021, https://www.nber.org/sites/default/files/inline-images/w29364.jpg.

[110] Richard Rothstein, *The Color of Law: A Forgotten History of How Our Government Segregated America* (New York: Liveright Publishing, 2018).

[111] Terry Gross, "A 'Forgotten History' of How The U.S. Government Segregated America," NPR, last modified May 3, 2017, https://www.npr.org/2017/05/03/526655831/a-forgotten-history-of-how-the-u-s-government-segregated-america.

[112] Ta-Nehisi Coates, "The Case for Reparations," *The Atlantic*, June 2014, accessed February 11, 2023, https://www.theatlantic.com/magazine/archive/2014/06/the-case-for-reparations/361631/.

[113] "The Segregation Myth: Richard Rothstein Debunks an American Lie," YouTube video, June 26, 2020, https://www.youtube.com/watch?v=2roWLzrqOjQ.

[114] "Explained | Racial Wealth Gap | FULL EPISODE | Netflix," YouTube video, April 17, 2020, https://www.youtube.com/watch?v=Mqrhn8khGLM.

[115] Cleve Mesidor, "Crypto Can Be a Driver for Racial Equity," *Boston Globe*, last modified May 12, 2022, https://www.bostonglobe.com/2022/05/10/opinion/crypto-can-be-driver-racial-equity/.

[116] "Lamar Wilson on the Basics of Bitcoin, Crypto's Impact on the Black Community + More," YouTube video, March 2, 2022, https://www.youtube.com/watch?v=UWfJzHi7AQE.

[117] John Lynch, "How Jay-Z and Jack Dorsey's Bitcoin Academy Provides Financial Inclusion and Breaks Down Barriers of Inequity," Insider, last modified September 7, 2022, https://www.businessinsider.com/jay-z-jack-dorsey-bitcoin-academy-marcy-houses-2022-9.

[118] Jon Logan, interview with the author, July 10, 2022.

[119] Bank Black USA, accessed December 5, 2022, https://bankblackusa.org/.

[120] Digital Financial Revolution Tour, accessed December 5, 2022, http://www.thedfrtour.com/.

[121] Sharon G. Smith et al., *The National Intimate Partner and Sexual Violence Survey (NISVS): 2010-2012 State Report*, April, 2017, https://www.cdc.gov/violenceprevention/pdf/nisvs-statereportbook.pdf.

[122] Adrienne E. Adams, *Measuring the Effects of Domestic Violence on Women's Financial Well Being*, May 17, 2011,

https://centerforfinancialsecurity.files.wordpress.com/2015/04/adams2011.pdf.
[123] "About Financial Abuse," National Network to End Domestic Violence, accessed December 6, 2022, https://nnedv.org/content/about-financial-abuse/.
[124] Oxfam International, "Women Rights Organisations Hit Harder by Funding Cuts and Left Out of COVID-19 Response and Recovery Efforts," accessed July 10, 2021, https://www.oxfam.org/en/press-releases/women-rights-organisations-hit-harder-funding-cuts-and-left-out-covid-19-response.
[125] Anita Posch, interview with the author, July 13, 2022.
[126] Human Rights Foundation, *2020 Annual Report*, 2020, https://hrf.org/wp-content/uploads/2021/05/2020-HRF-Annual-Report_FINAL.pdf.
[127] Oliver Williams, "Corrupt Elites Siphon Aid Money Intended for World's Poorest," *Forbes*, last modified February 20, 2020, https://www.forbes.com/sites/oliverwilliams1/2020/02/20/corrupt-elites-siphen-aid-money-intended-for-worlds-poorest/?sh=589bc5221565.
[128] Alex Gladstein, interview by the author, June 29, 2022.
[129] Troy Adkins, "Countries Using the U.S. Dollar," Investopedia, last modified June 10, 2022, https://www.investopedia.com/articles/forex/040915/countries-use-us-dollar.asp.
[130] Andrew Swiston, *Official Dollarization as a Monetary Regime: Its Effects on El Salvador*, June, 2011, https://www.imf.org/external/pubs/ft/wp/2011/wp11129.pdf.
[131] BTC Media, "El Salvador," Bitcoin Magazine, accessed February 10, 2023, https://bitcoinmagazine.com/tags/el-salvador.
[132] "List of Countries by Human Development Index," Wikipedia, accessed December 6, 2022, https://en.wikipedia.org/wiki/List_of_countries_by_Human_Development_Index.
[133] Ndongo Samba Sylla, "The CFA Franc: French Monetary Imperialism in Africa," *London School of Economics and Political Science* (blog), last modified July 12, 2017, https://blogs.lse.ac.uk/africaatlse/2017/07/12/the-cfa-franc-french-monetary-imperialism-in-africa/.
[134] Mawuna Remarque Koutonin, "14 African Countries Forced by France to Pay Colonial Tax for the Benefits of Slavery and Colonization," The Institute of the Black World 21st Century, last modified January 14, 2015, https://ibw21.org/editors-choice/14-african-countries-forced-by-france-to-pay-colonial-tax-for-the-benefits-of-slavery-and-colonization/.

---

[135] John Nichols, "Gotta Sequester? Or Was Cheney Right That 'Deficits Don't Matter'?," *The Nation*, March 1, 2013, https://www.thenation.com/article/archive/gotta-sequester-or-was-cheney-right-deficits-dont-matter/.
[136] "U.S. National Debt Clock," U.S. National Debt Clock.
[137] Thomas Grennes, Mehmet Caner, and Fritzi Koehler-Geib, "Finding the Tipping Point – When Sovereign Debt Turns Bad," *Policy Research Working Papers*, August 23, 2010, https://doi.org/10.1596/1813-9450-5391.
[138] "The United States Government Debt Is Estimated to Have Reached 137.20 Percent of the Country's Gross Domestic Product in 2021," Trading Economics, accessed December 3, 2022, https://tradingeconomics.com/united-states/government-debt-to-gdp.
[139] "Value of $1 from 1800 to 1899," CPI Inflation Calculator, accessed December 3, 2022, https://www.officialdata.org/us/inflation/1800?endYear=1899&amount=1.
[140] Maria Belen Liotti, "In Argentina, Mass Protests Demand Higher Wages, Lower Inflation," Reuters, last modified August 17, 2022, https://www.reuters.com/world/americas/argentina-mass-protests-demand-higher-wages-lower-inflation-2022-08-17/.
[141] Aya Batrawy, "Inflation Sparks Global Wave of Protests for Higher Pay, Aid," Associated Press, last modified June 25, 2022, https://apnews.com/article/inflation-middle-east-africa-56399743fe9ad28692c88c007bb901d6.
[142] "M1 (M1SL)," FRED St. Louis Federal Reserve, last modified November 22, 2022, https://fred.stlouisfed.org/series/M1SL.
[143] Edmund C. Moy, "Understanding the Money Supply Increase in the U.S. and Its Potential Consequences," Wheaton College, accessed December 3, 2022, https://www.wheaton.edu/academics/academic-centers/wheaton-center-for-faith-politics-and-economics/resource-center/articles/2021/understanding-the-money-supply/.
[144] "Consumer Prices up 9.1 Percent Over the Year Ended June 2022, Largest Increase in 40 Years," U.S. Bureau of Labor Statistics, last modified July 18, 2022, https://www.bls.gov/opub/ted/2022/consumer-prices-up-9-1-percent-over-the-year-ended-june-2022-largest-increase-in-40-years.htm.
[145] Walter J. Williams, "Alternate Inflation Charts," Shadow Government Statistics, last modified November 10, 2022, http://www.shadowstats.com/alternate_data/inflation-charts.
[146] "Median Sales Price of Houses Sold for the United States," FRED Economic Data St. Louis Federal Reserve, last modified October 26, 2022, https://fred.stlouisfed.org/series/MSPUS.

[147] "S&P 500 Index," TradingView, accessed December 3, 2022, https://www.tradingview.com/symbols/SPX/.
[148] Lydia Saad and Jeffery M. Jones, "What Percentage of Americans Own Stock?," Gallup, last modified May 12, 2022, https://news.gallup.com/poll/266807/percentage-americans-owns-stock.aspx.
[149] Ben Zeisloft, "Wall Street Firms Are Buying up Single-Family Homes," Daily Wire, last modified August 3, 2021, https://www.dailywire.com/news/wall-street-firms-are-buying-up-single-family-homes.
[150] Ryan Dezember, "If You Sell a House These Days, the Buyer Might Be a Pension Fund," *Wall Street Journal*, last modified April 4, 2021, https://www.wsj.com/articles/if-you-sell-a-house-these-days-the-buyer-might-be-a-pension-fund-11617544801.
[151] Lawrence Mishel, "Growing Inequalities, Reflecting Growing Employer Power, Have Generated a Productivity–pay Gap since 1979," Economic Policy Institute, last modified September 2, 2021, https://www.epi.org/blog/growing-inequalities-reflecting-growing-employer-power-have-generated-a-productivity-pay-gap-since-1979-productivity-has-grown-3-5-times-as-much-as-pay-for-the-typical-worker/.
[152] Juliana Menasce Horowitz, Ruth Igielnik, and Rakesh Kochhar, "Most Americans Say There Is Too Much Economic Inequality in the U.S., but Fewer than Half Call It a Top Priority," January 9, 2020, https://www.pewresearch.org/social-trends/2020/01/09/trends-in-income-and-wealth-inequality/.
[153] "Household Income Distribution According to the Gini Index of Income Inequality in the United States from 1990 to 2021," Statista, accessed December 3, 2022, https://www.statista.com/statistics/219643/gini-coefficient-for-us-individuals-families-and-households/.
[154] "Gini Index," The World Bank, accessed December 3, 2022, https://data.worldbank.org/indicator/SI.POV.GINI.
[155] Kevin Kelleher, "Gilded Age 2.0: U.S. Income Inequality Increases to Pre-Great Depression Levels," *Fortune*, last modified February 13, 2019, https://fortune.com/2019/02/13/us-income-inequality-bad-great-depression/.
[156] Christian Weller, "Wealth Inequality on the Rise during Pandemic," *Forbes*, last modified December 22, 2021, https://www.forbes.com/sites/christianweller/2021/12/22/wealth-rises-at-all-income-levels-but-faster-at-the-top/.
[157] Robert Frank, "Soaring Markets Helped the Richest 1% Gain $6.5 Trillion in Wealth Last Year, According to the Fed," CNBC, last modified

April 1, 2022, https://www.cnbc.com/2022/04/01/richest-one-percent-gained-trillions-in-wealth-2021.html.
[158] "Our Mission," FREOPP, last modified June 12, 2016, https://freopp.org/our-mission-3b16e8e8c656.
[159] Jackson Mejia and Jon Hartley, "Inflation's Compounding Impact on the Poor," FREOPP, last modified April 25, 2022, https://freopp.org/inflations-compounding-impact-on-the-poor-f82ea4d61d9b.
[160] "Consumer Prices," U.S. Bureau of Labor Statistics.
[161] Kathryn Watson, "Yellen Admits She Was 'Wrong' About Inflation in 2021," CBS News, last modified June 1, 2022, https://www.cbsnews.com/news/inflation-janet-yellen-wrong-treasury-secretary/.
[162] Jeff Cox, "Powell Warns of 'Some Pain' Ahead as the Fed Fights to Bring Down Inflation," CNBC, last modified August 26, 2022, https://www.cnbc.com/2022/08/26/powell-warns-of-some-pain-ahead-as-fed-fights-to-lower-inflation.html.
[163] "Inflation and Money," Farm Bureau, last modified May 12, 2022, https://www.fb.org/market-intel/inflation-and-money.
[164] "How Many Bitcoins Are There?," Buy Bitcoin Worldwide, accessed December 3, 2022, https://buybitcoinworldwide.com/how-many-bitcoins-are-there/.
[165] Brent Hecht, "Gold's Stock-to-Flow Ratio and Why It Matters," Seeking Alpha, last modified July 7, 2020, https://seekingalpha.com/article/4357409-golds-stock-to-flow-ratio-and-why-matters.
[166] Hecht, "Gold's Stock-to-Flow."
[167] Jose Oramas, "Bitcoin Stock-to-Flow (S2F) Model: What You Need to Know," CryptoPotato, last modified March 23, 2022, https://cryptopotato.com/bitcoin-stock-to-flow-s2f-model.
[168] Satoshi Nakamoto, "Bitcoin: A Peer-to-Peer Electronic Cash System," October 31, 2008, https://bitcoin.org/bitcoin.pdf.
[169] "Gold's Cost of Production Analysis," Bunker-Group, last modified February 18, 2022, https://bunker-group.com/en/blog/gold-s-cost-of-production-analysis.
[170] Richard Cantillon, *An Essay on Economic Theory: An English Translation of Richard Cantillon's Essai Sur La Nature Du Commerce En Général* (Auburn, Ala.: Ludwig von Mises Institute, 2010).
[171] Paola Boel and Peter Zimmerman, "Unbanked in America: A Review of the Literature," *Economic Commentary (Federal Reserve Bank of Cleveland)*, nos. 2022-07 (May 26, 2022): 8, https://doi.org/10.26509/frbc-ec-202207.

[172] Chad Stone et al., *A Guide to Statistics on Historical Trends in Income Inequality*, January 13, 2020, https://www.cbpp.org/research/poverty-and-inequality/a-guide-to-statistics-on-historical-trends-in-income-inequality.
[173] Patrick Henry, "Economic Inequality Has Deepened During the Pandemic. That Doesn't Mean It Can't Be Fixed," World Economic Forum, last modified April 7, 2022,
https://www.weforum.org/agenda/2022/04/economic-inequality-wealth-gap-pandemic/.
[174] Paul Vigna, "Bitcoin's 'One Percent' Controls Lion's Share of the Cryptocurrency's Wealth," *Wall Street Journal*, December 20, 2021, https://www.wsj.com/articles/bitcoins-one-percent-controls-lions-share-of-the-cryptocurrencys-wealth-11639996204.
[175] Michael Weymans, "Bitcoin Wealth Is Becoming More Evenly Distributed over Time," E-Commerce Institute Cologne, last modified March 29, 2022, https://ecommerceinstitut.de/bitcoin-wealth-is-becoming-more-evenly-distributed-over-time-3-4-2/.
[176] "Household Income," Statista.
[177] *Human Development Report 2010: The Real Wealth of Nations: Pathways to Human Development*, January 1, 2010,
https://hdr.undp.org/content/human-development-report-2010.
[178] Weymans, "Bitcoin Wealth," E-Commerce Institute Cologne.
[179] Peter S. Goodman, *Davos Man: How the Billionaires Devoured the World* (New York, NY: Custom House, 2022), 5.
[180] Fred Imbert, "Trump Says Dollar Will Get 'Stronger and Stronger,' Mnuchin Was Misinterpreted," CNBC, last modified January 25, 2018, https://www.cnbc.com/2018/01/25/trump-says-dollar-to-get-stronger-and-stronger.html.
[181] Saqib Iqbal Ahmed, "Trump Pivots to Embrace a Strong U.S. Dollar," Reuters, last modified May 14, 2020, https://www.reuters.com/article/us-global-forex-trump-dollar-idINKBN22Q31S.
[182] "Triffin Dilemma," Wikipedia, accessed December 3, 2022, https://en.wikipedia.org/wiki/Triffin_dilemma.
[183] Benjamin Landy, "Graph: How the Financial Sector Consumed America's Economic Growth," The Century Foundation, last modified February 25, 2013, https://tcf.org/content/commentary/graph-how-the-financial-sector-consumed-americas-economic-growth/.
[184] Greta R. Krippner, "The Financialization of the American Economy," *Socio-Economic Review* 3, no. 2 (May 2005),
https://www.depfe.unam.mx/actividades/10/financiarizacion/i-7-KrippnerGreta.pdf.

[185] Stephen G. Cecchetti and Enisse Kharroubi, *Why Does Financial Sector Growth Crowd Out Real Economic Growth?*, September 2014, https://www.bis.org/publ/work490.pdf.
[186] "World Reserve Currencies since 1450," Midas Gold Group, accessed December 3, 2022, https://www.midasgoldgroup.com/news/world-reserve-currencies-since-1450/.
[187] "Bretton Woods and the Birth of the World Bank," The World Bank, accessed December 3, 2022, https://www.worldbank.org/en/archive/history/exhibits/Bretton-Woods-and-the-Birth-of-the-World-Bank.
[188] E. F. Schumacher, "Multilateral Clearing," *Economica* 10, no. 38 (May 1943): 150, https://doi.org/10.2307/2549461.
[189] "London Gold Pool," Wikipedia, accessed December 3, 2022, https://en.wikipedia.org/wiki/London_Gold_Pool.
[190] James Chen, "Eurodollar: Definition, Why It's Important, and Example," Investopedia, last modified January 31, 2021, https://www.investopedia.com/terms/e/eurodollar.asp.
[191] "August 15, 1971 – Richard Nixon Closes the Gold Window," YouTube video, August 15, 2014, https://www.youtube.com/watch?v=7_Xw5tWsOQo.
[192] CMI Gold & Silver, "Historical Gold Prices Over 200 Years of Historical Annual Gold Prices," Only Gold, last modified 2022, https://onlygold.com/gold-prices/historical-gold-prices/.
[193] "Value of $1 from 1971 to 2022," In2013Dollars.com, accessed December 3, 2022, https://www.in2013dollars.com/us/inflation/1971?amount=1.
[194] Andrea Wong, "The Untold Story Behind Saudi Arabia's 41-Year U.S. Debt Secret," Bloomberg, last modified 2016, https://www.bloomberg.com/news/features/2016-05-30/the-untold-story-behind-saudi-arabia-s-41-year-u-s-debt-secret.
[195] Wong, "The Untold Story," Bloomberg.
[196] Michael Hudson, *Super Imperialism: The Economic Strategy of American Empire*, 3rd ed. (Dresden: ISLET, 2021), 201.
[197] "Crude Oil Prices – 70 Year Historical Chart," MacroTrends, accessed December 3, 2022, https://www.macrotrends.net/1369/crude-oil-price-history-chart.
[198] Wong, "The Untold Story," Bloomberg.
[199] US Department of State, *Sama Agrees to Purchase Treasury Issues*, doc. no. 1974JIDDA07310, December 12, 1974, https://aad.archives.gov/aad/createpdf?rid=270129&dt=2474&dl=1345.

[200] It is important to concede that the petrodollar system undoubtedly had an instrumental effect on helping the United States win the Cold War. That said, I'm not aware of any historical analysis that would claim the United States would not have eventually emerged as the sole superpower even without the petrodollar.
[201] A Joint Resolution Relating to the Disapproval of the Proposed Foreign Military Sale to the Government of the Kingdom of Saudi Arabia of M1A1/A2 Abrams Tank Structures and Other Major Defense Equipment., S. Res. 39, 114th Cong., 2d Sess. (Sept. 8, 2016), https://www.congress.gov/bill/114th-congress/senate-joint-resolution/39.
[202] John Sifton, "Resolution Seeks to Block US Arms Sale to Saudi Arabia," Human Rights Watch, last modified September 8, 2016, https://www.hrw.org/news/2016/09/08/resolution-seeks-block-us-arms-sale-saudi-arabia.
[203] A Joint Resolution Providing for Congressional Disapproval of the Proposed Foreign Military Sale to the Kingdom of Saudi Arabia of Certain Defense Articles., S. Res. 31, 117th Cong., 1st Sess., December 7, 2021, https://www.congress.gov/bill/117th-congress/senate-joint-resolution/31/text.
[204] Merrit Kennedy, "Trump Vetoes Bills Intended to Block Arms Sales to Saudi Arabia," NPR, last modified July 25, 2019, https://www.npr.org/2019/07/25/745200244/trump-vetoes-bills-intended-to-block-arms-sales-to-saudi-arabia.
[205] Mark Mazzetti, "Saudi Arabia Warns of Economic Fallout If Congress Passes 9/11 Bill," *New York Times*, last modified April 15, 2016, https://www.nytimes.com/2016/04/16/world/middleeast/saudi-arabia-warns-ofeconomic-fallout-if-congress-passes-9-11-bill.html?_r=1.
[206] U.S. National Commission on Terrorist Attacks upon the United States, *The 9/11 Commission Report*, July 22, 2004, 171, https://govinfo.library.unt.edu/911/report/911Report.pdf.
[207] Seung Min Kim, "Obama Vetoes Saudi 9/11 Bill," Politico, last modified September 23, 2016, https://www.politico.com/story/2016/09/obama-jasta-228548.
[208] "Justice Against Sponsors of Terrorism Act," Wikipedia, accessed December 3, 2022, https://en.wikipedia.org/wiki/Justice_Against_Sponsors_of_Terrorism_Act.
[209] Craig Unger, *House of Bush, House of Saud: The Secret Relationship between the World's Two Most Powerful Dynasties* (New York: Scribner, 2004).

[210] Chris Murphy, "Senate Passes Murphy's Resolution to End U.S. Involvement in Saudi-Led War in Yemen," March 13, 2019, https://www.murphy.senate.gov/newsroom/press-releases/_senate-passes-murphys-resolution-to-end-us-involvement-in-saudi-led-war-in-yemen.
[211] Shadi Hamid, "Middle Eastern Autocrats Embarrassed Biden at Will," Brookings Institution, last modified July 22, 2022, https://www.brookings.edu/blog/order-from-chaos/2022/07/22/middle-eastern-autocrats-embarrassed-biden-at-will/.
[212] "Assassination of Jamal Khashoggi," Wikipedia, accessed December 3, 2022, https://en.wikipedia.org/wiki/Assassination_of_Jamal_Khashoggi.
[213] Rebecca Falconer and Shawna Chen, "WaPo Slams Biden's Move to Shield MBS in Khashoggi Killing Suit," Axios, last modified November 18, 2022, https://www.axios.com/2022/11/18/biden-admin-saudi-prince-immunity-khashoggi-killing-lawsuit.
[214] Shobhit Seth, "Why China Buys U.S. Debt with Treasury Bonds," Investopedia, last modified October 23, 2022, https://www.investopedia.com/articles/investing/040115/reasons-why-china-buys-us-treasury-bonds.asp.
[215] Michael H. Fuchs, Daniel Benaim, and Blaine Johnson, "China Is Violating Uighurs' Human Rights. The United States Must Act," *Foreign Policy*, last modified November 28, 2018, https://foreignpolicy.com/2018/11/28/china-is-violating-uighurs-human-rights-the-united-states-must-act/.
[216] "United States' Share of Global Gross Domestic Product (GDP) Adjusted for Purchasing Power Parity (PPP) from 2017 to 2027," Statista, accessed December 3, 2022, https://www.statista.com/statistics/270267/united-states-share-of-global-gross-domestic-product-gdp/.
[217] "Currency Composition of Official Foreign Exchange Reserves," International Monetary Fund, accessed December 3, 2022, https://data.imf.org/?sk=E6A5F467-C14B-4AA8-9F6D-5A09EC4E62A4.
[218] John Antona, Jr., "88% of All 2019 Forex Transactions Are in US Dollars," Trader's Magazine, last modified January 24, 2020, https://www.tradersmagazine.com/am/88-of-all-2019-forex-transactions-are-in-us-dollars/.
[219] Barry Eichengreen, "Lessons from the Marshall Plan," April 2010, https://web.worldbank.org/archive/website01306/web/marshall_plan.html#.
[220] "Past Presidents," The World Bank, accessed December 3, 2022, https://www.worldbank.org/en/archive/history/past-presidents.
[221] Hudson, *Super Imperialism*, 161.

[222] "International Bank for Reconstruction and Development Subscriptions and Voting Power of Member Countries," World Bank, accessed December 3, 2022, https://thedocs.worldbank.org/en/doc/a16374a6cee037e274c5e932bf9f88c6-0330032021/original/IBRDCountryVotingTable.pdf.
[223] "IMF Members' Quotas and Voting Power, and IMF Board of Governors," International Monetary Fund, last modified December 3, 2022, https://www.imf.org/en/About/executive-board/members-quotas.
[224] Hudson, *Super Imperialism*, 186.
[225] "Robert McNamara," Wikipedia, accessed December 3, 2022, https://en.wikipedia.org/wiki/Robert_McNamara.
[226] Alex Gladstein, *Check Your Financial Privilege: Inside the Global Bitcoin Revolution* (Nashville, TN: BTC Media, 2022), 214.
[227] "United States Intervention in Chile," Wikipedia, accessed December 3, 2022, https://en.wikipedia.org/wiki/United_States_intervention_in_Chile.
[228] *CIA Activities in Chile*, accessed December 3, 2022, https://nsarchive2.gwu.edu/news/20000919/index.html.
[229] "Robert McNamara," Wikipedia.
[230] "Robert McNamara," Wikipedia.
[231] Dylan Matthews and Byrd Pinkerton, "'The Time of Vasectomy': How American Foundations Fueled a Terrible Atrocity in India," Vox, last modified June 5, 2019, https://www.vox.com/future-perfect/2019/6/5/18629801/emergency-in-india-1975-indira-gandhi-sterilization-ford-foundation.
[232] John Perkins, *The New Confessions of an Economic Hit Man*, 2nd ed. (Oakland: Berrett-Koehler Publishers, 2016).
[233] David E. Sanger, Alan Rappeport, and Matina Stevis-Gridneff, "The U.S. and Europe Will Bar Some Russian Banks from SWIFT," *New York Times*, last modified February 26, 2022, https://www.nytimes.com/2022/02/26/us/politics/eu-us-swift-russia.html.
[234] Sean Ross, "What It Would Take for the U.S. Dollar to Collapse," Investopedia, last modified March 23, 2022, https://www.investopedia.com/articles/forex-currencies/091416/what-would-it-take-us-dollar-collapse.asp.
[235] Eric Martin, "Ditch Bitcoin: IMF Urges El Salvador to Rethink Crypto," *Bloomberg*, accessed February 23, 2023, https://www.bloomberg.com/news/articles/2022-01-25/imf-board-urges-el-salvador-to-ditch-bitcoin-as-legal-tender.

[236] Kevin George, "El Salvador Opens the Door to Bitcoin Bonds," Investopedia, last modified January 12, 2023, https://www.investopedia.com/el-salvador-bitcoin-bond-7094463.
[237] *El Salvador: Staff Concluding Statement of the 2023 Article IV Mission*, 1, February 10, 2023, https://www.imf.org/en/News/Articles/2023/02/10/el-salvador-staff-concluding-statement-of-the-2023-article-iv-mission.
[238] Paul Bishop, "The Financial Costs of WWI," Kingston upon Hull War Memorial, accessed December 3, 2022, https://ww1hull.com/the-financial-cost-of-ww1/.
[239] Mathias André and Malka Guillot, *1914 - 2014: One Hundred Years of Income Tax in France*, July 2014, https://www.ipp.eu/wp-content/uploads/2014/09/n12-notesIPP-july2014.pdf.
[240] Julian Jackson, "The Politics of the Gold Standard in France, 1914-1939," Monthly Review, last modified July 17, 2010, https://mronline.org/2010/07/17/the-politics-of-the-gold-standard-in-france-1914-1939/.
[241] Leland Crabbe, "The International Gold Standard and U.S. Monetary Policy from World War I to the New Deal," *The Federal Reserve Bulletin* 75, no. 6 (June 1989): 426, accessed December 3, 2022, https://fraser.stlouisfed.org/files/docs/meltzer/craint89.pdf.
[242] Adam Fergusson, *When Money Dies: The Nightmare of Deficit Spending, Devaluation, and Hyperinflation in Weimar Germany* (New York: PublicAffairs, 2010).
[243] Glyn Davies, *A History of Money*, 4th ed. (Cardiff: University of Wales Press, 2016), 646.
[244] "Declaration of War with Japan, WWII," S.J. Res. 116, U.S. Senate, accessed December 3, 2022, https://www.senate.gov/about/images/documents/sjres116-wwii-japan.htm.
[245] "United States Declaration of War on Japan," Wikipedia, accessed December 3, 2022, https://en.wikipedia.org/wiki/United_States_declaration_of_war_on_Japan.
[246] "Timeline of U.S. Federal Debt since Independence Day 1776," Debt.org, last modified October 12, 2021, https://www.debt.org/faqs/united-states-federal-debt-timeline.
[247] "Take a Closer Look: America Goes to War," The National WWII Museum, accessed December 3, 2022, https://www.nationalww2museum.org/students-teachers/student-resources/research-starters/america-goes-war-take-closer-look.

[248] "Financing, World War II," Encyclopedia.com, accessed November 29, 2022, https://www.encyclopedia.com/defense/energy-government-and-defense-magazines/financing-world-war-ii.
[249] David Vergun, "First Peacetime Draft Enacted Just before World War II," DOD News, last modified April 7, 2020, https://www.defense.gov/News/Feature-Stories/story/Article/2140942/first-peacetime-draft-enacted-just-before-world-war-ii/.
[250] Tyler Bamford, "Steel Cents, Silver Nickels, and Invasion Notes: US Money in World War II," *The National WWII Museum*, last modified December 4, 2020, https://www.nationalww2museum.org/war/articles/united-states-money-in-world-war-ii.
[251] "Guns or Butter Social Policy: Essential Primary Sources," Encyclopedia.com, last modified November 29, 2022, https://www.encyclopedia.com/social-sciences/applied-and-social-sciences-magazines/guns-or-butter.
[252] "United States in the Vietnam War," Wikipedia, accessed December 3, 2022, https://en.wikipedia.org/wiki/United_States_in_the_Vietnam_War#1960s.
[253] Sherry G. Gottlieb, *Hell No, We Won't Go!: Resisting the Draft during the Vietnam War* (New York, NY: Viking, 1991), xix-xxii.
[254] Faisal Islam, "Iraq Nets Handsome Profit by Dumping Dollar for Euro," *The Guardian*, last modified February 15, 2003, https://www.theguardian.com/business/2003/feb/16/iraq.theeuro.
[255] Julian Borger, "There Were No Weapons of Mass Destruction in Iraq," *The Guardian*, last modified October 7, 2004, https://www.theguardian.com/world/2004/oct/07/usa.iraq1.
[256] "War Finance," Wikipedia, accessed December 3, 2022, https://en.wikipedia.org/wiki/War_finance.
[257] Linda J. Bilmes, "The Financial Legacy of Iraq and Afghanistan: How Wartime Spending Decisions Will Constrain Future National Security Budgets," HKS Faculty Research Working Paper Series RWP13-006, March, 2013.
[258] "Estimate of U.S. Post 9/11 War Spending, in $ Billions FY2001 - FY2022," Watson Institute International & Public Affairs Brown University, 2021, https://watson.brown.edu/costsofwar/figures/2021/BudgetaryCosts.
[259] U.S. Constitution, Amendments I – XXVII, accessed December 4, 2022, https://constitutionus.com/.

---

[260] "Synopsis of Each Ratified Amendment," List of Amendments to the United States Constitution, accessed December 4, 2022, https://en.wikipedia.org/wiki/List_of_amendments_to_the_United_States_Constitution.
[261] Eric Hughes, "A Cypherpunk's Manifesto," Activism.net, last modified March 9, 1993, https://www.activism.net/cypherpunk/manifesto.html.
[262] "U.S. National Debt Clock," U.S. National Debt Clock.
[263] Ray Dalio, *The Changing World Order: Why Nations Succeed and Fail* (New York: Avid Reader Press, 2021).
[264] Lyn Alden, interview by the author, October 19, 2022.
[265] A Resolution Impeaching Donald John Trump, President of the United States, for High Crimes and Misdemeanors, H.R. Res. 24, 117th Cong., 1st Sess., Feb. 13, 2021, https://www.congress.gov/bill/117th-congress/house-resolution/24/text.
[266] "Cynthia Lummis," GLAAD, accessed December 4, 2022, https://www.glaad.org/gap/cynthia-lummis.
[267] Sam Stein, "Kirsten Gillibrand Reached out to Gay Rights Group," Huffpost, last modified February 23, 2009, https://www.huffpost.com/entry/kirsten-gillibrand-called_n_160331.
[268] Lummis-Gillibrand Responsible Financial Innovation Act, S. 4356, 117th Cong., 2d Sess., June 7, 2022, https://www.congress.gov/bill/117th-congress/senate-bill/4356/text.
[269] Morgan Chittum, "Senators Compromise on Crypto Tax Provision; Bull Run Continues," Blockworks, last modified August 9, 2021, https://blockworks.co/news/senators-compromise-on-crypto-tax-provision-bull-run-continues.
[270] Awareness about Bitcoin in the House of Representatives also appears to be bipartisan, but perhaps with less momentum than what Lummis and Gillibrand are bringing to the Senate. The Congressional Blockchain Caucus was created as a platform for industry and government to understand the blockchain technology that Bitcoin pioneered, and the group is decidedly bipartisan with two of its four co-chairs representing each political party. Unfortunately, not much has come from this caucus and their website hasn't been updated since 2020. In 2021, the Digital Assets Working Group for Democratic members of Congress was announced with nothing of note being published or released since.
[271] "Watch Again: Texas Senator Ted Cruz Speaks at CPAC," YouTube video, August 5, 2022, https://www.youtube.com/watch?v=WwaRD0w2ReI.

[272] An Act to Amend the Environmental Conservation Law, in Relation to Establishing a Moratorium on Cryptocurrency Mining Operations That Use Proof-of-Work Authentication Methods to Validate Blockchain Transactions, S. S6486D, 2021st Leg., N.Y., Nov. 22, 2022, https://www.nysenate.gov/legislation/bills/2021/S6486.
[273] The Satoshi Action Fund, accessed December 4, 2022, https://www.satoshiaction.io/.
[274] Dennis Porter, interview with the author, August 22, 2022.
[275] "1905 French Law on the Separation of the Churches and the State," Wikipedia, accessed December 4, 2022, https://en.wikipedia.org/wiki/1905_French_law_on_the_Separation_of_the_Churches_and_the_State.
[276] "Supreme Governor of the Church of England," Wikipedia, accessed December 4, 2022, https://en.wikipedia.org/wiki/Supreme_Governor_of_the_Church_of_England.
[277] "Barack Obama Quotes Dr. Martin Luther King to Become President of the US by Filmmaker Keith O'Derek," YouTube video, April 3, 2018, https://www.youtube.com/watch?v=cUIAEGUdohk.
[278] Peter McCormack, interview with the author, June 16, 2022.

Made in USA - Crawfordsville, IN
98499_9798987636305
04.25.2023 1021